Freddie Dixon

THE MAN WITH THE HEART OF A LION

Freddie Dixon

THE MAN WITH THE HEART OF A LION

DAVID MASON

Haynes Publishing

To Bettie Mason
(1917–2008)

First published in July 2008

A catalogue record for this book is
available from the British Library

ISBN 978 1 84425 540 5

Library of Congress control no. 2008922586

Published in association with the Michael Sedgwick Memorial Trust.
This work is published with the financial assistance of the Michael Sedgwick Memorial
Trust. This Trust was founded in memory of the famous motoring researcher and author,
Michael Sedgwick, 1926–1983.
The Trust is a registered charity (charity no. 290841) set up to encourage the publication
of new motoring research and the recording of motoring history. Full details and contact
address can be found on the Trust's website www.michaelsedgwicktrust.co.uk.
The Trust welcomes suggestions for new projects, and financial donations to help with
future work.

Published by Haynes Publishing, Sparkford,
Yeovil, Somerset BA22 7JJ, UK
Tel: 01963 442030 Fax: 01963 440001
Int. tel: +44 1963 442030 Int. fax: +44 1963 440001
E-mail: sales@haynes.co.uk
Website: www.haynes.co.uk

Haynes North America Inc.
861 Lawrence Drive, Newbury Park,
California 91320, USA

Printed and bound in Great Britain
by J. H. Haynes & Co. Ltd, Sparkford

CONTENTS

Part Three – *The End of an Era*

PREFACE

My interest in Freddie Dixon began when I purchased on a whim my Riley Lynx, sadly no longer in my possession. If a car can have charisma that car had it. As I began to research the history of Riley, the name Dixon came up frequently. The interest was heightened because he was local to me. It has taken time and patience to tell the story which I hope will satisfy those who know of him and introduce him to a new audience.

Author David Mason at the wheel of his 1933 9hp Riley Lynx.

My object has been to tell the Dixon story as others remember him wherever possible, although I have had to rely upon published sources extensively, as can be seen. So far as possible I have tried to use original sources.

The story of Dixon's trial and imprisonment has, I believe, been set out accurately for the first time. The press cuttings were inaccurate and sensational (nothing has changed in seventy years). I was fortunate enough to find the original papers from the trial in the (then) Cleveland County Council archives, unopened for so many years. It was a thrill to handle originals so important to the story.

Some may be disappointed that I have not taken each Dixon car and detailed every nut and bolt, chassis number and induction system. That would be a task for a book in itself. Riley enthusiasts will I am sure appreciate that the 'Riley Years' are just part of the story. The motorcycle racing era forms another and Dixon's profound effect on his contemporaries yet another.

I am deeply grateful to all who have helped me. The mistakes and deficiencies are, of course, all mine.

David Mason
Darlington
July 2008

ACKNOWLEDGEMENTS

I have been helped so much by so many people in the writing of this book that it would be impossible to list everyone who has been involved. If your name is not mentioned please do not assume that you are forgotten or unappreciated.

My first contact was with Ted Zealand of Middlesbrough, who compiled a file on Dixon in 1981. I then contacted Frank Dixon's daughter, Mrs E Nixon, who introduced me to Gilbert Corduce, Dixon's doting nephew. Gilbert, a delightful man, who died before the research was long under way.

I have been much assisted by William Boddy, Robert Elliott, Charles Mortimer, Dr Joe Bayley, Mark Gillies, then of *Supercar Classics*, the editors of *Classic Cars* and *Classic and Sportscar* and the RAC Library. I am grateful to them all.

I am grateful too for the early assistance of the editor and staff of *The Middlesbrough Evening Gazette*. I should also mention the staff of the (then) Cleveland County Council archive office.

I am grateful to various officers of the Riley Register, the Riley Owners' Club and the Railton Owners' Club for their assistance from time to time.

When I have advertised my interest in Dixon I have been astonished by the response from people locally and otherwise, with many memories of him, his cars and his life. Again, many thanks. I have been very grateful for the help of people I wrote to without introduction who were so helpful. I should mention as a representative of this generous group Bob Thomas of the Isle of Man, who provided information and photographs.

Some people I have been in touch with stand out. I am indebted to Barbara Farquhar, a great Riley enthusiast and a stern but warm and kind critic.

Bert Hadley was a delight to be in touch with. His affection for Dixon
had survived Dixon's antics at Donington and elsewhere, when Bert was
witness to many Dixon excesses.

Martyn Flower, the Yarm amateur historian was enormously helpful
with the sand racing history. Without his help that aspect of Dixon's life
would have been almost impossible to illuminate.

I would like very much to give special thanks to Pat Ferguson, who was
so hospitable and helpful on two research trips to the Isle of Wight. His
company was a delight and of huge benefit. His help has, I hope, brought
to life Dixon's interest and achievements in four-wheel-drive technology
and the personalities involved.

It was a great pleasure to be in touch with the charming Ernest Lyons.
His affection for Dixon was palpable. In that connection, I was much
helped by Gordon Small of D C Thomson & Co, author of *Sweet Dreams, The
Life and Work of Rex McCandless*.

I must mention Robin Read, at times agent and potential publisher.
Robin has encouraged me and has wanted to see the Dixon story told
since he saw the great man at Goodwood as a young man.

AN INTRODUCTION TO
FREDERICK WILLIAM DIXON

'WHY WAS HE BORN SO BEAUTIFUL,
WHY WAS HE BORN AT ALL?'

… were the opening words of a favourite song of Dixon's racing friends and rivals, sung frequently in the bars of Weybridge and the Isle of Man when Dixon was leading the revels.

Charlie Dodson holds the bottle for ever-thirsty Dixon after gaining second place in the 1935 Mannin Beg race. Frank Dixon stands on left.

Short, squat, cherub-faced in youth, Churchillian in later years, immensely strong, ugly, pugnacious, hard drinking, charming, aggressive, secretive, brilliant, master of meticulous engineering, prankster, hell raiser, skilled but at times reckless rider and driver, visionary. Freddie Dixon was all of these.

Dixon was a man who secured for himself a unique place in the history of motor sport and engineering. He was an innovative thinker, with an unsurpassed ability to see engineering problems in their simplest terms.

Everything Dixon involved himself in had to be reduced to first principles, redesigned and redeveloped, and meticulously executed. Only ten tenths was good enough for Dixon. Dennis May knew Dixon well in later life and was to say that he owed his success to:

'Plain straightforward engineering knowledge and experience; an unusual capacity for sustained and concentrated thought and a refusal to side-step a problem until he has it ten tenths licked (faced with an enigma he goes off into interminable grunt-punctuated musing, oblivious to those around him); the ability to see the job in its first principles; a gift for orderly progression in applying his ideas which he commits to paper before something else crops up to crowd them out of his mind; disinclination to accept a practice or precedent on the mere grounds that that's how it's always been done in the best of circles; an unfailing turning-to-account of his failures and setbacks. Why does this or that happen? What's the reason behind it?'

A whole mythology developed around Dixon. The popular press adored him, as a constant source of dramatic material. Dixon did nothing to dispel the myth that he was a magician. If others thought he possessed superhuman powers, why should he shatter the myth? The truth is that Dixon was a man of immense talent, even genius, but that his successes were the result of meticulous attention to detail, together with profound powers of original thought. He was never afraid of work, and would often work almost ceaselessly for days on end. When perfection was attained, he would strip his work down again and try for something even better.

Dixon loved practical jokes. He carried fireworks with him whenever possible, and was never more delighted than when they were stuffed down the trousers of an unsuspecting victim and lit, often causing more damage to the wearer of the garment than to the trousers.

Dixon's exploits off the track were as legendary as his exploits on the track. After the racing finished, Dixon would celebrate (whatever the result) and was always the centre of the party. A favourite haunt of racing drivers and their entourages at Brooklands was The Ship at Weybridge, run by Henry Crane. He managed to keep a balance between his regulars and the rumbustious Brooklands crowd. Dixon, who haunted the place, with his friend Charles Brackenbury, became a leader of the revels. Crane was always assured of being over compensated for the damage which inevitably followed from the celebrations. Dixon was always prepared to pay for his amusement. Another favourite was the Hand and 'Spike' (Hand and Spear), again near Brooklands.

There are too many stories of Dixon's madcap exploits to tell without the subject becoming tedious. However, some cannot be missed. At Shelsley Walsh one day, Dixon was so drunk that his friends undressed him and put his stocky frame to bed. They then returned to the bar to find a naked Dixon standing at the bar swigging a large Scotch. He was not a man to give in.

In 1935 Dixon found himself at the Casino at Dieppe, where a celebration was to take place. Part of the fun was to be a swarthy gentleman stripped to the waist and wearing a turban, who was to carry a pretty girl into the room on a tray. This was too much for Dixon, and he marched into the kitchen, where the unfortunate girl sat on her tray, picked up the tray and swept into the dining room, the terrified girl hanging on to Dixon's neck.

Britain in the Twenties and Thirties was a class ridden society, and this was no more evident than in the world of motor racing. It was the era of the rich amateur. Dixon was the scourge of class divisions. He divided the world into the 'haves' and the 'have nots', and, at least in the early days, regarded himself as a 'have not'. Although he proved to be a successful businessman in later life, he could not compete with the titled and wealthy who dominated the sport. He was, however, a great leveller. Charles Mortimer remembers an incident in the paddock at Brooklands when Earl Howe who, in his role as President of the British Racing Drivers' Club, a body which somewhat reluctantly accepted Dixon as a member, addressed a recumbent Dixon, half under his racing car, with words on the lines of 'Morning! How's Dixon this morning?' to which Dixon, climbing out from under the car, replied without blinking,

'Awreet. 'Owe's 'Owe?' His Lordship loved it, and related the tale for many years. This unlikely pair were to be friends, on first name terms. Dixon was always prepared to recognise courage and skill in others.

Dixon became a hero on the Isle of Man for his exploits on two and three wheels. When he turned to four, he was again the idol of the Island. He could do no wrong, even when he turned up to a prize giving reception in his overalls, and covered in oil when his hosts and fellow guests were in their best. He insisted on shaking his oily hand with every dignitary, holding in his massive paw a tube of toothpaste, which he squeezed over each unfortunate.

Dixon's language was rich in expletives. His favourite word usually rhymes with luck, but was made by him to rhyme with book. He could be blunt far beyond the point of mere rudeness. He was quick with his fists, and ever ready for a fight if he thought he or his machines had been slighted. He could clear a bar in a twinkling. Dixon is remembered as a hard drinker, but always a happy one, never maudlin nor unpleasant. He was a non-drinker in his early competitive years, but took a fancy to Pimms No. 1 in his Brooklands days, although beer remained his favourite drink until he turned to gin later. A large Scotch would help him through the long nights of toil on his machines.

Dixon's driving was said to be wild, always giving the impression, perhaps deliberately, that he was about to have an accident. It was also effective, skilled and determined. A glance at his results confirms this. Winner of the Tourist Trophy on two, three and four wheels, twice winner of the arduous Brooklands 500, once driving entirely on his own, a remarkable feat of endurance, winner in the Isle of Man of the round the houses race – the list goes on.

Dixon is remembered above all as a warm, kind and generous man, always willing to help. He may have masked his warmth in his at times aggressive and blunt manner, but those who remember him do so with genuine affection and respect.

No-one who met Dixon was unaffected by the experience. He was a unique product of a sport in its heyday, before the advent of vulgar commercialism and politics destroyed it. Of the band of courageous, talented, colourful exponents of a sport full of drama, tragedy, achievement and spectacle, Dixon will be remembered as a unique and brilliant example.

PART ONE
TWO WHEELS
AND THREE

To celebrate the 75th Anniversary of the Isle of Man TT motorcycle races, the Manx Post Office issued a series of stamps featuring famous riders on the Mountain Circuit. Here, Dixon rides his 1927 Junior TT-winning 350cc HRD-JAP.

CHAPTER ONE

EARLY YEARS

Frederick William Dixon's parents, John and Martha Dixon, were natives of Goathland, North Yorkshire, but moved to Stockton-on-Tees two years after their marriage on 11 May 1885. They were a hard-working Victorian couple, with a successful business as market gardeners and small shopkeepers, although on Dixon's birth certificate his father is described as a general labourer.

They were to bring up eight children in the small County Durham town of Stockton. Fred Dixon was often referred to by the press as a bluff Yorkshireman. Bluff he may have been, but he was a County Durham

Dixon was called up in 1914 and joined the Army Service Corps, serving in the Motor Transport depot at Grove Park.

man, and only formed his Yorkshire connections when he moved to Middlesbrough in his teens.

It may be useful at this stage to consider the name Dixon himself used. The press always called him Freddie, or Dixon. He is still almost universally referred to as Freddie Dixon. Laurie Denny, who built the banking sidecar, referred to him as Dixon. In his famous 'Is it true what they say about Dixon?' articles, Dennis May, who knew him well, referred to him as Dixon, although interestingly in one caption to a photograph, probably prepared by an editor, Dixon is referred to as Freddie.

It must be said that Dr Joe Bayley, the Brooklands motor racing authority, refers to Dixon as Freddie. Charles Mortimer referred to him as both Freddie and Dixon. In his articles for *The Autocar* 'My Plunge into Car Racing' Dixon (or his ghost writer) refers to Dixon as Freddie, but that is consistent with that being his public name. In advertisements Dixon refers to himself as Freddie, but again that is a public use of the name.

Dixon's great friend and admirer Ernest ('Ernie') Lyons refers to him as Freddie or as Dixon. The names seem to be interchangeable. Despite all these contradictions it is most probable, from the recollections of people like Pat Ferguson (of whom more later) who knew Dixon well, that the forename used by family and friends was Fred. Dixon's autograph was always *Fred* and his garage business used the shortened form, too. Freddie was largely an invention of the press.

Dixon shared his parents with three brothers and four sisters. Harry, the eldest, emigrated to Australia, and played little part in the Dixon story. Frederick was the second, born on 21 April 1892 and was followed by Frank, who will appear often in the narrative, and then Wilfred. The sisters were Helen, Olive, Emily (Cissy) and Edith. The family home was 31 Alliance Street, Stockton. Little is known of Dixon's early years, except that he attended Borowsfield School, and presumably led the normal life of a young boy in late Victorian County Durham. He left school, as was customary for the time, at the age of thirteen.

Stockton's main claim to fame is as the town at one end of the Stockton and Darlington Railway, opened in September 1825 as the world's first public railway. The story of the railway has often been told, and will not be repeated here, except to say that the railway was originally designed to give access via the River Tees to the sea for the coal of South Durham.

Stockton-on-Tees in late Victorian England was a market town as well as a railway town, and no doubt the market was the outlet for John Dixon's produce. It boasts the widest main street in Britain. It must have been a pleasant, semi-rural environment for a young boy, no doubt one of high spirits, to grow up in.

There would be few motor vehicles in Dixon's early years, but as the century drew to a close, motor cars and motor cycles were increasingly part of everyday life. We do not know when motor vehicles first took hold of young Fred's imagination, but by the time he left school in 1905, he had decided on a career with motor vehicles, and after being apprenticed briefly to a local firm of electrical engineers, which gave him a lifelong interest in the electrical side of motor vehicles, the young Dixon went to work at the garage of Kit McAdams in Yarm Lane, Stockton. He was later transferred to the Middlesbrough branch of the firm, beginning his first association with that town.

The young apprentice's first association with Riley occurred in 1906 when he was only about fourteen. He was sent by his employer to recover a Riley which had lost its front axle whilst descending Clay Bank, a then notorious hill. His instructions were to find a local farmer with a horse to tow the car back to the garage. A willing farmer was found and with much heavy breathing and cursing the car was pulled and pushed back on to the road and the front end strapped to the cart for support.

Dixon sat at the wheel, and the unfortunate horse began the long tow home. When a gradient came, Dixon and the farmer, who was driving the cart, would jump down to assist the straining horse. This gave the curious Dixon the chance to look at the engine of the Riley, which lay under the seat. Young Dixon knew that a much steeper hill was imminently approaching and that the horse would need more assistance than merely being relieved of their weight. He checked the coils and other essentials and startled both the horse and its driver as he let in the clutch, the poor horse then being subjected to even more weight. He then caused even more consternation as the engine leapt into life, accelerating the poor animal furiously. They trundled home, the horse trotting happily with the help of the restored-to-life Riley.

At about this time Dixon was entrusted with the task of driving a pair of prim old ladies over the desolate Whitby moors in a Gnôme car. The battery was flattened by some defect when the party was about ten miles from the nearest garage. The still young Dixon remembered from his brief time with the electrical engineers that the addition of an acid substance might bring a battery back to life. He disappeared into the foliage and filled up the battery from his own resources. The old ladies continued their journey, never knowing what substance had brought the vehicle back to life.

Fred's proficiency with batteries was tested again when he was sent to restart a Studley, one of the first cars with a reasonably functional dynamo and starter motor. Dixon knew that shaking a battery sometimes brought enough life to start the car. He saw no point in removing the battery for that purpose. The startled owner was nonplussed to see his precious vehicle being violently shaken by the hood sticks by the muscular young apprentice. He showed little gratitude for being made mobile again.

There was an election in Stockton in 1906. Dixon was seconded to drive a candidate around the constituency in a Beeston Humber. His political colour is not known and would not have troubled Dixon, who regarded all politicians with equal suspicion. Local hooligans caused Dixon trouble by hanging on to the vehicle. Dixon again used his electrical skills to rig up a contraption which caused the vehicle body to be live in relation to anyone standing on the ground and holding on to the body. It certainly rid him of the local youths, but brought retribution upon him when the aspiring MP came to the vehicle unexpectedly and seized the body of the car to hoist himself in. The idea for this trick may have arisen from Fred's habit of wiring up door handles to give his Sunday school teachers a shock!

Dixon was resourceful even in those early days. Kit McAdam had a Ford agency and Dixon was entrusted with a pre-Model T car. It was soon apparent that the main bearings were breaking up. The sump on that model was nondetachable, and there were panels in the side of the crankcase to give access to the crankshaft. Dixon peered in. His suspicions were confirmed. The contemporary leather faced clutch slipped wildly at the slightest contact with oil. Why, therefore, should a big end lined with leather not act in a similar way? Dixon took a piece of leather from the hood strap. His repair got him home and kept going for a few days until a proper repair could be carried out.

Middlesbrough, unlike Stockton with its ancient origins, is an ugly creation of Victorian commercialism, resulting from the extension of the

Stockton and Darlington Railway to the mouth of the River Tees in December 1830. It is now a town with its wealth based on chemicals, but in Dixon's youth steel and heavy engineering, including shipbuilding, was its lifeblood. This was the bustling, hard-living steel town of Dixon's early life, and he was no doubt excited by the rapid progress made in engineering around him.

Late Edwardian motorcycles were relatively crude devices, although often beautifully finished in nickel plate. Dixon acquired his first motorcycle in 1909, an ancient machine, presumably of one cylinder and without gears.

The early years of the century saw not only astonishing improvements in motor vehicles, which established the supremacy of the internal combustion engine, but also great enthusiasm for the young sport of motorcycle and car racing. Throughout the country there were thriving motor clubs, usually centred around motorcycles, which were more available to the mass of people than were cars. Middlesbrough was no exception. Young enthusiasts would meet on their machines and hold unofficial competitions. Dixon was one of them. Bowsefield Lane, Middlesbrough was one of the favourite meeting places, and then the company would travel on their primitive machines on the dusty and windy roads of the day to some field, perhaps at Yarm, or Hutton Rudby, where events would be held with the consent of the farmer.

Very little is known about Dixon's exploits then. It is easy to accept that the wild determination which drove him in later life was then present, and what is known is that Dixon came to the attention of William Egerton Price, manufacturer of the Cleveland motorcycle in Middlesbrough, and later to be Mayor of the town. The Middlesbrough and District Motor Club is one of the oldest motor clubs in the country, and has its origins in enthusiasts meeting at a roundabout in Middlesbrough on motorcycles. The Club held events for motorcycles in the hilly countryside around Middlesbrough and Dixon was the rising star of these events. It was probably in those events that Alderman Egerton Price saw Dixon excel. He must certainly have impressed Egerton Price, because he persuaded Dixon to take one of his company's machines to the Isle of Man for the Tourist Trophy Race of 1912. It will be recalled that this was only three years after Dixon acquired his first motorcycle.

The idea of holding a British road race was conceived at the annual dinner of the Auto Cycle Club (later the Auto Cycle Union) in January 1907. The original Tourist Trophy was presented to the ACC by a great pioneer enthusiast, the Marquis de Mouzilly St Mars. English roads could not be closed for racing, and there was a blanket speed limit of 20mph. Facilities had to be found elsewhere for the race. The more enlightened Isle of Man was chosen and the Manx government gave permission for the race. The original course was triangular and started and finished in St Johns. In the early years there was a limit on the amount of fuel a bike could carry, but this was abandoned in 1909. In 1911 the Mountain circuit was introduced, and the St. Johns circuit abandoned. The field was divided for the first time into Junior and Senior events. The Mountain circuit was 37.75 miles long, and gave many vantage points to the enthusiastic audience. The weather on the Island was to say the best unpredictable, the surface of the roads was dusty or muddy, according to the weather, and always bumpy. The machines which roared around the circuit had primitive springing and brakes. Only the strongest succeeded.

It was to this exciting, tough and challenging scene that Dixon travelled in 1912 at the age of twenty. There is a story, uncorroborated, that Dixon did not tell his parents where he was going, and simply said he was going away for a couple of weeks, taking with him the new boots of one of his brothers. On his return the boots were ruined. As compensation he took his brother for a ride on his motorcycle, and promptly lost his brother's cap!

The Cleveland motorcycle was a single cylinder belt driven machine. Egerton Price insisted that Dixon did not change anything on the bike, and that it competed in its standard form. There is a suggestion, again uncorroborated, that Dixon had modified its brakes to the extent that they were impossibly severe, but if this was the case it was against the instructions he had been given, and is an early example of rebelliousness.

The machine was not up to the task. A rubber company had entered the belt making business, and to promote its new product, gave each competitor a dozen new belts. These were distributed at two sites, the present site of the pits, and Ramsey. Dixon's riding was so enthusiastic that he managed to tear two belts to pieces on each lap. The motorcycle simply fell apart on the arduous circuit, and Dixon had to retire, although the precise cause is not known. Dixon returned home scratched and bruised, but he had made his debut. The remarkable feature is that Egerton Price, no doubt a hardheaded businessman, had thought that Dixon showed sufficient promise to sponsor him in this premier race. He cannot have expected him to win, but that he competed was a tribute to the young Dixon.

Dixon is remembered as a restless young man, constantly changing his motorcycle steed from Norton to Harley-Davidson and Accord. He seems to have eventually formed an affection for the eight valve V-twin 998cc Harley-Davidson, manufactured by the great Milwaukee company, and we will hear more of this machine.

The war interrupted Dixon's life in 1914, as it interrupted so many others. He was called up, and must have shown particular engineering skills, because he rapidly rose to the rank of Staff Sergeant in the Army Service Corps, serving at the Motor Transport depot at Grove Park, London. This was a significant event in Dixon's early life, because he was responsible for the maintenance of the complete range of military vehicles, and must have learnt a great deal. Also, on leaving the army, he was not content to go back to being someone else's servant, and on his demobilisation set about creating his own business in the motor vehicle world of Middlesbrough. His first premises were a wooden shed which he built himself, but later he constructed the Park Garage in Linthorpe Road, Middlesbrough which survives, but not as a garage.

There can be no doubt that Dixon had business skills as well as engineering skills. He had many contacts in the towns around Yorkshire, and had no difficulty in selling cars and motorcycles for himself and for others. He built up a successful business, helped by his brother Frank, who it seems never became a partner in Dixon's enterprises, but was his manager for many years. By 1919 Dixon had created the basis of his successful future.

In 1919 Dixon took part in the Scottish Speed Championship, but no success is recorded, although in 1920 he carried off the prizes for the solo and sidecar events, beating a local champion. He continued to compete in local events organised by the Middlesbrough and District Club, and others. There were hill climbs on the notorious hills of North Yorkshire, such as Rosedale, said to be the steepest hill in England, and the equally challenging Sutton Bank, with its twists and turns. Of all the enthusiasts who took part locally, Dixon was dominant.

CHAPTER TWO

THE FIRST VICTORIES

W e do not know precisely when Dixon was demobilised, but like so many others who had fought in the ill-named 'Great War', he faced a new world. The country was on the verge of the Roaring Twenties and it has been said that Dixon helped to make the Twenties roar. There was a

Dixon on the Indian on which he came second to Howard Davies (on a 350cc AJS) in the 1921 Isle of Man Senior TT race. The 500cc sidevalve Indian was a highly successful, if somewhat improbable adaptation of the 1000cc V-twin, using only the rear cylinder.

new mood of optimism, a feeling, probably misguided, that a war had been fought which would change the world. Dixon had cause to have emerged with a feeling of confidence.

The Isle of Man Tourist Trophy series did not get under way again until 1920. Dixon competed in the 1920 Scottish Speed Championship at Saint Andrews, carrying off the honours for the sidecar and solo events. It is highly probable that Dixon took part in local events organised by the Middlesbrough and District Motor Club and other clubs in 1919 and 1920, but no records appear to have survived. It is known that he had success at Chatsworth and Sutton Bank. He was victorious in the 200 mile trial for the Gjiers Cup, organised by the Middlesbrough Club over a course in the Lake District. His competition mount was by now the eight valve V-twin 989cc Harley-Davidson, but for the Tourist Trophy of 1920 he rode an Indian, coming twelfth in the Senior race. His mount may have been a works machine, and if this was so it suggests that Dixon was becoming a national figure in motorcycle competition.

The course was altered in 1920, presumably to add interest. The Senior race was won by T C de la Hay on a Sunbeam at an average speed of 51.48mph, which contrasts well with the winning speed in 1914 of 49.49mph. D M Brown was second on a Norton, with W R Brown third on a Sunbeam. Dance on a Sunbeam set up the fastest lap at 55.62. The length of the race was 226.5 miles, as opposed to 225 for the 1914 race. The post-war racing scene had begun. Brooklands opened for racing in April, after extensive repairs were carried out to cure the damage caused by the lorries of the Royal Flying Corps. Brooklands never regained the relative smoothness it had shown before the war.

In 1921 Dixon began competing in earnest. He rode in April 1921 in the York Motor Club's hill climb at Sutton Bank, making the record time of 1 minute 17 seconds. Dixon also competed in the Otley speed trials at East Chevin, where he astonished his fellow competitors by riding up a few minutes before the start on a travel-stained Harley-Davidson combination, demanding to know where the hill was. On being shown it, Dixon made a hurried survey and immediately on coming down took off the sidecar and won the solo race. He then re-attached the sidecar and won the sidecar race, setting up a new record, and immediately mounted his combination and set off for Middlesbrough, leaving questions like

'How does he do it?' behind. He made fastest time of the day in the sidecar event at Horton Scar on Whit Monday. It was reported that he had been a prolific prize winner in events held by the Middlesbrough and District Motor club.

It was in 1921 that sand racing was first organised by the Middlesbrough and District Motor Club, following a suggestion from its President, William Ryan. The races were organised over the beach at Saltburn, which came to be called the Brooklands of the North. On 9 July 1921 the first meeting was held, and there was an excellent entry of 228 riders. Three Yorkshire Championship races were held. Dixon achieved fastest time of the day and a win in the 1000cc Championship.

Dixon formed his first association with the Douglas company, which we will see was a long and prolific one, in 1921. He was offered a ride for Douglas in the 1921 French Grand Prix over the Circuit de Provins, about eighty kilometres from Paris. Dixon was one of several Douglas entrants, his team-mates being Alfie Alexander, Jack Emerson, Teddy Kickham, Reuben Harveyson, and a Frenchman whose name Dixon later forgot. He later said that he then first experienced what he described as the Douglas Feeling, a sensation of effortless speed, with a lack of vibration, and good acceleration. Dixon also wrote that the Douglas machines lacked the acceleration and steering to make them competitive. Douglas experts and fans will have to decide which of these contradictory opinions is correct. Dixon was unplaced. The engine size of his mount is unrecorded.

Dixon later recorded that towards the finish of the race, on a particularly rough 'S'-bend, the spectators waved frantically at him, as though signalling Dixon to stop. He could see no reason for doing so, and ignored the signals of the crowd. He later discovered, he said, that the spectators had arranged the attendance of a doctor at the corner to deal with the Dixon mishap they thought inevitable. It must be remembered that this was recorded some years later, and the episode may have grown in proportion by the passage of time. The significance of the race was that Dixon had begun his long and as it will be seen, not always happy association with Douglas. The race was marred for Dixon by a serious accident involving Teddy Kickham.

Dixon came second in the Isle of Man Senior TT on an Indian after an exciting duel with Howard Davies on a 350cc AJS. Dixon's style in practice was described as meteoric and he was said to have frightened everyone. He was expected to break records if he did not crash. Le Vack, also on an Indian, was strongly fancied to win and to break records.

The race began at 9.30am in glorious weather. De la Hay made a good start, as did Dixon, who was described as adopting his unusual riding style, with his head over towards the left-hand side. Last to leave was Dance on a Sunbeam, receiving a rousing cheer. By 9.55 Davies on the AJS was in the lead, with de la Hay second. Davies completed his first lap in 41 minutes, 17 seconds, slower than the expected speed. Dixon completed the first lap in 41 minutes 16 seconds, but of course he had left after Davies. Dixon's second lap was completed in 42 minutes 9 seconds, and he was therefore slowing down. He was fourth fastest. Davies lay second, and Edmond on a Triumph was first. Davies was a favourite of the crowd, because of the small capacity of his machine, and because he had already come second in the Junior race, having broken the lap record and he had been unlucky not to win.

At the end of the third lap Dixon lay fifth, with Dance in the lead, Davies second, Bennett on a Sunbeam third and Le Vack fourth. Dance fell back to seventh place after crashing his machine and damaging the gearbox, forcing him to complete the race in top gear. Edmond broke the course record on the fourth lap. Bennett had moved into the lead, with Davies second, riding wonderfully, Le Vack third and Dixon fourth. Davies moved into the lead on the fifth lap, and Dixon lay fourth, Bennett second and Edmond third. Bennett slowed down, and Davies moved further ahead, and received a tremendous reception as he came home, not yet the winner as Bennett still had 3.5 minutes to run, and Edmond had some chance of catching Davies's time if he rode a splendid lap. Bennett was slowing, due it was said to concussion suffered in a practice crash. Edmond developed an oil leak and lost all the oil from his tank. At 2.07pm Davies was declared the winner. Le Vack received a tremendous cheer as he finished, but he was 31 seconds behind Dixon's time. Dixon came second after riding a race without incident. His cornering was as it had been in practice, bold and dramatic, and the high average speed of the race was more a result of fast cornering than of high speed on the straights.

1921 was an historic year for motorcyclists in Britain. For the first time in Britain a motorcycle exceeded 100mph, and a motorcycle race of 500 miles was won at a speed of over 70 miles per hour. The potential of the motorcycle for speed and reliability was convincingly shown.

It was Douglas Davidson, riding a specially imported Harley-Davidson who on 28 April broke the 100mph barrier, in strong competition with Claude Temple, also on a Harley-Davidson, and Bert Le Vack on *The Camel*, his 994cc eight-valve Indian. That story must be told elsewhere.

In March 1921 the British Motor Cycle Racing Club (Bemsee) announced that it would hold a 500 mile race for solo bikes on 2 July 1921. A G Miller commissioned Sydney Garret, the rider and professional silversmith, to produce a 200 guinea cup for the race. BMCRC awarded silver cups for the second- and third-placed and Victor Horsman donated a cup for the winner of Classes A and B (350cc and 250cc).

Five hundred miles at racing speeds on a motorcycle on the banked and bumpy Brooklands track was a formidable challenge, and a 500 mile race for motorcycles would not be held in Britain again until 1958. The 500 was declared by *Motor Cycling* to be a stiffer test than the TT.

There were five classes: 250cc, 350cc, 500cc, 750cc and 1000cc. In Class E, 1000cc, which included Dixon's eight-valve Harley-Davidson, there were 20 competitors including Le Vack on an Indian, Temple and Harveyson on Harley-Davidsons. Zenith was represented by an entry of eight bikes, two with JAP engines, Matchless had an entry of three in this Class and there were three Indians. The Class was made up by a Sunbeam-JAP, a Martin and a DOT-JAP The total entry for the race was sixty four. Pits were arranged at the Fork, and any part of the motorcycles could be replaced, other than the cylinders and crankcase, which were sealed.

It was a colourful sight as the competitors lined up shortly before 7.00am. To assist the spectators in following the race each class wore a differently coloured jacket. The front row was in white (250cc) or blue (350c), the second rank yellow (500cc), the third rank green (750cc) and the rear rank was in red (1000cc).

Dixon must have had problems staying in the saddle of his Harley in practice, and came up with the idea of covering the seat of his bike with emery paper. As the race progressed Dixon found that his tail end was covered in blood. The emery paper had worn through his leathers, his underpants and then his skin, producing more blood than even Dixon was prepared to tolerate. He roared into the pits and tore off the seat covering, then set off again. This was one of the many trials he suffered in the race.

Promptly at seven the flag fell, and the riders pushed their mounts into action, with a roar from the exhausts. The organisers had erected a board at the Fork which had a card for each rider showing how many laps he had completed.

It was a gruelling race for man and machine. Half of the field failed to finish, as chains, belts and tyres failed to stand up to the punishment. After thirty-seven laps Le Vack led the 1000cc class at 80.77mph. Speeds were much higher than predicted. At 45 laps he suffered a deflated tyre, and Douglas Davidson took over the lead on his Harley-Davidson. However, after 200 miles Dixon had taken over the lead of the 1000cc class at 74.34mph. This lasted until shortly after 10.30am and the 300 mile stage, when Davidson had taken the lead at 72.75mph. The strain must have been showing, because speeds were decreasing. At about this time Dixon had a disastrous blow-out on the Railway Straight, skidding the whole kilometre of its length, then falling from the Harley-Davidson. Dixon was shaken, but unhurt, and the bike had survived. He motored to the pits and changed the wheels, then screamed back into battle. Dixon's crash almost ended the race for Milner on his 250cc Levis, who after breaking his frame and lashing it back together, lost the leading position in his class, and then having suffered gear change problems, collided with Dixon's riderless machine, hurling both bike and rider from the track. He was not injured and set off again, finishing second in the 250cc class.

Le Vack, after many tribulations managed to re-take the lead in the 1000cc Class. He was not challenged and eased off. Meanwhile, Dixon stopped to make a precautionary wheel change, losing only three minutes, then set off to catch the leader. By 2.00pm Le Vack looked like a certain winner, but on his 182nd lap he failed to appear at the pits. One of his team-mates, Reuben Harveyson, signalled to the pit that he required help, and the pit staff roared off on a sidecar combination to the Byfleet aeroplane sheds where Le Vack had stopped. Excitement rose in the

Harley-Davidson camp. Could Dixon win? Then a red dot was seen on the
Byfleet Banking, and as it increased in size it revealed itself to be Le Vack,
streaking towards victory.

Le Vack then developed oiled sparking plugs and hurriedly changed
these in the pits. He was then off on his final lap. Dixon could not catch

For the 1922 Senior TT Dixon again rode one of the ingenious single-cylinder versions of the
1000cc V-twin Indian. The forward-facing Schebler carburettor and tankside gear lever are
two of the Dixon modifications to this machine, on which he ran second for some time before
a burst tyre put him out.

him. Such was the drama of the finish that the flagman failed to lower his flag for Le Vack at the end of his winning lap, and he went on to complete an extra lap. Dixon was ten minutes behind, and came in an honourable second. Le Vack's winning speed was 70.43mph. Dixon's speed was 68.86mph. Over twenty miles per hour separated him from the winner of the 250cc Class. The race had seen several records broken, including the Class E record for 200 miles by Dixon at 74.31mph.

Dixon was said by 'Carbon' of *Motor Cycling* to be the freshest finisher, who came off the track as cheerful as if he had just gone out for a five mile sprint. It must be said that another observer saw Dixon staggering slightly at the finish. The race must have been an enormous physical and mental test of endurance. Dixon rode again in the 1922 M&DMC sand event at Saltburn. There was another good entry, of 301 riders. He was again victorious in the 1000cc Championship.

Dixon was back on the Isle of Man for the 1922 Senior Tourist Trophy, held in June. He again rode an Indian, modified to his own specification with footboards, American style, instead of pedals, a modified front brake, tankside gear lever and a Schebler carburettor. Whilst a close second to Bennett on the 5th lap a crash caused by a burst tyre put him out of the race. The tyre makers, Hutchinsons, awarded Dixon the money he would have received for a runner up's place.

Again the weather was magnificent and the course was watered. Davies, the winner in 1921 took up the place reserved for the first to start when the race began at 10.00am precisely. Davies was quickly away. Dixon, who had again distinguished himself in practice, made a good start. Most of the competitors wore brightly coloured waistcoats, with the Indian team in red: it must have been a dazzling sight. At the end of the first lap Dixon lay sixth. Bennett on his Sunbeam was in the lead, with Langman second on a Scott, and Brandish's Triumph third. Dixon had moved up a place on the next lap, with Bennett still in the lead and by the third lap Dixon lay in third place to Bennett and Wood, on a Scott. Dixon was improving his position as the fourth lap progressed and lay second at its end and then paused briefly as he was about to set off on his fifth lap, receiving a rousing cheer from the crowd. There was sympathy from the crowd when the announcement was made that Dixon had retired with tyre trouble, and he was said to be badly shaken. It could so easily have

been another second place for Dixon, and he might even have caught
Bennett to take his first win in a TT. Bennett came home the winner on
his Sunbeam, with Brandish second on Triumph and Langman third on a
Scott. Dixon's performance was impressive as usual.

Saturday 17 June saw the first of the 200-mile sidecar series of races at
Brooklands, organised by the enterprising Ealing and District Motor Cycle
Club. Effectively, there were three races run together: for the 350cc
combinations starting at noon, the 600cc machines starting an hour later,
and the 1000cc machines starting at 2.00pm. This meant that the most
exciting racing took place whilst the largest crowd was present and meant
that the small machines were not still fighting long after the larger
machines had finished.

The classes were identified by the colour of the sidecars, 350cc blue,
600cc red and 1000cc yellow. All combinations had to be fitted with a
skid to support the sidecar if it should lose its wheel. In the event, the
race started late and the 350cc machines did not leave until 12.10pm,
and all other classes set off correspondingly later. Dixon rode his eight-
valve Harley-Davidson, and had incorporated a drive to the sidecar
wheel from the countershaft sprocket, with the shaft lying parallel to
the sidecar axle. He had used this arrangement in hill climbs, and had
found that it relieved side drag and reduced rear wheel spin. It
effectively gave two wheel drive. Dixon's was the most unusual machine
in the race.

The event attracted a very good field, including Kaye Don and Bert Le
Vack. Le Vack, Charlesworth and Don rode Zeniths with side-by-side ohv
JAP engines. Packman's Packman was similarly powered with a bulbous
fronted sidecar carrying a long tail.

At 2.10pm the 1000cc machines roared off into the fray, among the
smaller machines which had been buzzing around already for two hours.
Longman made one of the best starts, but Packman and Claude Temple
(Harley-Davidson) were slow in starting. Kaye Don had tyre trouble
within 500 yards of the start and had to fit a new cover. Davidson on an
Indian and Le Vack fought a battle between themselves, thundering
around for lap after lap within yards of each other, whilst Dixon and
Packman fought their own battle behind. Charlesworth on a Zenith and
Longman on an Ariel-MAG were also locked in a struggle. At the end of

the first hour Le Vack had covered 26 laps, Davidson 25, Temple and Allchin 24 each, Dixon 22 and Kaye Don 21. Don then broke a piston but managed to replace it and was soon away again. On his 44th lap Le Vack burst his rear tyre, and limped for almost a lap on the flat to his pit. The wheel change took 1.5 minutes, and it took him only five laps to recover the lead. Then he had a fuel pipe break, and found the replacement had the wrong sized union. By his 57th lap he was three laps behind Davidson who had made steady progress.

The race went on, and then Dixon was forced to retire with a broken piston said not to be of Harley-Davidson manufacture. There must have been no time to change the piston because Dixon would not have retired willingly. The closing stages were exciting, although by this time Dixon was only a spectator. Le Vack was clearly the fastest, but Davidson had built up a substantial lead because of the problems Le Vack had suffered. They passed the Fork almost together, with Davidson having covered 71 laps and Le Vack 70. Le Vack was five or six miles per hour faster than Davidson, and he rapidly caught up on Davidson, but failed to win by half a lap. There was only 1 minute 38 seconds between the two, and Allchin, third, was thirteen minutes behind Le Vack. Several records were broken, and the first 200 mile sidecar race was a success, although not for Dixon, who had been forced out by mechanical failure.

The Essex Motor Club held an event on Saturday 22 July. There were three motorcycle events, all with a Fork start and a long finish. Dixon competed in the solo race on the Harley-Davidson, lapping at 90mph, but was not among the winners. He then attached his sidecar for the 3-lap Passenger Machine Handicap. There were also cyclecars in the race, and the spectacle must have been bizarre, as Dixon stormed around on his powerful machine among these lightweights. He won at 75.74mph. There had been difficulties over noise with the residents, and warnings had been issued by Colonel Lindsay Lloyd that machines had to be properly silenced. These warnings went unnoticed in this race, and the noise was enormous.

This was effectively the end of Dixon's season. He had gained more experience and his reputation was high as a rider and as a tuner of fast machines. No doubt he looked forward to the 1923 season.

CHAPTER THREE

1923, THE YEAR OF THE BANKING SIDECAR

The most prolific year of Dixon's motorcycle career was 1923. He achieved remarkable success, and demonstrated his genius for original engineering. His greatest success of the year was undoubtedly the creation of a banking sidecar for the 1923 Sidecar TT, the first to be held,

Dixon with an apprehensive Walter Denny and the banking sidecar.

and his riding of it to an impressive victory. Dixon later described his success in the 1923 sidecar TT as 'A kind of joke with a lucky break in it'.

The racing year began on 7 April with the first Bemsee meeting of the year, at Brooklands. Brooklands had been closed for three months over the winter, and opened for testing in February. There was a new grandstand for spectators at the Fork, and increased shed accommodation for competitors' machines. In March it was announced that motorcycle speeds would be calculated from the 50-foot median line, the line used for cars, rather than the 10 foot median line which had been used for motorcycles.

There were nine events for the first meeting of the year, which attracted a small field for six handicap and three scratch races, all held over three laps and starting and finishing at the Fork. Dixon had a good win in the Solo Handicap on the 989cc eight-valve V-twin Harley-Davidson which he had ridden so successfully in the past. Dixon had blown up his better engine the day before, and fitted a spare engine, which he only just had time to test. His winning speed was 93.71mph. His fellow scratchman Oliver Baldwin came second on a 994cc Matchless, with Turner on his Indian third. Dixon had an exceptionally large carburettor, hidden from prying eyes by a metal shield. This was an early example of Dixon's obsessive secrecy. He used all his skills to tune his machines, with considerable success, and was unwilling to share his secrets. He carried a leather gauntlet which, in the absence of anything else, could be used to cover up the carburettor and which he would remove only at the last possible moment as the race began.

Dixon again was very fast in the 1000cc Solo Handicap, covering a standing start lap at 89mph. Dixon's second lap was covered at 97mph, and the second man, Oliver Baldwin on a 994cc Matchless-MAG was half a mile behind on the second lap. Dixon's win was convincing at 94.05mph, Baldwin coming second well behind, with Lieutenant R T Grogan third on a 988cc Zenith-JAP, having been almost lapped by Dixon.

Dixon also competed that day in the 600–1000cc Passenger Handicap. Four machines entered, with Dixon on the eight-valve Harley-Davidson. Peaty entered a Bleriot-Whippet cyclecar, and Jacobs rode a Norton in full touring trim, including club badges. Dixon had an easy win, despite losing his crash helmet, which nearly led to his disqualification, especially when the Bleriot-Whippet almost came to grief by colliding with the discarded headgear. Dixon was relaxed enough to slow down to talk to his sidecar passenger, steering the combination single handed.

The last race of the day was a scratch event for the large machines. Dixon was very fast, with a standing start lap of 89mph and then a flying lap of 97mph, which left the opposition well behind. He almost lapped Baldwin's Zenith and won at an average of 94.5mph.

Brooklands was frequently used for record breaking, despite its notoriously bumpy surface, which would eventually drive the fastest men to the Continent for their record breaking attempts. The first record breaking attempts of 1923 were held on 16 May. Dixon had problems when his float chamber came apart in an early run, but despite side winds which caused him to sway and swerve, set up records of 85.87mph and 82.72mph for the Class G, 1000cc with sidecar record, flying start 5 mile record and the 10 mile standing start record. The 5 mile record had been held by L Parkhurst, an American, who had established the record at 83.91mph at the much smoother Daytona Beach in Florida. Dixon also established a flying start mile record at 93.88mph.

The second BMCRC meeting of the year was on 5th May. The meeting opened with two 100 mile races, with the idea of allowing competitors to try out TT machines. Dixon did not compete in these long distance races, but did well in the Senior three lap Handicap on the Harley-Davidson. Pickering won on a 984cc BSA, but Dixon did well to come from scratch to second place. Gill's Indian was third.

The year was packed with activity. On 26 May the BMCRC held its third monthly meeting of the year at Brooklands. Dixon was entered for the three lap Solo Handicap on the 989cc Harley-Davidson, but failed to start. Whatever problem he had had was resolved by the time the 1000cc Passenger Handicap began, but it was not Dixon's day. Fred Hatton on a 736cc Douglas with a sidecar had a magnificent ride and came home a convincing winner, with G N Morris on a 1074cc Morgan-Blackburne second and Dixon trailing home third. The 500cc scratch race lacked spectacle as there were only five starters, but the spectators were then given the thrill of Claude Temple, Fred Dixon, Bert Le Vack and Oliver Baldwin battling out the 1000cc Solo Scratch Race. This was a race between the leading exponents of the day. All made a good start, and Temple on his 996cc British Anzani led after the first lap, which he covered from a standing start at 91mph. Le Vack was close behind, with Dixon third and Baldwin fourth. Temple rode a magnificent second lap at 101.23mph. Le Vack had a misfortune and dropped out, leaving Temple to win at the excellent average of 97.85mph, with Dixon second and Baldwin third.

In 1923 the organisers of the Isle of Man TT held a sidecar race for the first time. Dixon entered on a remarkable machine, a Douglas with banking sidecar. The engine of the Douglas was designed by Stephen Leslie Bailey and it was later said that it was first drawn only three weeks before the race. This is probably not correct, in the light of what Dixon later wrote about the machine. It was claimed to be 'a triumph for calculation as opposed to experiment' as it had been handed over to Dixon without testing. This may have some truth, but the reality is that the engine was probably more developed than was said at the time. Douglas had introduced a new TT bike for 1923, and how Dixon's machine differed from these is not clear. The machine showed many of Dixon's idiosyncrasies, as we will see.

A view of the famous Dixon banking sidecar outfit in later years, without the vital sidecar, but showing its lightweight construction and the ingenious system of levers by which the hardworking passenger canted the third wheel.

The engine had a one inch hole at the bottom of the crankcase, sealed to the oil tank under the frame by a rubber ring. The oil tank was of cast aluminium and formed the clamp to hold the engine to the frame. The oil pump was contained in the oil tank, and operating a lever pulled a piston against a spring forcing oil through a tell-tale visible to the driver, who could measure the rate at which oil entered the engine. It was necessary to operate the lever only once every three or four miles. Four bolts went through from the bottom of the tank to secure the engine to the frame. The carburettors were AMAC and were fed air through a 'letter box'. They were operated by a twist grip coupled to a cross bar, connected to the carburettor slides by piano wires.

Dixon had arranged to ride for Douglas in the sidecar race. He visited the Bristol factory shortly before the race to see what the factory was preparing for him. He found that the factory was working on a sidecar with a leaning body. Dixon was not completely happy about this, and after one or two sleepless nights he came up with the idea of a banking sidecar. He applied to patent the concept on 5 June 1923, jointly with Bailey, giving as their address the Douglas factory in Bristol.

The banking sidecar fulfilled a simple purpose. When a motorcycle with sidecar turns to the left it can turn much faster if the motorcycle leans towards the sidecar, and if the machine leans outwards a right-hand corner can be taken very much faster. This advantage was conventionally achieved in racing by the sidecar passenger and the rider of the motorcycle leaning to left or right on bends, the passenger often hanging out over the side of the sidecar, or scrambling behind the rider of the motorcycle.

Dixon already had a formidable reputation as an engineer and tuner, and this was enhanced by his invention of the banking sidecar. It was claimed that from conceiving the idea to creating it as a working example took Dixon only ten days. The actual construction was carried out by Laurie Denny, the Redcar motor engineer. He much later said that the frame was drawn out in chalk on the workshop floor. The chassis was made up with Reynolds tube and had brazed lugs. Welding equipment was not yet available. The front fitting was machined from a bar and went through the lower tube of the cradle frame.

There was no convenient cross tube on the rear of the frame to secure the rear bar of the sidecar, and a plate was brazed on to the rear to accept

The action of the banking sidecar allowed it to rise on right turns; Denny pulling on the outside lever here at Quarter Bridge, in 1925.

it. By taking off two nuts it was possible to remove and refit the sidecar in minutes, with perfect alignment.

The main feature of the banking sidecar was the arrangement of the wheel and axle. There was a central transverse chassis member which formed a hollow casing, inside which the axle was allowed to rotate. The axle was also tubular. A spindle ran through it to operate the sidecar brake. On the outer end of this was a seven inch arm which formed a crank web, with the wheel spindle as the crank pin. There was a lever on each side of the body from the axle, projecting vertically on the left-hand side and roughly forty degrees forward on the right-hand side. When the levers on the sidecar were pulled backward by the passenger the axle rotated, taking the arm with it. As the wheel was firmly on the ground, that end could not go down, and the sidecar was tilted towards the outside. If the lever was pushed forward, the axle dropped and the whole machine tilted inwards for left-hand corners. There was a simple locking peg to hold the sidecar in the normal position, released by depressing a knob on the left-hand lever. Because the weight of the body would tend to cause the machine to lean inwards if the levers were released, a strong spring was fitted to take the weight off the passenger's arms.

The sidecar seat was unique. It slid on runners, like an oarsman's seat, allowing the passenger to lie down with the seat back lowered, and returning it to the vertical as he pulled himself up, giving the correct position to operate the levers.

The axle was hollow, with a rod passing through it to operate the Fibrax ring brake by a lever on the right-hand side. The Fibrax ring was spoked to the hub and also clipped to the wheel spokes. The ring itself was aluminium, with the Fibrax friction material fitted by brass wood screws. It was known as the Research Association Brake. The brake lever was later removed and replaced by a pedal operated by the driver's left foot when operation by the passenger proved too exciting. The body was pivoted front and rear and sprung on quarter elliptic springs. It was covered in aluminium, sand blasted on the top to prevent glare from the sun. As can be seen from the patent (page 210), Dixon had even more radical ideas for the banking sidecar, including a system of replacing the lever which operated the banking mechanism with a steering wheel.

The Auto Cycle Union tried to prevent the machine from running, as it was untried, and at first Dixon was obliged to practise with the mechanism locked. He pleaded with the officials, and was allowed to demonstrate the sidecar over one lap, with a close scrutiny being kept at different points on the course. Dixon was allowed to use the machine for the race in full working order.

It was said that Dixon did not like wire controls. He modified the Douglas to exclude as many as possible by having the exhaust lifter operated by a lever on the crankcase, the clutch by a pedal, the front brake interconnected with the rear. The throttle was operated by twist grips on each side of the handlebars, so that Dixon could operate the throttle even when leaning so far that he could not reach one side of the handlebars. The foot operated clutch and twin twist grips made for faster gear changes, although clutchless gear changes were quite easy with the gearbox employed. There was a scoop to cool the rear cylinder, extra heavy wheel spokes and six security bolts to each wheel. Everything was sweated, wired or fitted with split pins. For the race the sidecar had a small aero screen. Dixon had a similar screen on the motorcycle, attached to the handlebars. He rode without goggles.

This was an early example of the way in which Dixon achieved success by sheer ingenuity and attention to detail. He was a prodigious worker, and it will be seen as his exploits are related that it was his capacity for work and attention to detail which separated Dixon from his contemporaries. Laurie Denny was later to remember how the team would work all night in the stable which was Dixon's workshop on the Island. The team would stay at the Queen's on the Prom. It was Denny's job to collect coffee and sandwiches (and no doubt beer) on his Velocette. Practice was in the early morning with sleep grabbed when possible, and the promise of a high time if the team won.

Dixon grew used to working through the night, whether at his Middlesbrough base, or on the track. He also had from his early days a reputation for his off track activities, resulting in wildly excessive celebrations before, and particularly after races. Dixon said later in life that half of what he won for racing he kept, and half went on his celebrations, which often involved compensating publicans and hotel keepers for the results of his excesses. However, whatever his reputation, Dixon does not appear to have allowed his pleasures to interfere with the serious business of winning races. He would work obsessively into the night, and would not sleep until whatever project engaged him was complete. We shall see that Dixon frequently drove himself to exhaustion in preparing for racing.

Dixon's brave passenger for the TT was T W (Walter) Denny, Laurie Denny's cousin, and it was his task to operate the banking sidecar. Great strength was necessary to operate the banking mechanism, particularly on right-hand corners. It gave tremendous benefits in cornering, but only if the passenger was very strong, and if he was in accord with the rider as to the course to be followed.

The levers were set at different angles to allow the passenger to use his right arm to assist in raising the sidecar, as the left would be in a difficult position to operate the lever, which would finish up behind him.

Dixon and Denny practised together for the race, learning to use the banking sidecar. Coordination between the rider and passenger was crucial, and Dixon signalled to Denny when it was necessary to tilt the sidecar. At first, Dixon later wrote, they proceeded carefully, but when Dixon found the motorcycle was working well, and that he and Denny were functioning together soundly, he could not resist the temptation to increase his speed. As the team passed Ballaugh Bridge at high speed the machine took off, a combination of high speed and Dixon's late signal to bank the sidecar for a left-hand bend. Dixon could not steer an airborne machine, and a nasty wall confronted them. There was a risk that the combination would be seriously damaged, and Dixon braced himself to take the impact with his shoulder, shielding the vulnerable handlebars. Dixon and Denny negotiated the bend successfully in this way, and quickly alighted to examine the damage. This was limited to a missing footrest and a damaged mudguard. The pair set off gingerly to ride quietly home. The footrest was later found, but Dixon did not claim it, as he did not wish to admit the incident. This near disaster persuaded Dixon to practice more sedately, and may have influenced his later decision on tactics for the race.

There were fourteen starters and the race was held over three laps giving a distance of 113.25 miles, as against the 226.5 miles of the solo races. The first man away was Harry Reed on a DOT, followed by Hatton. Langman (Scott) made the best start. It was noted that Denny leapt acrobatically into the sidecar having pushed off the machine. The position clocks moved slowly round, showing the arrival of the riders at various points. Dixon was soon signalled from the Bungalow. He completed the first lap in 42 minutes 23 seconds, despite a problem with a slipping clutch, which cured itself, but was beaten into second place by Langman who circled at 41 minutes 36 seconds.

Dixon had decided as a matter of tactics not to go flat out on the first two laps. There were those who had predicted that Dixon's machine would not survive the course, while others predicted that the result would be between Dixon and Langman. Dixon had the more advanced engine, but was at a disadvantage when opposed by the proven reliability of Langman's Scott. The banking sidecar was unproved in competition.

Graham Walker on a Norton lay third with A C Taylor fourth on an OEC Blackburne. Langman's first lap was a remarkable achievement and Dixon realised that he would have to ride fast to catch up. He had been astonished to find Langman, who had started later, closing up on him on

At Braddan, Denny can be seen pushing hard on the inner lever to allow Dixon a 'solo' stance as he sweeps to the right and out towards Union Mills.

the first lap. Dixon's decision not to overstress his machine might have been his downfall, as clearly Langman was going all out. Dixon came in at the end of each lap to refuel, losing valuable time, as Langman did not stop at the end of his first lap.

Three machines dropped out on the first lap, with Scally crashing at the Bungalow after his forks collapsed. Montgomery took eighty minutes to complete the first lap, and arrived at the pits with the sidecar's tail damaged. At the end of the second lap Dixon was in the lead, but again stopped to refuel, with Langman storming through. Dixon's pit stop was very brief, but Langman led him on time, having started later. Dixon's second lap was thirteen seconds faster than his first, but Langman had taken twelve seconds off his time and had a minute and a half advantage over Dixon. Walker remained in third position, and there were only three minutes between him and the leading Scott. The race was still wide open. Langman was signalled as having stopped at Ballacraine, and there was speculation that he might have run out of fuel, not yet having stopped for replenishment. Then the news was received that Langman had crashed at

Braddan Bridge. Dixon arrived at the scene seconds after the accident, and found Langman's machine upside down and sliding. Dixon avoided a collision, but he later said that he did not know how. Luckily Langman and his passenger were unhurt, but Langman was out of the race.

Dixon was going very fast, and raised his pace in case there were others he had miscalculated over other than Langman. He seemed certain to win if he could finish and was well ahead of Walker, his main remaining rival. The telephone operator at Creg-ny-Baa, whose job it was to report the positions of the riders, rang up, and asked to be relieved as Dixon had twice ridden at him and he was afraid that the third time Dixon would land on his roof!

Walker and Tucker on Nortons were chasing Dixon but had little chance of catching him. Dixon roared on. Despite the tilting sidecar, it was reported that fresh air was seen under the sidecar's wheel at times. Dixon was signalled at Governor's Bridge, then was seen on the straight heading for victory at terrific speed. This was despite the fact that his frame had collapsed and that the motorcycle was permanently leaning towards the sidecar. Dixon later speculated that this was a result of the crash in practice. It was only the handlebar resting against the sidecar body which prevented total collapse. Denny manipulated the banking mechanism to see the combination home. Dixon came home to victory to massive applause, looking perfectly relaxed and fit, and ready for another lap.

There was still a battle for second place. Tucker was next home, but Graham Walker, also on a Norton, had four minutes advantage due to his later start and he beat Tucker with a minute to spare. Dixon's speed for the race was 51.15mph. It would have been better still had he not had to stop on every lap for fuel. Walker's time was 52.5mph, and Tucker's 52.07mph. Langman put up the fastest lap at 54.69mph. Had Langman survived the race, Dixon would have been fighting to win and his crash was fortuitous for Dixon. This does not detract from Dixon's marvellous victory on his unique and ingenious machine, but Dixon himself was later to record that Fate had been kind to him. He said that he had no problems other than the collapse of the frame in the closing stages. He regretted accepting the advice he had been given by others to hold back on the first two laps, and admitted that this would have been a serious, even fatal, mistake if Langman had not crashed. Denny reported that he had a lively time, but felt perfectly fit, although his arms were aching with pulling the levers. The design of the banking sidecar had allowed him to remain seated.

Whether the banking sidecar was a huge success, and a real step forward, or just a fruitless deviation from conventional design can be debated. Dixon won the race, but arguably only because of Langman's misfortune in crashing. The banking sidecar was in a very damaged condition at the end. It is not generally appreciated that Dixon used the banking sidecar outfit again in the 1924 and 1925 TTs, but without the same degree of success. When it is recorded to have been used later, it was not by Dixon and was in the locked position. Douglas and Dixon never sought to market the idea, nor to offer it to other competitors. However, it was a brave try and an innovative and brilliant attempt both conceptually and in its construction, to make a huge leap forward in sidecar technology.

Dixon returned to the Indian team for the Senior race, although he later said that he regretted his commitment to Indian as he would have

Dixon came third in the 1923 Senior TT, again riding an Indian, but this time with a lighter, vertical single-cylinder engine rather than the earlier truncated V-twin.

preferred to ride a Douglas. The weather was wet and overcast for the race with mist on the mountains. The race started, as usual, with the machines leaving at short intervals to space out the field on the narrow roads of the Island. Dixon made a good start and was said to look as though he was off on a short sprint. The crowd settled down to watch the scoreboard 'clocks' which were the only indication they had of the position of the riders over the 37.75 mile circuit. There was drama at the start as Veasey's Douglas burst into flames. The Pyrene operators sprayed him as he passed and the flames were put out. George Dance discovered a nail in his rear tyre at the start and had to replace the cover. The officials announced he would be credited with the time taken, to the delight of the crowd, to whom he was an idol. Dance eventually got away. Dixon was going well and did a good first lap. The positions at the end of the first lap were Whalley first, Bennett second, Alexander third and Sheard fourth, all on Douglas, a remarkable achievement. Dixon was fifth. As Whalley came into the pits to refuel there was a further cry of 'Fire!' as either his machine or Bennett's burst into flames. There were clouds of smoke, but the flames were quickly extinguished and both men were off again.

There were several retirements due to tyre troubles. It was speculated that this was because the overstressed wooden-framed sidecars had left bodywork tacks on the course during the sidecar race.

At the end of the second lap the Douglas machines still dominated the field, holding first, second and third places. Whalley still led, with Sheard second and Alexander third. Dixon had moved his position up to fourth, at an average speed of 57.57mph. Whalley's speed was 59.43mph, then Dixon was delayed at Quarter Bridge with tappet trouble. Only a little over three minutes separated the nine surviving riders. The weather was deteriorating with heavy rain and mist shrouding the mountain. The speed of the machines was remarkable in these conditions, which made the race more a test of the rider, as speeds were necessarily reduced, relieving the stress on the machines.

Stanley Woods on a Scott was disqualified for taking on fuel at an unauthorised place. Barker's Norton was not allowed to continue after a scrutineer's inspection of a broken fork. There were many mechanical casualties in the race. Dixon's tappet trouble meant that he had slipped back, and was not in the first six on the third lap. Whalley still led, with

Sheard second and Black's Norton was third. Whalley's speed had been reduced to 58mph by the weather, still a remarkable achievement. Then Whalley had to stop to change a sparking plug, but this did not cure the problem, and he limped along on one cylinder with damaged rocker gear. Sheard rapidly took over the lead. Ollerhead on a Douglas stopped to tie up his exhaust with string, it having been trailing on the ground for almost a lap. The race was still dominated by Douglas machines, with Sheard in the lead, Whalley next, Ollerhead third, and Alexander fourth. Howard Davies retired with engine trouble on the mountain, where the weather was improving, although the stand was still drizzled upon. By the fifth lap Sheard still led, but Douglas had lost its dominating position as Shaw and Walker had moved into second and third places on Nortons.

The crowd watched Sheard's clock intently as it moved round relentlessly. Then news was received of a fatal accident to J H H Veasey, the first fatality since the races resumed after the war. He had lost control and collided with a stone wall at Greba Bridge when his handlebar caught the stonework.

At the end of the fifth lap Dixon moved up the field to take fourth place. Sheard led at 56.26mph, Black was second on a Norton at 55.43mph and Alexander on a Douglas was third.

Sheard kept up his steady pace, and was cheered enormously by the crowd as he came in to win. He was not only a Manxman, but also the only man at the time to have won the Senior and the Junior race. The race was still full of excitement, because there was a real battle for second place. Only seconds separated Black on the Norton and Alexander's Douglas. These were the last two to start. Dixon was still going well, his yellow scoreboard disc dropped and a moment later he flashed past the post. When the calculations were done Black, the last man to start, was second, with Dixon third only one second ahead of Walker. If Dixon had not suffered tappet problems he might well have come home second or even first. In any event he had ridden a fine race. To have come third so soon after his remarkable performance in the sidecar race was a wonderful achievement.

Sheard's winning speed was 55.55mph, a time of 4 hours 4 minutes for the 226.5 miles of the race. Dixon's speed was 55.00, remarkably close to that of the winner. His time was 4 hours 7 minutes. Whalley put up the fastest lap of the race at 59.74mph, and was unlucky not to be among the winners. Norton won the Manufacturers' Team Award, although the Douglas was undoubtedly the star machine of the race.

Dixon next rode a Douglas in the 1923 Grand Prix de France. He took with him the motorcycle combination, carrying a 350cc engine which he fitted for his solo entry in the Grand Prix. He had never seen the circuit before and suffered from a weight penalty and must have ridden well to come third. Whalley was first on a 500cc Douglas. Dixon did not return home immediately, as his next commitment was the Spanish Twelve Hour race. He lingered at the French circuit to watch the car Grand Prix which followed the motorcycle Grand Prix. The sidecar was refitted to the Douglas, and Dixon later related how his riding attracted the attention of a local gendarme. He chased Dixon without success at first, but eventually caught him at a local garage whilst Dixon refuelled. Dixon made good his escape having shaken the astonished gendarme warmly by the hand.

Dixon and the rest of the Douglas team set off for Madrid and the Twelve Hour race. They suffered from the intense heat as they laboured to prepare their machines. Dixon was to ride his sidecar combination. The road surface was abominable and Dixon and Denny made wry faces at each other over its condition. No proper steps were taken to close the roads, even for the race, and cattle were a constant hazard. Machines and riders took a battering and Dixon said he was relieved when mechanical trouble, later shown to be a damaged camshaft bearing, put him out of the race. Dixon had run seven of the twelve hours and comfortably led his class. He was later told that if he had run a further mile he would have beaten the previous best time for twelve hours and would have won the race. Whalley won the race on a 500cc Douglas, which was some consolation to Dixon.

Dixon riding an Indian had a superb victory in the Belgian Grand Prix in July. There was a terrific thunderstorm on the morning of the race as the town of Dinant was awakened by the roar of open exhausts. Part of the enormous scoreboard was blown down, and the timing box was struck by lightning leaving the timekeepers running for cover. These were bad omens, but by the time the race started at 10.30am, having been delayed for half an hour, the weather was fine and the sun shone on the competitors and the crowds. Dixon rode in the Senior class for machines up to 500cc. After the first lap he was in the lead, with Hassall second, Jackson third and Kaye Don fourth. Longman led the 350cc class, and Handley the 250cc. It was a British onslaught. Dixon remained in the lead at the end of the eighth lap, with Dance second, Breslau third and Jackson fourth. Longman led the 350cc class and Davison the 250cc.

Dixon was said to have ridden with superb judgement, a high compliment for a man whose riding style sometimes had a look of recklessness about it. At the end of the twenty-fourth lap Dixon still led from Stoddart and Vidal. Longman retained the lead in the 250cc class, and they started their last two laps almost together. Longman suffered appalling luck when he was forced to retire with a broken sprocket. He had looked an easy winner. The Junior race was won by a Belgian, Huynen, and Dixon roared home an easy winner in the Senior class, with Stoddart second on a Sarolea and Vidal third on a similar machine. They had held on well during a gruelling race, but could not catch the flying Englishman.

The organisers made the mistake of giving pistols as prizes. Dixon celebrated after the race in his usual way, and decided to test the pistol he had won. He did this without leaving the hotel bar, and customers, and no doubt the management, were horrified to see and hear Dixon blasting the ceiling. Dixon could be relied upon to pay for the havoc he created and no doubt the hotel keepers were well compensated for the results of Dixon's high spirits. He always aimed to take home half of his winnings, spending the other half on celebrations and reparations.

Dixon put up the fastest lap in the Senior class at 65mph, with de la Hay fastest in the Junior race at 61mph. It was said that the wins by the Britishers in the Senior and Lightweight classes were well received. The race came to a wet end as the deluge began again as Dixon finished.

A few days after his Belgian victory, Dixon was at Brooklands for the BMCRC 200 mile races. The 1922 200-mile sidecar races had proved so successful that it was decided to hold solo races over the same distance in 1923. It was Le Vack's day, after he had competed in two 200 mile races and won them both, an astonishing feat of skill and endurance. Dixon rode a Harley-Davidson in the 1000cc race, along with Frank Longman and Kaye Don. Le Vack rode a new Brough Superior-JAP, the frame of which had only been delivered from the Nottingham factory the week before. It was fitted with a side-valve V-Twin JAP engine. Le Vack had already won the 350cc race on a New Imperial-JAP. He was a favourite to win the 1000cc race if he had the stamina.

The 1000cc race was held at the same time as the 500cc and 750cc races. Each rider in the 1000cc race wore a red jumper as the machines lined up in the back row for the start at 2.00pm. Le Vack's first win was in the morning, and he must have been hardly rested by the time the afternoon race started. There was a barrage of noise as the riders revved their engines to prevent the hard plugs from oiling. There was a total of twenty-five starters, including eight in Class E, the 1000cc machines. Le Vack was slow off the mark, and G N Norris shot into the lead as the large machines roared off. He was quickly passed by Dixon on the Railway Straight. Norris then had to call in to the pits to remove a damaged shock absorber. Kaye Don went in complaining about his steering.

The field spread out, Le Vack having taken the lead and Dixon having slipped back to third place, with Temple in between. After ten laps Dixon moved back into second place, but had been lapped by Le Vack.

Kaye Don developed tyre trouble, and then Dixon pulled in with a sight feed lubricator he had fitted himself broken away from the tank. He taped it up and set off again to challenge Le Vack, but he was badly splashed by oil. Le Vack was lapping at just under 90mph, with Grogan's Norton second. Temple had retired and that, with Dixon's pit stop, allowed Humphries, a complete outsider, to take second place on an Indian. After thirty-eight laps Le Vack pulled in to refuel, and was quickly away. At forty laps Le Vack remained in the lead with Humphries two laps behind and Dixon another lap behind. Dixon, by superb riding, was catching up on them both, riding close in on the banking, and leaning at an alarming angle. He quickly passed the outclassed Humphries and by the forty-fourth lap was only a lap behind Le Vack.

This remained the position, although on Le Vack's fifty-fourth lap Dixon pulled in for fuel. He was quickly away, and made a determined effort to catch Le Vack, who was level with Humphries on the track, although two laps ahead of him. Dixon was lapping at 87mph, and eventually caught Le Vack, who then shot away. Dixon then had further misfortune when his engine began to misfire. He dropped back and Le Vack coasted to his second victory of the day, and a tremendous ovation.

Dixon finished second nine minutes later, with Humphries third. Le Vack's winning speed was 83.44mph, whilst Dixon's was 78.91. We can only speculate on what Dixon might have achieved had he not suffered mechanical problems. July 28 saw the fifth BMCRC meeting of the year. There were four three lap handicaps and five two lap scratch races. Dixon entered the Harley-Davidson in the three wheel handicap, and was easily the fastest, effortlessly overcoming his six second handicap, beating Norris's 1098cc Morgan. Dixon was to race Norris again in a scratch race, but this race, along with others, was abandoned.

There were eleven entries for the 1000cc scratch race, but only eight lined up for the start. Le Vack rode the Brough Superior which had excelled in the recent 200-mile race. Dixon had the eight valve Harley-Davidson and Longman a sidevalve machine of the same make. Dixon lost a tappet rod on his first lap, and came into the pits on one cylinder. Le Vack had an easy victory at 90.63mph. Dixon was beaten in the 1000cc handicap by Lieutenant Grogan on a Norton, no doubt with a very advantageous handicap. Dixon did well to come second from virtually scratch, and it was said that he was an awe-inspiring sight as he streaked around the banking, head nodding on the vicious bumps.

The BMCRC held a meeting on 18 August. Dixon entered the three lap 1000cc Solo handicap and came second, with a lap at over 100mph, only the third time this had been done since racing resumed in 1920.

Dixon continued his busy year competing in the Ealing Club's 200-mile sidecar races on 25th August, the second in the series. Again the sidecars were painted in colours according to their class, the 350s light blue, the 600s red and the 1000cc machines yellow. The same colours were used on the scoreboard. Again the start was staggered, with the 350cc race starting at noon, the 600s at 12.30pm and the largest machines at 1.00pm. The idea was to ensure that all the classes would finish approximately together.

Many competitors had shown considerable ingenuity in using the sidecar to house an extra fuel tank, as stopping for fuel was clearly a waste of time if it could be avoided, and could affect the outcome of the race. Baxter's Rex-Acme had its tank hidden in the nose, whilst Greening's was carried on the side of the sidecar. It is not known whether Dixon adopted any similar means of increasing his overall speed.

Five minutes before the start the machines which were first off lined up. The competitors were pushed off with engines dead, which avoided the smog which usually accompanied the start. The smaller machines screamed off. Dixon and his fellow 1000cc competitors had an hour to wait before they set out to do battle. At 12.30pm the 350s were waved over towards the Vickers sheds so that the 600cc machines could start, and at 1.00pm the same procedure was adopted to allow the largest machines away. Dixon had a bad start on the Harley-Davidson, and the rear wheel had to be lifted on to a stand to allow the machine to be started after Dixon stalled it. He was off very quickly. Again it was Le Vack's race. He took the lead from the start, crouching over the tank of the Brough Superior, sheltering behind the small screen. After two laps Le Vack was half a lap ahead of the field, lapping at 80mph. Dixon was next, with Temple third, also on a Harley-Davidson.

After six laps Le Vack had a lead of a full lap, and Dixon had dropped to third place, although on the track Dixon and Le Vack were separated by only a few yards. Bridgeman came into sight and astonished everyone when his sidecar came adrift and ran alongside his Indian. On the sixteenth lap Le Vack still led, with Temple second and Dixon third. On his thirtieth lap Dixon limped into the pits to change a flattened rear tyre. The machines in this class ran without incident in this order, and after fifty laps Le Vack had a lead of five laps, a remarkable achievement in this competitive field. Temple and Dixon battled it out behind.

Temple gained two laps on Dixon. The quiet scene was shattered as Jepson arrived balancing his Zenith on two wheels, as a result of a broken sidecar axle. Then there was a cry of 'Fire!' as Humphries' Indian burst into flames. The flames were quickly put out, but the machine was too damaged to continue. Dixon stopped for fuel, as did Temple, and the final result was a good win for Le Vack, at 75.32mph, Temple second at 70.30mph and Dixon trailing into third place at 65.8mph. Le Vack had broken several records, including the 50 miles, 100 miles and 200 miles. The race was not one of Dixon's best, but a third place was creditable in this competition.

Dixon's busy year was drawing to a close. On 22 September he rode at Bemsee's sixth meeting of the year. There was a heavy rainstorm as the racing was about to begin, but it did not last and the racing was under way on time. Dixon was entered in the 1000cc sidecar race, competing against his main rival, Le Vack. Dixon rode the Harley-Davidson and Le Vack competed on his Brough Superior. It must have been a close and dramatic race, because Dixon led off the Byfleet Banking, but it was Le Vack who stormed home to victory.

On 9 September the Motocycle Club de France held its records meeting in the Bois de Boulogne. The course was a kilometre long. Two runs were made and the mean taken. Honours for the day went to Dixon and Bert Le Vack. Dixon rode a Harley-Davidson in the 1000cc sidecar and solo classes. In the solo event. Dixon's speed was 171.8kph, or about 107mph, and in the sidecar event he managed 143.769kph, or about 89mph. Dixon's time on the solo was the fastest ever recorded for a motorcycle over the kilometre. Dixon's one way times had broken the British records, and his mean times were a world record. Le Vack broke records in the 350cc classes.

September 29th saw the Essex Motor Club's meeting at Brooklands. Dixon concluded the day's events by racing E P Dowey's Leyland, the fastest car at the meeting, on his Harley-Davidson. Because of the handicapping, which gave Dixon a start of only twenty-five seconds, he would have had to lap at 100mph for the three laps of the race to win. This was an impossible task, but Dixon put up a fine show for the spectators, catching the Leyland on the Banking only to be passed again, and lapped at very close to 100mph on his second and third laps to come a very good second at an average speed of 94.88mph. Dixon was defeated by the handicapping.

The final major event of the year at Brooklands was the Bemsee Championship Meeting on 20th October. This was just after the Olympia show, and there were many innovative machines at the meeting. Le Vack rode an overhead valve 1000cc twin to considerable effect. All events were over five laps, and Dixon did five laps at 100.01mph, a record speed, and the first time a motorcycle had run a race of this distance at over 100mph.

Dixon rode a Harley-Davidson in the 1000cc sidecar championship. There was disappointment when Temple and his British Anzani did not turn up for the race, as it was rumoured that he intended to compete vigorously. There was an excellent field, with Dixon, Le Vack and Riddoch on the starting line. Le Vack was second to Dixon after the first lap. There was a large gap between these two and the rest of the field. Le Vack took over the leading position on the second lap and maintained it to the end, winning at 83.7mph, with Dixon three hundred yards behind. Riddoch was third.

The big race of the day was the 1000cc solo championship. Temple and the British Anzani turned up. Dixon again rode a Harley-Davidson. It has been suggested that this was the same machine that Dixon rode in the sidecar Championship, but this is probably incorrect. The machine used for the 1000cc Solo race was an eight valve Harley-Davidson with a modified loop frame. The front down tube and saddle tube were cut off just below the points where the crankcase was attached to the frame. The loop passing below the crankcase was removed and replaced by two massive engine plates attached to the front down tube and the saddle tube, as well as the crankcase bolts. The frame was probably one of two brought from the USA in November 1920. They then had no sprung front forks, and were unrideable at over forty miles per hour. The engines were fitted in normal loop frames. Dixon later fitted normal sprung front forks and modified the frame. He liked short wheelbase machines and had no difficulty in achieving his excellent result in this race.

Dixon could only run second to Temple on the first lap, although his average speed for the lap was over 100mph! These were astounding speeds for motorcycles, and would not be beaten for some time. Temple and Le Vack disappeared from the race, presumably with mechanical problems, and Dixon raced to victory, without serious competition, but it was no hollow victory. His speed of over 100mph for the five laps was proof of that. Dixon had taken the championship from Le Vack, a wonderful victory.

Dixon ended the victorious 1923 season on the highest note possible. He had further victories to come, but 1923 must be seen as the high point of Dixon's motorcycle racing career, proof that he could compete with the best, like Le Vack, and that he was a master of racing technology, the best tuner and engineer of his day, at a time when there was a great deal of competition. His name is still remembered on the Isle of Man, especially at the time of the TT, when the Fred W Dixon trophy is still competed for and awarded to the winner of the Sidecar TT Race for two-stroke machines of 301–350cc and four-strokes of 401–600cc

CHAPTER FOUR

1924–1926,
THE WASTED YEARS

1924

For the 1924 season, Dixon deserted the Indian team and formed an association with the Douglas company. He not only rode their machines, but also became closely involved in the development of the company's products.

During the early Twenties, Dixon made a number of outings on a 1000cc Harley-Davidson, the other American motorcycle. Dixon usually rode this fire-eater solo, as here at Saltburn, but also with a sidecar on occasion. Note the characteristic inlet-over-exhaust valve arrangement, Dixon footboards, and virtual absence of brakes.

Dixon's interest in Douglas is said to have begun in 1922, when a Douglas machine came second in the Senior TT. There were, in fact, five companies involved in the Douglas story, from its early days in 1907 to the demise of the final company in 1957. The history of the companies was firmly rooted in the City of Bristol. In popular memory, Douglas is remembered for its motorcycles, but in its fifty years the company was involved in the production of cars, tractors, Vespa scooters, industrial engines, dirt track racers, TT machines, lorries, aero-engines of its own design, electric floats, drain covers, and improbably, a giant wheel in which sat a man.

The Douglas family was originally involved with foundries, but in 1907 joined up with J J Barter, who had been producing rather unsuccessful motorcycles with flat twin engines, a configuration with which Douglas became strongly identified. In 1911, when the Mountain circuit was used for the TT for the first time, two of the four Douglas entries finished. Douglas had considerable success in the 1912 TT, coming first, second and fourth. The war saw the production of 25,000 motorcycles for the War Department, and by 1922 Douglas produced a 500cc ohv, a 733cc ohv and 350cc and 595cc side valve machines. The reality was that the company had too large a model range. Sheard had won the 1923 Senior TT on a Douglas, and of course, Dixon's victory in the 1923 sidecar event with the banking sidecar was with a Douglas.

The Douglas company had seven model changes between 1921 and 1931, far too many for financial health, and probably reflected an excess of enthusiasm over good management. The company had further financial vicissitudes, until Douglas's fortunes were again boosted by war. After joining Douglas in 1924, Dixon intermittently worked for the company over a period of several years. He left in 1926 to work for the JAP engine organisation, when he became disillusioned over restrictions on his work, to which he was not temperamentally suited.

Douglas suffered a disastrous fire in 1927, and in 1928 Cyril Pullin, Douglas's other great designer left. He was interested in designing machines to fill an order for the Spanish Army. This required machines with single cylinder engines, which the Douglas company was unwilling to produce. Pullin left to pursue the project on his own behalf. Dixon, together with Rex Judd, was persuaded to rejoin the company.

Dixon did not totally abandon his Harley-Davidson in this period, as we shall see, but most of his competitive efforts were on Douglases. The machines were undoubtedly fast, and no doubt Dixon made them faster, but they were not reliable in Dixon's hands, perhaps suffering from a combination of over complication and the undoubted pounding Dixon gave to every machine he rode. There were those who said that Dixon was destructive of engines, and that no engine could stand the treatment he gave it. However, Dixon had enjoyed success on the Harley-Davidson and on the Indian. Dixon no doubt asked a lot of his mounts, but equally he gave a lot in terms of engineering skills and meticulous preparation.

The 1924 season opened at Brooklands on 22 March. There was more spectacle than usual at the first meeting of the season, which had traditionally been marred by the inability of handicappers to ensure close finishes because of a lack of information, and the unwillingness of the top riders to reveal their form so early.

Dixon entered the 1000cc scratch race, making an excellent start on the Harley-Davidson. Longman also made a good start, taking the lead on his Harley-Davidson, but rapidly disappeared from the running. Temple, the third star of the race, made a poor start, with only one cylinder of his British Anzani firing. Dixon had a remarkable first lap, at 91.03mph from a standing start, and came around for the first time well in the lead. Koehler on a Zenith was a poor second. Dixon's second lap was faster still, at 103.33mph, but Temple, who had continued to have misfiring problems found the solution, and began to ride furiously to catch Dixon. The race was between these two, but Dixon looked a sure winner until he failed to reappear, and Temple roared home an easy winner. Dixon's problem was a sheared magneto drive key. There is another report that Dixon retired because he lost his crash helmet as he passed under the Members Bridge, but it seems unlikely that Dixon would allow this to deter him. Dixon's best lap of 103.33mph had been officially timed, and therefore constituted a lap record.

Dixon and Temple resumed their battle in the 1000cc handicap race. Dixon had six seconds over Temple, but after the first lap they were level on the Railway Straight. Temple finished 100 yards ahead of Dixon, but neither could catch Koehler on his Zenith.

There was a challenging entry for the Expert Handicap, as would be expected, including Temple, Dixon, Denly and Horsman. They were obviously severely handicapped, and at the end of the second lap Baxter on a Rex-Acme was in the lead, with Horsman fourth, and Dixon and Temple coming up through the field. Dixon was rapidly gaining on Horsman, but could not catch him in the distance available, and Horsman had a fairly easy win. Denly took third place, in what was said to be one of the best handicap races.

Dixon must not have immediately left Brooklands, because on 25 March he was at the track for the first record breaking of the season. He set records for the standing start kilometre and mile in Class C (1000cc with sidecar) on the Harley-Davidson. For the kilometre record his mean speed was 64.41mph, with a speed in one direction of 65.5mph, and for the mile his mean speed was 50.9mph, with a best one way speed of 51.37mph. The faster speeds stood as British records, whilst the mean speed was a world record.

The BMCRC Easter meeting was held on 19 April. There was an enormous crowd, estimated at 8000 people. The rule against the pusher off pushing a machine over the foul line, thirty yards from the start, was enforced properly for the first time, and there were several disqualifications because of it.

Dixon's first race of the day was a five lap 1000cc scratch race on the Harley-Davidson. He led for four laps, and then burst a tyre at over 100mph on the Railway Straight, hanging on until the machine slowed right down, and then jumping off just as it toppled over. A T Koehler was in second place on a 976cc Zenith. He had been riding well, and moved into the lead. The only other riders to finish were Longman on a 989cc Harley-Davidson and Horsman on a 599cc Triumph, but they were disqualified for crossing the foul line at the start, and the race had the probably unique result of having a first place winner only from a field of six.

Dixon's next race of the day was the three lap Expert Handicap. There was a good field of ten riders, including Temple. Dixon had fitted a standard Harley-Davidson wheel to his machine with a great deal of effort, and was ready for the start. Dixon's race was short. On the first lap a stone got between the rear chain and the sprocket, jamming his transmission. It was not Dixon's day. Temple put up a spectacular performance, covering his second lap at 107mph, but the race was won by Maund on a 344cc Zenith, despite a magnificent battle between Bowles and Temple.

June 7 saw the BMCRC's Whitsun meeting. There had been no meeting in May because of a strike by the Brooklands riders. The Brooklands authorities had been under constant pressure from local residents over noise from the inception of the track. They had not wanted the track to be built back in 1907, and there were constant threats of injunctions. This caused the authorities to take a strict line with competitors over noise, although there was no precise definition of a noisy machine. The motorcycle racers felt particularly victimised, and rebelled when Dougal Marchant was refused permission to go on to the track on the grounds of excessive noise. The riders got together, and despite an offer from the BARC to observe at the meeting on 10 May to see if the machines were excessively noisy, the riders refused to race despite attempts to persuade them by 'Ebbie' Ebblewhite, the legendary starter and timekeeper. Dixon's part in all of this is not recorded, but it would seem likely that he would make his views known. The dispute was resolved by a compromise, and more precise regulations over silencers were introduced.

There were thirteen races for the Whitsun meeting. Dixon was entered for the five-lap 1000cc Solo Scratch race but failed to start. Temple won the race on a 996cc Montgomery – British Anzani. Dixon did not take part in any other race, and it may be that he was having serious mechanical problems. No explanation has been found for Dixon's failure to start.

Dixon's mount for the 1924 Sidecar TT was again a Douglas banking sidecar combination. Dixon had to do a last minute repair to a cracked frame lug, and was working on the machine as the riders lined up for the start. He made a good start despite this, and went into the lead, passing through Ramsey before anyone else had reached Sulby. Mist and rain began to descend on the mountain. Dixon went all out and completed his first lap to be greeted by roars of approval as he raced on, his spare tank enabling him to do several laps without stopping for fuel. Grinton on a Norton held second place until he had trouble with his controls, and had to continue by holding the throttle wire. Dixon's lead was sixteen seconds, his first lap time being 43 minutes exactly, a speed of 52.65mph. Tucker was third at the end of the second lap on a Norton, with Alexander fourth on a Douglas. Grinton dropped back, and Tucker moved into second place, but three minutes behind Dixon's flying Douglas.

Dixon's next lap (the fastest of the race) was completed at 53.23mph, a time of 42 minutes 32 seconds. Tucker's speed was 51.34mph. There was then a sensation, as Dixon stopped between Ballacraine and Sulby and Tucker passed him. Dixon struggled on for a short distance, but then retired at Kirkmichael with a broken piston. This was reported to be due to defective heat treatment of the piston. Most of the piston escaped through the exhaust, but Dixon struggled on for another half lap before giving up, a remarkable achievement. Alexander's Douglas also suffered engine failure.

On his third lap Tucker had a twelve minute lead over Taylor on an OEC, with Reed third on a DOT. Tucker came in to win, a popular victor. After such a brilliant start Dixon must have been bitterly disappointed. He would have been a certain winner if the machine had lasted and must have started favourite. It was not to be his last bad luck with a Douglas.

Dixon again had a Douglas mount for the Senior TT. Dixon later suggested that the Douglas company did not officially enter the TT in 1924 and that his was a private entry. It has not been possible to verify this. The competitors waited in a state of tension for the lightweights to start their race. Then the large machines were wheeled out. Dixon was cheered as he wheeled out his Douglas to the start. No doubt he had the sympathy of the crowd after the events of the sidecar race.

Alexander made the best start on a Douglas with a windscreen and a handlebar controlled wiper. Langman's Scott also made a good start, with a tremendous buzz from the engine. Dixon roared past the grandstand at over 75mph at the end of his first lap, a streak of black, yellow and aluminium. The reverberations of his engine could be heard as the machine was lost from view and roared up the straight to Ballacraine. From a standing start Dixon almost took the lap record at 35 minutes 31 seconds. Bennett was next on his Norton, then Wood on a Scott, then a bunch of riders within feet of each other. As Hassall and Emerson passed the grandstand their handlebars touched, and the crowd craned their necks to see the crash, which never came.

Out of the thirty-five starters in the race twenty-four completed the lap in less than forty minutes. Dixon's average speed was 63.75mph, with

Bennett's 62.23mph. The machines roared on over the mountainous and twisty course, bouncing on the poorly made roads, setting up exceptional times. Dixon remained in the lead over the second lap, which took him 36 minutes 30 seconds; slower than his first. Bennett was 1 minute 7 seconds behind, but at the end of his second lap Dixon was forced to stop. He maintained first place, whilst Bennett had trouble with his filler cap, forcing him to stop after every lap.

Dixon's third lap was completed in 36 minutes 21 seconds, at a speed of 63.23mph. Bennett was still second, but by half distance had lost his filler cap, and was no doubt blinded by fuel spray.

At Governor's Bridge on his fourth lap Dixon had a fall, caused by oil on the track dropped by another competitor, which had been covered by a layer of dust, and which Dixon was unlucky enough to be the first to encounter. He carried on, but slowly, having had a shaking, which caused a plug to oil. Dixon stopped to change the plug, but found that his bag of tools had disappeared, presumably having fallen off in his spill at Governor's Bridge. He had the frustrating experience of having two spare plugs fastened to his tank, but no means of fitting one, having for the first time raced without a spanner in his pocket. Bennett was still second with Langman third on a Scott and Shaw fourth on a Norton. Sheard, the Manxman, retired, to the disappointment of the locals.

Dixon was still riding as hard as he could on his fifth lap, despite the oiled plug but was passed by Bennett, who arrived at the pits first, and having started later than Dixon, had a good lead. Whalley's Douglas retired. Bennett stopped to refuel, but was quickly off into the race. Dixon appeared several minutes later, lying down flat behind his windscreen to gain speed.

On the final lap, spectators who could see the scoreboard concentrated on the discs showing the position of Bennett and Dixon, tracing their progress. A back marker in the form of Langman moved rapidly up the field on his Scott, and there were only five minutes between the first three riders. Bennett drew away on the last lap. He was at Craig-ny-Baa when Dixon was at the Bungalow. Langman moved into second place on time, having started several minutes later than Dixon. Bennett came home to victory, a popular winner, to be cheered. Dixon came in second on the road with a grin on his face, but Langman had second place on time.

Dixon found that a piston had completely disintegrated, and had been expelled through the exhaust pipe. Bennett had ridden a well planned race, staying within catching distance of Dixon until Dixon began to have mechanical problems in the form of the oiled plug. Clearly Dixon's promise in the race up to the fourth lap suggested he should have been victorious. Again Dixon was robbed of a deserved victory.

Dixon was back in action for sand racing at Saltburn. He raised the flying kilometre speed record to 101.68mph, the first time 100mph had been exceeded on sand. The record was to stand until 1926, when A Greenwood on a 998cc Brough Superior raised it to 105.52mph. Dixon came second in the 1-mile 1000cc event to Greenwood.

On Sunday 13 July the Belgian Grand Prix was held on the Spa Circuit, over the roads joining Francorchamps, Malmédy and Stavelot in the Belgian Ardennes. The weather was hot, which made the course very dusty. The course was 9.37 miles, with several difficult corners and some steep hills. There were effectively four races, the 500cc class, the 350cc class, the 250cc class and the 175cc class. No less than forty riders started, with the 500s going off first, then the 350s, 250s and the 175s leaving together. Dixon rode an Indian in the 500cc class, and at the end of the first lap was third to Burlage on a Norton, who led, and Stobart on a Sarolea. Dixon created a drama when a fuel pipe broke, causing a fire. He found that if he slowed down the flames became vertical and threatened him, but that if he kept up his speed the flames were swept away from him. Dixon roared on, with flame streaming from his machine, until his fuel was almost used up, then screamed into the pits and leapt from the blazing machine. The flames were extinguished, a repair was effected and Dixon set off in pursuit of the leaders. He could not catch them and the 500cc race was won by Alec Bennett on a Norton, with Bonvert second on a Sarolea and Whalley third on a Douglas. There were wins for other British riders in the other classes.

Dixon probably remained abroad, because on Wednesday 30 July he competed in the French Grand Prix, held over the new Lyon circuit, riding an Indian. British machines and riders were again well represented. Again, effectively, four races were run together, for 500cc, 350cc, 250cc and 175cc machines. Dixon rode in the 500cc Class. The 175cc machines had to cover 231.45 kilometres, the 250cc machines

277.74 kilometres, the 350cc machines 324.03 kilometres and the 500cc machines 370.32 kilometres.

The race started at 7.00am. At the end of the first lap Bennett passed his team-mate Hassall in front of the grandstand to take the lead, with Gramand third on a Peugeot and Dixon's Indian fourth. At the end of lap two Dixon still lay fourth, with Bennett leading the 500s at an average speed of 95.55kph, with Longman averaging 92kph in the 350cc class. Dixon stopped for a brief replenishment, amusing the French spectators with the size of his oil squirt. He then roared off.

A violent thunderstorm half way through the race drenched the course, making it treacherously wet. The race went on, and Dixon came in to second place in the 500cc class, behind Bennett. Bennett's time was 3 hours 54 minutes, and Dixon's 3 hours 59 minutes. Dixon cannot have been a serious challenge to Bennett. Crabtree on a Peugeot was third in this Class. Longman won the 350cc Class, which meant he had won the three premier races of the year, the TT, the Belgian Grand Prix and the French Grand Prix.

On 23 August the Ealing and District Motor Cycle Club again held its 200-mile sidecar races at Brooklands. The day was showery, but successful. Again the various classes were distinguished by the colours of their sidecars, the 350s blue, 600s red and the 1000s yellow. Dixon had a new Harley-Davidson and Bert Le Vack a Brough Superior of 996cc. There were nine starters, as they lined up at 1.00pm. From the start Le Vack and Dixon fought it out in front, exchanging first and second places.

On lap three Le Vack led but then the positions were reversed. Temple had taken up third place shortly after the start. This was very much a race of champions. Unfortunately, the champions were not to finish. On his tenth lap Le Vack had engine trouble when a piston broke, and he retired. Dixon led at 78.3mph, with Temple second and Allchin third. These three were well ahead of the pack. Temple had a flat tyre, and came in to replace the wheel, and was quickly away. Then Dixon retired with valve trouble, letting Allchin into first place. Temple lay second, with Humphreys third and Longman fourth.

There was an exciting duel between Temple and Allchin for the lead, which was brought to an end when Allchin retired with clutch trouble. Temple took the lead, but shortly afterwards was halted with another puncture, allowing Humphreys into the lead. Temple rejoined the race, but soon retired with further problems. Only Humphreys, Allchin and Longman were left in the race, and this was the final order. Several records were broken at the meeting, including the Class G three hour record by Humphreys.

Dixon did not take part in the 200-mile solo races in September, but was back at Brooklands on 11 October for the BMCRC Championship Meeting. The event was marred by rain and was partially postponed. Racing began at 1.00pm.

All races were scratch races over five laps. Le Vack was in France, as was Marchant. Dixon rode a Douglas in the 600cc sidecar championship, fitted with a very low bullet-shaped sidecar. Nine of the fourteen entrants started, and after the first lap Dixon was in the lead, only a yard ahead of Horsman on a Triumph. Both were well ahead of the third man, Judd, on a Douglas. However, the Douglases were soon in trouble, as first Dixon, then Judd and Jewitt, the other Douglas rider, pulled in to the enclosure with engines firing on only one cylinder, presumably caused by the wet state of the track. Horsman was first, over half a lap ahead of Tucker, the only other man to finish.

Dixon entered the 1000cc sidecar championship, although it is not clear what his mount was. On the third lap he was fourth, but he did not appear again among the leaders, and the race was won by Riddoch on a Zenith, with Temple second and Longman third. The rain grew worse, flooding the track, and the meeting was abandoned.

This wet and disappointing day brought to an end Dixon's season for 1924. It cannot have been a year from which Dixon drew much satisfaction. He had put up some exceptional performances, often leading by impressive margins, but had been defeated so many times by mechanical breakdown. He must have hoped for better in 1925.

1925

1925 saw new noise regulations at Brooklands. It was compulsory to have fishtail ends of specified dimensions on the exhaust. The first Bemsee meeting of the year was held on 21 March, but Dixon does not appear to have taken part. He did not take part in the first record breaking attempts of the year, or the second BMCRC meeting of the year on 11 April, the

Easter Meeting. There was more record breaking on 14 April, but without Dixon. There is no obvious explanation for his inactivity.

On 23 May the Ealing Club again held its 200-mile sidecar event. The weather was dull and threatened rain, and the crowd was small. Dixon took part in the 600cc sidecar event on a 596cc Douglas with sidecar, and set up a tremendous performance in the early stages. Very shortly after the start he had to swerve violently to avoid another competitor's assistant. This was in the wet, as a drenching shower of rain had fallen shortly before the race began. The sidecars for the 600cc class were painted red, as had become customary.

Dixon's tactics seemed to be to force the pace, to attempt to cause his main rivals to retire with mechanical faults, a dangerous tactic in view of the apparent fragility of the Douglas.

On lap twenty-one Staniland on a Norton briefly took the lead from Horsman, but Horsman was soon back in the lead, with Tucker on a Norton running third, and Dixon now fourth. Dixon had not been able to keep up the pace, and it may be that the Douglas was not performing as it should.

On his twenty-third lap Dixon went into the pits to replenish his fuel. This did not take long, but the engine refused to restart, and it took Dixon some time to make the necessary adjustment to get it going again, slipping further back in the running. Horsman and Staniland were drawing away from the rest of the field. After thirty laps Dixon was not in the first six. Horsman led, with Staniland second, Tucker third, Prestwich fourth, Anstice fifth and Munday sixth on a New Hudson. Horsman and Staniland continued to swap places. Tucker had to retire with problems with his sidecar chassis. It was then announced that Dixon had retired. The cause was not revealed.

Staniland was in the lead, and remained there without serious opposition when Horsman had to retire with piston trouble. Staniland rode on despite two broken front shock absorbers, and came in an easy winner, with Lawson second on a Sunbeam, and Munday third on a New Hudson. Dixon's decision to force the pace may not have been a wise one.

For 1925 Dixon entered the Junior, Senior and Sidecar TTs. Again his determined and dashing riding was marred by mechanical failure. Dixon was, of course, contracted to Douglas, and his mount in each race came from that company. There was a threat of rain as the machines were readied for the Junior race. The motorcycles were kept in a marquee after scrutineering, and were wheeled from there to the start at 11am. Twemlow, the winner of the Junior in 1924, was first off, misfiring slightly as he reached Bray Hill. Sheard rode a Douglas, and was cheered as he started, but Dixon received the largest ovation. Dixon set off at a fast pace, and was signalled at Sulby before Woods, who had left the start a minute before him on his Royal Enfield.

Twemlow took the lead followed by Porter, with Dixon close behind and going well. Twemlow was first through the start, but Dixon had gained two minutes on him to take the lead. Dixon's time for the first lap was 34 minutes 38 seconds, a lap record by twenty-seven seconds. Handley on a Rex-Acme did the lap in 34 minutes 39 seconds, just a second behind Dixon on time. 'Paddy' Johnston took third place on a Cotton.

Dixon was first through Sulby on the second lap, with Twemlow a few seconds behind. Dixon maintained his lead up to the Bungalow, again with Twemlow close behind, and Handley forging through the field.

At the end of his second lap Dixon pulled in for fuel and oil. This delayed him for only 1.5 minutes, and he roared off. Handley went in to replenish, and there was a buzz of excitement as his time was awaited, because he was obviously close to Dixon on time, and took less time to fill up. When the times were posted Handley had taken over the lead, with Dixon second and Simpson third on an AJS. Dixon had lapped at 65.37mph, with Handley only .03 of a second slower. Handley's time for both laps was astonishingly identical at 34 minutes 39 seconds. Dixon flashed through at the end of his third lap, waving to his supporters, but by this time he had dropped to third place, with Simpson second and Handley in the lead.

There was more bad news for Dixon's supporters, as it was reported that he had gone through Ramsey riding very slowly. His indicator remained at Ramsey. Handley was pressing on, despite a stuck marker board which indicated otherwise, and broke the lap record on his fourth lap at 34 minutes 23 seconds. He pulled in to replenish and change his fly-spattered goggles, and was rapidly away again. At the end of the fourth lap Dixon was not among the first six, with Handley first, Davies second on a HRD and Simpson third. Handley's lead over Davies was 2 minutes

27 seconds, and he looked a certain winner. Dixon's race was over, another retirement, although the cause is not known. Again the Douglas had proved unreliable, letting Dixon down after a brilliant start.

Handley came home to win, with Davies second and Simpson third. Handley's speed for the race was 65.02mph, a terrific performance for a competitor in the Junior. Dixon's cornering was said to be the fastest of the day, but it was Simpson who provided the great thrill when he entered into a terrific skid when his rear brake rod fell off. It was another disappointing outing for Dixon.

The sidecar race was again run immediately after the Lightweight event. Tucker, as the winner in 1924, was first off the line. Most of the riders, including Dixon on the banking sidecar, made a good start, and Dixon led on the first lap, completing it in 40 minutes 17 seconds. Hatton was second after the first lap, with a time of 40 minutes 29 seconds on a Douglas, with Parker third also on Douglas. On the second lap Langman, the favourite for the race, went out with gearbox trouble. Dixon went in to replenish his oil, but had only a short stop. He broke the lap record on the second lap at 39 minutes 36 seconds, a speed of 57.18mph.

The race was not entirely Dixon's. Parker on a Douglas was challenging him for the lead, with Tucker and Grinton close behind. Dixon could not afford to relax. At half distance Dixon was still in the lead, with Parker second and Taylor third on a Norton. Grinton had dropped back to fourth. Disaster was not far away for Dixon, as he was forced to retire at Laurel Bank with engine trouble. Parker, Grinton and Tucker battled it out for the lead, and Grinton soon took up a commanding position. Only seven seconds separated the first three riders at the end of the third lap. The first three flashed past the grandstand flat out over their tanks, as though in a Brooklands sprint. The race turned into one between Parker and Taylor, with the crowd carefully timing them as they battled for first place. It was Parker who came home first, with Taylor second and Grinton third.

Dixon had ridden another superb race, full of excitement and drama, particularly as his machine and sidecar leaped into the air at Ballig Bridge. Had Dixon's machine the stamina to finish the course, he would have been a very likely winner, in the light of his performance in the early stages of the race. No one could catch him as he streaked around the course. The unreliability of the Douglas had cost Dixon another race.

The weather for the Senior race threatened rain, but improved as the machines lined up for the start. 'Ebbie' Ebblewhite sent the riders off, with Bennett away first. He was first at Ballacraine, with Dixon there one and a half minutes later, and already challenging. Howard Davies passed Dixon on the mountain road, and then Dixon pulled in for adjustments. At the end of the first lap, Dixon was not in the first seven. All of the first seven bettered the lap record for the previous year's Senior. On the second lap Dixon's marker stuck at Ramsey for some moments, a depressing sight for his supporters. Simpson then broke the lap record at 32 minutes 50 seconds.

At the end of lap two Dixon was not in the first six. He never appeared among the leaders, and again was forced to retire after crashing in Parliament Square when his engine seized. The race was won by Howard Davies on a HRD-JAP, with Longman second on an AJS and Bennett third on a Norton. Howard R Davies was, of course, the creator of the HRD, and rode his machine to win at 66.13mph, a very good performance.

The race was a dismal affair so far as Dixon was concerned, with no real prospect of victory and a dramatic end when his engine seized. The 1925 TT season was one of disappointment for Dixon. He had again proved that he was able to make motorcycles travel very fast, and that he was a skilled and determined rider, capable of setting the pace in races. The TTs were marred by unreliable machines, unable to stand up to the pace Dixon set for them.

July 11 saw the very popular sand racing at Saltburn. Dixon was the winner of a Yorkshire Championship, although his mount is not known. He also was successful in the Welsh Sidecar TT and achieved fastest solo and sidecar times of the day at Kop Hill.

Dixon was at Brooklands on 15 August for the 200-Mile Solo races organised by the BMCRC. The weather was perfect, and a large crowd enjoyed exciting racing. There was a new scoreboard at the Fork, which helped spectators to follow the progress of the riders. The morning saw the combined race for the 250cc and 350cc machines (Class A and B), whilst the combined races for Class C and D (500cc and 1000cc) were held at 3.00pm. Dixon rode a Douglas in Class C. There was a tremendous battle over twenty laps between five of the stars of Brooklands racing, Horsman (Triumph), Dixon, Denly (Norton), Judd (Douglas) and the brilliant Le Vack on a HRD-JAP. The effect of this was a number of retirements when the machines could not stand the pace. By lap nineteen Dixon had taken second place to Judd, but by lap twenty-three Dixon was in the lead to Judd, with Le Vack third. Dixon then dropped out, although the cause is not known. Horsman took the lead, but then also dropped out, allowing Driscoll into the lead, and he came in to win, with Hough second on an AJS and Guyler third on a DOT. None of the stars who had set the initial pace was among the winners.

The Brooklands Championship meeting should have been held on Saturday 19 September, but was postponed because of bad weather, and was held on 10 October. Attendance was poor, although the racing was reasonably exciting. Dixon competed in Class F for 600cc machines with sidecar, on a Douglas. It was a one-man race, with Horsman assuming the lead from the start on his Triumph, and retaining it to the end, with Dixon following for the whole of the five laps, apparently without sufficient speed to catch Horsman. Dixon did manage to put some pressure on him, so Horsman could not relax, with Dixon three yards behind at the end of the first lap, 100 yards behind after four laps, and 75 yards behind at the finish. Tucker had gearbox trouble throughout and could not engage top gear. He did well to come in third. Horsman's winning speed was 80.89mph.

Dixon then took part in the race for 750cc machines, but had to ride the 596cc Douglas due to problems with his larger machine. He complained that the bike was unsuitably geared as the correct sprocket was not available. Walters on a Zenith-JAP led on the first lap, with Horsman second on his Triumph and Dixon third. Horsman put in a spectacular second lap at 103.11mph to gain the lead, which he battled for against Walters, and lost on the fourth lap. Walters came in an easy winner at 97.65mph.

Dixon was forced to ride the 596cc machine in the 1000cc event for which there were seven starters. Knight made a good start and led on the first lap on his Zenith-JAP. Wright lay second on a similar machine, with Dixon a creditable third on his much smaller Douglas. By the end of the second lap, Dixon had fallen some way behind, with Wright only just in the lead over Knight. On the next lap, Dixon had lost third place to Baldwin, and Wright eventually came home well in the lead, half a mile ahead of Knight, the second man, with Baldwin third, despite problems with his carburettor. The Championship Meeting ended just as darkness fell and a slight fog appeared over the track. Thirteen records were broken.

There was record breaking at Brooklands in October, with Dixon making an attempt in Class F on October 14th. Dixon rode a Douglas of 596cc with sidecar to take the records for the flying start five miles at 85.38mph, standing-start ten miles at 83.9mph, the flying start 5 kilometres at 137kph, the standing start 10 kilometres at 133.84kph and 50 kilometres at 135.84kph.

The final BMCRC Meeting of 1925 was held on 24 October. The weather was perfect again, but the crowd was small. There had been criticism that Brooklands, because of its size, did not provide a spectacle for the spectators. There were several aggregate cups, awarded for the performance of competitors over the season, not yet won, and there was every incentive for riders to compete hard. Dixon's performance was marked by a display of his characteristic unselfishness. Rex Judd had a spectacular accident when his machine fouled a footrest of Victor Horsman's mount at over 100mph. The two machines were locked together, then separated. Judd parted company with his machine, and was seen by the horrified spectators to be rolling along the track at high speed. He eventually came to a halt, and lay motionless on the unforgiving concrete. Dixon had been going splendidly and was in the lead, but sacrificed his chances of winning by stopping to assist Judd. Baldwin won the race, with Knight second, both on Zeniths. Judd had avoided serious injury, miraculously, thanks to his crash helmet and leathers.

Dixon, Horsman and Denly had a battle in the 500cc Solo Scratch Handicap, the three of them drawing ahead of the rest of the field. Denly was put out of the race when a rocker broke after six and a half laps. Dixon then slowed down, his engine misfiring, and Horsman took the lead. Dixon's machine cured itself temporarily and he was still a force in the race, but the misfiring recurred, and Horsman came in to win on his Triumph at 92.55mph, to take the Pullin Cup.

Dixon's consolation was to come first in the unlimited passenger handicap over Riddoch on a Zenith combination and Fitzgerald on a similar machine. Several records were broken. Unusually, and only because of the spectacular mishap Judd had suffered, the popular press reported the meeting. It was generally thought that motorcycle racing at Brooklands was ignored by the press, which even then was only interested in sensational drama, which Judd had provided.

The course could again be used for record breaking. On 27 October Dixon broke long distance records in Class F for machines up to 600cc with sidecar on a 596cc Douglas. He took the hour record at 74.07mph and several other records up to 200 miles at speeds up to 78mph. Not content with this, Dixon was back on 31 October with a 499cc Douglas to take records in Class C for solo machines up to 500cc. These included 50 kilometres at 150.925kph, 50 miles at 93.87mph, 100 kilometres at 143.42kph and one hour at 89.92mph. After completing the first 50 miles Dixon went into the pits and changed both sparking plugs, refuelled and was off again to take the hour record. Dixon's record breaking for the year continued on 13 November, when he set new records in Class F (600cc with sidecar) for the kilometre and the mile at 66.54mph and 71.51mph from a standing start.

An eventful racing year, although lacking any major wins for Dixon, was over. Speeds had risen over the year, despite the restrictions placed on riders and their machines, particularly to combat noise at Brooklands. There is no evidence that Dixon was not still a favourite of the crowds, despite his lack of a major win. He had led in several races until put out by mechanical failure, and the crowds loved Dixon's riding style, full of excitement, drama and determination. Dixon's reputation did not depend on final results, but on the thrilling performances he put up as he battled to win whatever the circumstances, and on his abilities as a tuner. Dixon and his supporters, of which there were many, could look forward to 1926 with new anticipation, although it was a year which contained many difficulties.

1926

The year 1926 began with Dixon's marriage on Tuesday 19 January to Margaret (Dolly) Thew, a native of Middlesbrough. St. Barnabas's Church was emblazoned with a sign pronouncing 'Flying Start' and Dixon's home with one announcing 'Finish'. Several well-known motorcycle racers were there, including Rex Judd and Reuben Harveyson. Handley sent a message of congratulation. The best man was fellow motor dealer and TT

Dixon's wedding on 19 January 1926 was attended by the cream of the Brooklands two-
wheeled racing fraternity, including (to his right) Dougal Marchant and Rex Judd and
(towering over his left shoulder) the incomparable Bert Le Vack.

racer, Stan Jones. Dixon and his bride departed for a motoring
honeymoon in Devon and Cornwall.

The marriage may not have been successful in the long term. However,
Dolly did support Dixon in his racing exploits, and preferred to travel to
the circuits to watch her husband than to sit at home waiting for a
possibly devastating phone call. She had enormous faith in his abilities as
a driver and engineer, which comforted her in the belief that Dixon would
leave nothing undone which affected his safety.

When Dixon later acquired his first racing car Dolly was persuaded to
travel in it. She displayed her innocent lack of knowledge of machinery

when looking at the rev counter, which registered 40, she told Dixon that the car was not very fast and pointed out that his own car would reach 40. They were in fact doing about 80mph, but to Dolly there was just fast and slow. She had no enthusiasm for the workings of cars. Her preoccupation was her husband's safety, tempered by her understanding of his need to win.

The couple had one child, a daughter called Jean who seems to have been born in the year of their marriage. Although when she was eight her mother described her as her father's greatest fan, the sad fact seems to be that she and her father drifted apart. Jean later emigrated to South Africa.

Locke-King, the creator of Brooklands, died in January 1926. He left a troubled course, with increasing resentment over noise from local residents, increasing the pressure for more effective silencers, which riders and manufacturers felt affected performance. Also, in 1926 the ACU banned the use of alcohol fuel for the Isle of Man TT races. Manufacturers were unwilling to make the necessary changes to carburation and compression ratios to allow their machines to compete first in road races, then at Brooklands. Alcohol was the favourite fuel, as it assisted cooling and increased performance. If the bikes were modified to run in the TT, tuners, including no doubt Dixon, were unwilling to make all the necessary changes to run at Brooklands. Riders then tended to fall into two camps, track racers and road racers, although Dixon continued to race in both, presumably because he had the Douglas company behind him.

1926 saw new economic gloom, and the General Strike. This all affected the motor cycle industry. J A Prestwich Ltd, manufacturers of the JAP engine, announced they were pulling out of motor racing. Bert Le Vack decided to concentrate his efforts at Montlhéry. There was a general atmosphere of gloom around at the beginning of the season in 1926.

Dixon did not take part in the first BMCRC meeting on 20 March, which was held in freezing weather. The weather had very much improved for the second meeting of the year at Brooklands on 11 April. There was a good programme of eleven races. Dixon rode a Douglas in the five-lap scratch event for machines up to 1000cc. Wright enhanced his growing reputation by leading from the start and coming in first on his large Zenith. His speed was 108.51mph, the fastest speed at which a

Brooklands event had been won. Dixon's Douglas ran badly for the first two laps, putting him out of the leaders, but the machine recovered, and Dixon at least had the satisfaction of completing the distance. Patchett was second on a McEvoy and Knight third on a Zenith.

Dixon rode the old TT Douglas in a three-lap handicap in classes C, D and E. He had a remarkable escape when a lower shacklepin in the forks broke at almost 100mph. Dixon had become a master of self survival in such situations, and after hanging on to the machine for about a quarter of a mile, flung himself off, seeing that a crash was inevitable. He escaped what could have been a horrifying incident with only cuts and bruises. Patchett won the race on his McEvoy, with Quinn second on a Triumph and Gibson third on a Sunbeam. Dixon, no doubt shaken, did not compete further that day. His motorcycle may have been a victim of the notorious and deteriorating Brooklands surface.

1926 was not as active a year as those which had gone before. Dixon was still very much involved with the Douglas company, and was concerned with the development of its products. No doubt part of his involvement was in promoting Douglas's products on the track, but Dixon's results so far on Douglas machines may have discouraged too much exposure. Dixon's reputation as a tuner of motorcycles for races remained unsurpassed. It was recognised that Dixon could always gain the extra vital few miles per hour from a machine which made the difference between success and failure. It was no doubt this reputation which encouraged the Douglas organisation to retain his services. There was no doubt that a Dixon-tuned and ridden motorcycle was formidable opposition in competition and Dixon would inevitably have won more races had the machines stood up better to the stresses imposed by racing.

Dixon competed in the Junior and Senior Isle of Man TT races, but without great success. The Junior race, as was customary, took place first in the series. There was no sidecar race, which had been discontinued after the 1925 race. The reason is not obvious, but it may have been that the race was felt to lack spectacle. It was unfortunate, because Dixon undoubtedly excelled at sidecar racing, and had shown this by his record breaking attempts with sidecar combinations.

The day of the Junior race dawned with brilliant sunshine, but clouded over as the Island was inclined to do. Mist gathered on the mountain as

'Ebbie' Ebblewhite began to line the machines up for the race. Handley, the winner in 1925, held the prime, but lonely, position on the central square of the grid before Ebbie sent him off first. The race was over 264 miles. There was immediate excitement as Twemlow fell off on the first lap, but was quickly away again on his HRD. The Douglas machines, including Dixon's, showed a reluctance to start. One by one the machines roared. Handley held his lead, and broke the lap record for a standing start. Bennett was next to complete the first lap, stopping for ten seconds to refuel, but lay third to Simpson, who had started later. Dixon was lying fourth, with a lap speed of 63.8mph, against Handley's 65.88mph on a Rex-Acme.

Handley had a good second lap, but Bennett was catching him. Dixon rode without goggles or gloves. He had a 55 second stop for fuel on his second lap. Dixon retained his fourth position on the second lap, with Simpson leading, Handley second and Simpson third on an AJS. Alec Bennett then took over the lead on his Velocette. Dixon's progress was seen to be relatively slow, as marked around the course by his indicator. Handley was experiencing mechanical troubles, and Bennett was building up a good lead. Dixon remained in fourth position. On the sixth lap Bennett had an eight minute lead over Dixon and Simpson, Dixon having moved briefly into third place behind Bennett and Simpson. Handley, with damaged gears, had dropped to fourth place.

Bennett created a sensation when it was announced that his speed over six laps was faster than that of the winner in the Senior in the year before. Dixon and Simpson were battling for second place, creating one of the most exciting duels of the race. On his last lap Simpson had a lead over Dixon, but was nine minutes behind Bennett, who had ridden a remarkable race. The last lap was a procession, with Bennett the convincing leader. Dixon had slipped back to fourth place, Handley having moved rapidly up into third place behind Simpson and Bennett. Bennett, the 29-year-old Irishman, with a reputation as the best long distance road racer, came in to win. Simpson was second, Handley third and Dixon fourth. The Velocette team won the team prize. Dixon had a disappointing race, but had been a serious challenger throughout. Bennett was a formidable opponent, and had the superior machine, although Velocette's history was mainly associated with two-stroke

machines, until it produced the overhead camshaft model which Bennett
had ridden so well.

Next came the Senior race. It was a cool and misty morning, but
visibility on the mountain was good. Howard Davies, the winner in 1925
rode again, and there was clearly going to be a battle between him and
Handley. Dixon again rode a Douglas, having spent a sleepless night
repairing a broken valve and its consequences. Dixon had problems on the
first lap. Simpson broke the lap record from a standing start, a remarkable
achievement. After the first lap Dixon was not in the first six, and he very
soon retired at Ballig. Dixon later blamed his demise on a gudgeon pin,
which he found was oversize. He had worked on the machine for months,
he said, and for once his careful attention to detail had failed. Woods won
the race on his Norton with Handley second on a Rex-Acme and Longman
third. It was a very disappointing race for Dixon, having retired so early,
and clearly having had problems almost from the start.

Dixon did not take part in the 1926 Brooklands 200 mile solo or sidecar
races. He did take part in the BMCRC Grand Prix races on 9 October, the
closing race of the season for the Bemsee. A Grand Prix circuit of 1.7 miles
was improvised at Brooklands with the start on the Finishing Straight. It
provided an exciting day's racing. Dixon had success in the 600cc sidecar
race on a 596cc Douglas with sidecar, winning at 50.38mph, faster by a
narrow margin than George Patchett's time in the 1000cc sidecar event.

Dixon took various records in 1926. On 27 October he took the world
records for Class F (600cc machines with sidecar) over two, three and four
hours, as well as the records for 100 miles and 200 miles, all on Douglas
machines of 596cc. For the two hour record he covered 155 miles 90 yards,
with 231 miles 1482 yards for the three hour record and 282 miles 389
yards for the four hour record, all very good speeds.

Dixon would ride again for Douglas in 1928, his last year as a
competitor on two wheels, but 1926 brought an end to his main period
of riding for Douglas. It may be a harsh judgement to describe this
period as 'The Wasted Years', and the reader must judge for himself
whether it is properly described in this way. The fact is that Dixon was
repeatedly beaten by the failure of his mount to complete the distance,
and it will be seen that his return to the Douglas fold in 1928 was not
universally approved.

CHAPTER FIVE

1927 – THE HRD YEAR

Dixon abandoned Douglas for the 1927 season. His mount in the TT was to be the HRD. He also rode Brough Superiors at Brooklands. Whether Dixon had fallen out with Douglas is not clear. He may have been disillusioned by the failures he had suffered on Douglas machines, losing races because of mechanical failure when victory was within his grasp. We know that Dixon had ceased temporarily to work on the development side of Douglas's product by this time. There appears to have been a major rift, but we shall see that it was later healed.

A happy gathering after victory in the 1927 Junior TT. To left and right of the winning HRD-JAP stand Howard R Davies, the manufacturer, and Fred Dixon, the victorious rider. Seated far left are Alec Bennett and Jimmy Simpson, two other TT giants.

The life of the HRD company was short but spectacular, and was crowned by Dixon's success in the 1927 Junior TT on a HRD 350. HRD was the creation of Howard Raymond Davies, still very much alive when his obituary was printed in *Motor Cycling* on 1 May 1927. Davies, described as an intrepid airman had crashed behind German lines, and survived a second air crash within two months. Before the war Davies had established himself as a rider of ability and courage. In 1914 he was a member of the winning Sunbeam team in the Senior TT, finishing joint second with Oliver Godfrey. On his return from the war Davies took a job with the firm of Amac, carburettor manufacturers, as a sales representative, but then in 1921, was employed by AJS as racing manager. In 1921 Davies became the only man to win the Senior TT race on a 350cc (AJS) machine, but then fortune deserted him, and he had several years of defeat through mechanical problems. Davies may have decided that the solution was to produce a motorcycle himself, to his own high standards, and in 1924 HRD Motors Ltd was created, based in Heath Town, Wolverhampton. This was actually a converted house, and was quite unsuitable. E J Massey was enlisted to help with the design of the new HRD machine. Massey had been involved with the rival firms of Massey and Massey Arran. Davies booked space at the 1924 London Olympia Show, and his three models created a sensation. The machines boasted a seven inch front brake and an eight inch rear brake, with JAP engines. The whole design was attractive and well built. Davies entered the 1925 TT, coming second himself, and his team-mate Harry Harris fifth, in the Junior. In the Senior he was beaten by Alec Bennett, but mainly due to Bennett's superior pit organisation. Bert Le Vack broke various records at Brooklands on a 500cc HRD in 1925. The marque was rapidly establishing itself, and was advertised by the slogan *Leaders in Design and Speed*. More suitable premises had been found, again in Wolverhampton, and production was ten or fifteen machines per week. A TT Replica was advertised.

Davies must have seen the obtaining of Dixon's services in 1927 as a major promotional coup, as Dixon was a national figure. Dixon's first step was to adapt his racing machines to his own specification, by fitting the footboards which he favoured, together with a windscreen and a backrest for the saddle.

Dixon's racing activity in 1927 was not as prolific as in previous years. He may have had other interests, but he entered again for the Junior and Senior TT. The weather for the race was perfect as G L Reynard, number one, took up his position in the first square. The riders set off at half-minute intervals. After the first lap Dixon lay in second place to Handley (Rex-Acme). Handley's time for the lap was 33 minutes 11 seconds, with Dixon's time at 34 minutes 9 seconds. Dodson lay third on a Sunbeam. Dixon was riding a fast and uneventful race. He was still in second place on the second lap, again behind Handley, by 1 minute 22 seconds. Bennett on a Velocette had moved into third place. Handley did not stop for fuel at the end of his third lap, causing comment. He then crashed, bending his footrest, but not damaging himself, and continued. Dixon continued his dogged race in second place. At the end of the third lap Handley was still in the lead, Dixon was second and Bennett remained the third man.

The procession of the first three continued on the fourth lap, and the positions were unaltered at its end. On the fifth lap Bennett retired with engine trouble and was replaced by Simpson on an AJS. The first two positions were unchanged. Dixon may have been reconciling himself to second place. The indicator system was malfunctioning, and it was difficult to follow the race from the grandstand. It did show that Handley had remained at Kirkmichael and that Dixon had moved to Craig-na-Baa. Then Dixon was shown at Governor's Bridge. The crowd rose to cheer as Dixon flashed past, a popular winner. It transpired that Handley had retired at Ballaugh, but he was reticent about the cause. H J Willis was second on a 348cc Velocette, but was 10 minutes 45 seconds behind Dixon, such was the strength of Dixon's, and the unfortunate Handley's, position. Simpson came home third on the AJS. Dixon's wife witnessed his victory, and was said to be delighted. Dixon had achieved his ambition to win a solo TT. His greatest ambition then, and one he was not to achieve, was to win the Senior TT, but he had established now the first two victories which would make him the only man to win the TT on two, three and four wheels. He had also shown that given a machine capable of finishing, he was a winning rider.

The weather for the Senior was unpromising, with mist on the mountain. Mainwaring on a Scott took up the number one position. There were fifty-seven entrants, and fifty-one left the line. As Dixon started the band played the hymn tune which had been sung at the

MIDDLESBROUGH   & DISTRICT
MOTOR   CLUB
CLUB TEAM PRIZE   SENIOR T.T. RACE
WINNERS   1927

J. GUTHRIE, 2ND

F. W. DIXON, 6TH   R. F. PARKINSON, 15TH

Middlesbrough and District Motor Club was proud of its local heroes, and of Dixon in particular. In 1927 they published this commemorative postcard of the M&DMC Senior TT Club Team prize winners.

presentation for his Junior victory. Dixon must have started as a popular favourite. Howard Davies competed on one of his own machines. At the end of the first lap Woods lay first on his Norton, with Dixon second, 53 seconds behind, and Simpson third.

The road had dried, and cornering speeds were rising. Despite this, Dixon's second lap was 18 seconds slower than his first, although he still lay second, with Woods in the lead, and Simpson third. Dixon was described as going like a madman to catch Woods, but without effect. As Dixon descended Bray Hill on his second lap at over 90mph he hit a bump, skidded broadside and jumped several feet into the air, calmly straightening out and passing a competitor as though he was touring.

At the end of the third lap Dixon still lay second behind Woods on his Norton, with Bennett third, also on a Norton. Woods was lapping well within the previous lap-record speed. Bennett was riding fast, completing his fourth lap in 32 minutes 44 seconds. Dixon was slowing down. His fourth lap took 40 minutes, and he was rapidly losing his lead over Bennett. Wood's pointer stuck, and Bennett took the lead. It was then reported that Dixon had lost his gear lever, but was continuing. Bennett retained the lead over Spann on a Sunbeam and Simister on a Triumph third. This remained the position for the fifth and sixth laps. Bennett came in to win at the record average speed of 68.41mph, despite the wet and treacherous roads in the early stages. Guthrie was second on a New Hudson, with Simister third on his Triumph, Dixon limped home into sixth place, having suffered serious problems with his gear change mechanism. It was an achievement simply to have finished in those circumstances.

Dixon was guest of honour when he and Davies returned to Wolverhampton and climbed on to the balcony of the Victoria Hotel to receive the ovation of a crowd of two thousand. The police band played as the winning machine was paraded on the back of a lorry. Dixon was reported to have said:

'I want to dispel an illusion about the terrible strain of riding in the TT. If there had been another ten laps I might have begun to feel a bit groggy, but riding an HRD machine, I finished the seven laps and I finished perfectly fresh. It has been my life's ambition to win a solo race, and I have been trying for fifteen years, and I want to thank Mr Davies publicly for building the machine that has enabled me to realise that ambition.'

Davies is reported to have said:

'It is a great thing to have made a machine that will stand up to the thrashing Freddy (sic) gives them.'

Despite the publicity attracted by Dixon's success and the undoubted quality of its product, the HRD company was not to survive 1927. It displayed its 1928 models at the Olympia Show of 1927, but by the time the show was over, the company was in liquidation. We can only speculate on what Dixon might have achieved if the company had continued.

August saw Dixon in action in the Hutchinson Hundred at Brooklands, riding a Brough Superior, but he crashed after only one lap. The race was

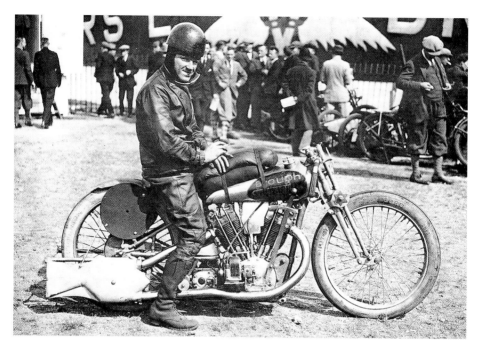

The splendid one-off ex-George Brough, Le Vack, Mavrogordato 996cc Brough Superior used in
1927 by Dixon, seen here astride it at Brooklands (27 August, Hutchinson 100 – ret.). Later ran
in the September Speed Trials at Arpajon, where he unofficially (timing strip failure) exceeded
130mph on three occasions. Note concealed carburettors and ingenious hand-change gear
linkage to the horizontal Sturmey-Archer gearbox. Peter Lancaster is the present-day owner.

won by Willis on a 348cc Velocette, with Ventura second on a Cotton-
Blackburne, and Longman third on a Harley-Davidson.

Dixon also rode a Brough Superior to establish new records for Class G
(1000cc and sidecar) on 26 October. He took the five kilometres at
103.25mph, the standing start ten kilometres at 97.24mph and the flying
start five miles at 103.05mph.

The BMCRC held its annual dinner at the Connaught Rooms, London
on Friday 16 December. Special Gold Star Badges were presented to those
who had lapped Brooklands at over 100mph. Dixon received his Gold Star,
along with several others, including Rex Judd, Le Vack, Claude Temple
and Tommy Allchin.

Dixon's year ended on a high note, but above all, it had seen him
achieve his ambition to win a TT on two wheels.

CHAPTER SIX

1928 – THE RETURN TO DOUGLAS

W hen Cyril Pullin left Douglas in 1928 Dixon was persuaded to return to the company as a development engineer. This meant that he also rode for the Douglas company in 1928. The HRD organisation had, of course, gone into receivership, and it may be that Dixon had little option other than to return to Douglas. It was not a move which was met with much enthusiasm by Dixon's followers and supporters, who remembered 'The Wasted Years'.

It was reported that by this time Dixon was living in Bristol, paying occasional visits home. One press report commented:

It is doubtful, however, if his admirers are wildly enthusiastic at his decision to return to the Douglas fold.

Bad luck dogged Dixon during virtually the entire period of his partnership with the flat twin. Admittedly he got more out of the engine than any other expert who handled it, but the fact remains that he failed repeatedly to go the full distance of either road or track events.

It was reported that Dixon had not lost his faith in the flat twin. He was reported to have said:

It can be got right, and once right, will wipe the track with the one lungers.

It must be remembered that Dixon was very much involved in the development of the Douglas product and he said that he had to take at least some responsibility for the apparent mechanical frailty of the machines. It may be that the flat twin was fundamentally flawed when disposed fore-and-aft in the frame, and that the technology of the day was better suited to singles. However, Dixon and Douglas persevered with the engine layout with which Douglas was so closely associated Dixon's contract required him to ride only for Douglas. He could not ride the Brough Superior he had ridden in 1927, and this was regretted by his admirers. The machine was returned to George Brough, but only after the enthusiasts of Middlesbrough had been exhorted by the press to examine it, an invitation which would not find favour with Dixon. Because of the fire in 1927, Douglas had not competed in the TT for that year. Dixon became heavily involved in developing the machines for the 1928 Senior and Junior TTs. He said that there would not be time to produce anything radically new, but it was expected that Dixon would prepare the machine in his usual meticulous way. It is believed that the machines Dixon prepared were not the new overhead cam designs, which were insufficiently developed. Dixon had faith in the 1926 ohv engine.

Dixon did not, it seems, race at Brooklands in 1928. This may be because he was too heavily engaged at the Douglas works, or that Douglas was not prepared to supply machines for Brooklands, because of the fuel problems. Dixon's racing in 1928 was exclusively concerned with the TT.

The Junior was run in perfect weather on Monday 30 June. It was so hot that the tarmac melted, and this caused problems for the riders. It was a colourful sight, with bunting at the start and brightly dressed riders and shining machines. Every vantage point was black with people long before the official car closed the road. The playing of the National Anthem announced the arrival of the Governor of the Isle of Man. Paddy Johnston was first away as the maroon went off at 10.00am. At the end of the first lap Sunbeams ridden by C J P Dodson and Arcangeli were in the lead. By the end of the second lap Bennett led on a Velocette, with Simpson second on an AJS and Arcangeli third. There was no sign of Dixon among the first six. A large number of machines could not stand the pace, and dropped out. Only the Royal Enfield team survived intact. Norman Black fell near Kirkmichael, and broke an arm. Frank Longman dropped out after thirteen miles with mechanical problems. Still Dixon was not among the leaders. His presence seems to have made no impact upon the race at all, and only his name in the record books shows that he took part. It may be that the machine had mechanical problems, or it may be that it was simply not competitive.

Bennett led at the end of the third lap, with Simpson second and Willis third on a Velocette. Bennett was riding fast, and broke the lap record several times. He still led at the end of the fourth lap, but Willis had taken over Simpson's position, and Arcangeli had moved back into third place. There was a scare on the third lap when it was reported that Arcangeli had suffered serious injury. It transpired that he was stunned, but not seriously injured. He was out of the race. Bennett pulled into the pits at the end of his fifth lap, but was quickly away. He had lapped at 70.28mph.

Bennett was well ahead at the end of the sixth lap. Willis lay second and Twemlow third on a DOT. Simpson had retired. Bennett came home a popular winner, with Willis second and Twemlow third. It was then the fastest Junior ever. Twenty-one finished, with Dixon eighteenth. Bennett's time was 3 hours 50 minutes 52 seconds whilst Dixon's was a poor 4 hours 45 minutes 33 seconds. Dixon's failure to show his usual form is inexplicable, except in terms of his mount being inadequate.

In contrast to the Junior, the Senior was run in the wet. It was the slowest Senior which had been run up to then. Brockbank was first away on a Cotton. Langton made the best start. Bennett, the Junior winner, was cheered as he left. At the end of the first lap Simpson was in the lead on an AJS, with Craig second on a Norton and Simcock's Sunbeam third. Simpson's lap time was 33 minutes 20 seconds.

On the second lap Dixon's marker on the scoreboard stuck. He had fallen at the Gooseneck after a skid in the wet, and was discussing matters with J W Shaw who had also fallen from his Norton. Bennett was having trouble with his machine, and was stuck on his first lap. The fatal 'R' appeared next to the names of Dixon and Shaw. Presumably their discussions had ended in a decision to retire. It must be assumed that Dixon's machine was damaged beyond repair, as it is unlikely that Dixon would be deterred merely by a fall and a wet course. Simpson led after the second lap, with Craig second and Simcock third. Dodson took over the lead on the third lap on a Sunbeam, with Simcock now in second place. Dixon was no doubt a discouraged and disappointed observer of the damp scene. Dodson came home to win with a time of 4 hours 11 minutes 40 seconds, with Rowley second on an AJS and Hatch third on a Scott.

It was a disappointing result for Dixon on what proved to be his last appearance on two wheels in the Isle of Man.

Dixon continued his involvement with the Douglas company, but disappeared from view until he reappeared when his interest in four wheel racing was awakened. A Douglas machine never appeared among the first three in any subsequent TT.

Part Two
The Motor Racing Years

A smartly dressed Dixon in his Riley Six, ready for the
1934 BRDC International 500.

CHAPTER ONE

PREPARATIONS

Fred Dixon never lost his love of speed and excitement, nor his self-confidence and supreme engineering skills. When his thoughts turned to car racing, typically he thought that manufacturers involved would flock to his door to secure his services. Equally typically, Dixon was not deterred by the indifference of the established racing manufacturers such as Alvis, whose only response to a request for a works car was a polite refusal, not necessarily politely received, and the suggestion that he lay out £700 or £800 to purchase a car from the company.

Dixon, as we have seen, ended his motorcycling career in 1928. He had a successful car dealership in Middlesbrough, managed mainly by his brother Frank, and he had made some money from motorcycle racing. In addition, he had earned a formidable reputation as an engineer, and on his retirement from motorcycle racing had gone, as we know, to the Douglas factory at Bristol. There he was concerned with the development of motorcycles, which he tackled with his usual verve and vigour. By 1930 he was worn out, probably bored, and looking for new horizons. These new horizons consisted mainly of taking a sabbatical. Dixon contemplated returning to two wheels, but decided that at the age of thirty-eight he did not have the stamina or strength for it, although one may wonder at this. Setting aside 'a fairly substantial packet of rupees', he was to say, labelled 'amusement only' Dixon looked for a cure for the blues. All of this was from Dixon's much later account, and a degree of embellishment cannot be discounted. He was to say that this was a 'stag interlude' without his family. Whether his family was with Dixon in Bristol is not recorded, but whatever the domestic situation, Dixon's plans for 1930 did not include his wife and daughter. In his article 'My Plunge into Car Racing' published in *The Autocar* in 1945, Dixon described how he prepared a list of places to visit. According to him, he stuck a pin in the list to decide where to go next. One trip was to Paris. The history of the Paris trip is not recorded, except that it was in the company of Geoff Daybell. No doubt it was memorable for Dixon, and the barkeepers of Paris. Dixon's knowledge of how to enjoy himself was surpassed only by his driving and mechanical skills

Also on the list was the 1930 Ards Tourist Trophy race in Belfast. A little more is known about the Ards trip. Between Paris and Belfast, said Dixon, he continued to stick pins in the list and to have a good time. In August 1930 Dixon found himself, again with Daybell, heading for Ulster.

Motor racing has been illegal on public roads in England almost from the dawn of motoring history. It was this lack of facilities to develop the infant motor car that led H F Locke-King to provide the nation with Brooklands in 1907. There was no law that allowed the closing of public roads for racing, although the police might turn a blind eye to small local events like hill climbs. The law was different on the Isle of Man and in Ulster, and there roads could be closed for motor sport. The Isle of Man was, of course, used for the motorcycle TT, and was the scene of triumphs by Dixon on two and three wheels. In 1927 Harry Ferguson, (later the tractor magnate) then chairman of the Ulster Auto Club, and Wallace McLeod, head of the motor engineering department of the Ulster Technical College, travelled to Brooklands, and obtained promises from several prominent racing drivers that they would support a race in Ulster if a course could be found.

The Tourist Trophy for cars had not been run since 1922. A party from the Royal Automobile Club travelled to Ulster to make an inspection of the proposed Ards circuit. The race was to be run by the RAC, although detailed organisation was left to the Ulster Race Committee. The circuit chosen was a tortuous thirteen and two thirds of a mile route, taking in the streets of Dundonald, Newtonards and Comber, with a combination of fast straights and difficult bends. The first bend was Quarry Corner, of which we will hear more later. A system of handicapping operated throughout the series, refined as the years went on. The theoretical object was to allow cars of different capacities to finish together. The apparent leader might not be the actual leader, and the race was robbed of the drama of a mass start. Following the progress of the race was therefore difficult.

The first of the series was held in 1928, and won by Kaye Don. The winner of the 1930 race was Tazio Nuvolari, driving a supercharged Alfa Romeo. Campari was second on a similar car, and Varzi third, again on an Alfa Romeo. Dixon witnessed this crushing Alfa victory.

The journey to the circuit proved exciting. Dixon and Daybell travelled in Daybell's 30/98 Vauxhall, a prospect which Dixon found more exciting than travelling in his own Essex saloon, which he said looked as though it had strayed from a funeral procession.

Dixon was not disappointed by the journey with Daybell at the wheel, Dixon beside him, no doubt urging him on to drive as fast as possible. On the way home, whilst Daybell was driving flat out, a heavily built policeman signalled to them to stop. Daybell asked what he should do. Dixon, for once showing regard for authority, advised him to stop. The officer took Daybell's details, accusing him of excessive speed. As they set off the officer shouted that Daybell had not told him the make of his car. 'An Austin Seven' shouted Daybell. He heard nothing more about the incident. Perhaps a sceptical senior officer doubted whether an Austin Seven was capable of the speed complained of.

On arriving at the circuit, Dixon, who knew little of high performance racing cars, carefully inspected the cars in the paddock. For the race he stationed himself on the inner part of the circuit, so that he could run from corner to corner to take in as much as possible of the technique involved. Dixon was not impressed. His view was that in his own Essex he could do better than the (in some cases) famous drivers he had observed. It is doubtful whether at this stage Dixon could have beaten Nuvolari, probably the greatest ever, but the seeds were sown.

After the race, Dixon returned to Middlesbrough, resolved to concentrate on his business, and on developing a four cylinder motorcycle he had designed. Sadly, the bike never reached production.

At about this time Dixon met up with one Len Ainslie, a marine draughtsman and trials rider, with a passion for cars. Ainslie assisted with the drawings for the motorcycle. The Depression was affecting trade of all kinds, including, presumably, Dixon's trade at Park Garage Middlesbrough, and he began to run out of money for the motorcycle project. Dixon's thoughts turned more and more to car racing, and it may be that this was partly inspired by the need to make extra money, although it is difficult to believe that even a winning team made much hard cash from motor racing in the 1930s. Dixon claimed to have made money at motorcycle racing, despite his post-race excesses.

Disregarding warnings and observations from others, perhaps including his wife, and with reservations because he could not accept failure, Dixon began to look around for a car. As we have seen, he did not receive the rapturous reception expected. Dixon had been a brilliant and successful motorcyclist, but to the car world he had nothing obvious to offer. These were the days of the wealthy amateur, where a rich man might pay his own expenses just to drive in a race. Very few had contracts with a team. Men like Malcolm Campbell and Lord Howe were typical of the wealthy and famous who raced only for fun and excitement.

1932

Dixon had a Riley agency at his Middlesbrough garage. He respected these cars, and he knew that the Brooklands Nine had done well. By the time Dixon had been rejected by the companies he had approached, and arrived at this train of thought, it was spring 1932. He had to move fast to compete in the 1932 (Car) TT, which was to be held on the Ards circuit in August. Entries had to be in by June.

The Riley company, along with many famous makes, was based in Coventry, and Dixon travelled there in June 1932. As an agent of the company he was, he felt, entitled to access to the factory and to the Riley family, who owned the company until its crash in 1938. By this time the company was in the midst of preparing its entries for the TT. Having hung around the factory for two days, without meeting anyone with the power to help him, Dixon made the acquaintance of a man called Pritty, of Glacier Metals, who supplied the Riley company with bearing materials. Dixon had intended to gain access to Victor Riley, head of the company, and the eldest of the Riley brothers. Pritty advised him instead to talk to Percy Riley, who ran engine production. Percy Riley was a talented engineer, and a man Dixon could admire. It is surprising that Dixon did not himself think of making this approach. Percy Riley had designed the high camshaft, crossflow hemispherical head 1100cc Nine engine, which was to play an important part in the history of the Riley company. Dixon was introduced by Pritty merely as an agent of the company. Racing plans were not mentioned. He was shown around the plant by Percy Riley himself, and saw some engines which caught his attention. They were 1100cc Nine engines in preparation for the TT. Riley confided that he had been asked to provide five engines, but had built eight.

Dixon went to the plant the next day, and asked for, and no doubt demanded, an interview with Victor Riley. This was promised for later in the day. Hours dragged by and eventually Dixon was told that Victor Riley had left the office and would not return that day. Dixon, volatile as he was, no doubt exploded. It is easy to imagine that the staff were treated to his invective, delivered in a broad north country accent. Whatever he said appears to have worked. A 'phone call was made to Riley's home, a call in which Dixon insisted on taking part. Riley, who knew, presumably, of Dixon as a motorcycle racer, and perhaps as an agent, agreed to return to the plant.

The day was not yet won. Victor Riley made it clear that he would not give Dixon a works car for the TT. Four cars were entered: for Captain George Eyston, Cyril Whitcroft, Chris Staniland and AWK von der Becke, later Riley's competition manager. There was to be a fifth engine (Victor Riley did not know of the eight that had been prepared) but no fifth chassis. The suggestion came from Dixon that he would purchase a Brooklands model if the factory would let him have an engine, if one was spare, and any other parts he needed. Perhaps surprisingly, but probably bearing in mind that Dixon would be no competition for the works team, Victor Riley agreed, but immediately began to discourage Dixon by pointing out the odds against him.

Dixon was shown the plans for the TT cars, showing how much had been done to reduce weight. Every part which could be drilled had been to the limit of safety. As would be expected, Dixon was not deterred. He asked if Riley knew of a suitable car. Victor Riley knew that Victor Gillow, the London car dealer and racing driver's 1930 Brooklands car was for sale. Twelve hours later Dixon was at Holland Park Avenue, London, where Gillow had his premises.

Gillow did not know Dixon. At that stage he was just another customer. Perhaps in an attempt to keep the price down, Dixon did not reveal his plans, but said that he was looking for a sports car in which he might do some racing. Gillow was unwilling to commit himself to a price, and Dixon was to say that 'cat and mouse' negotiations followed, which as a car dealer, were probably familiar to Dixon. Eventually the price was tentatively agreed.

Victor Gillow's patience was then stretched beyond endurance. Dixon related later how he fired questions about the gear ratios, the back axle ratio, the compression ratio and the type of fuel used. Even Dixon had to later admit that he had gone too far, bearing in mind Gillow's mercurial temperament. Dixon's recollection was that Gillow said:

'You think I want to tell you my racing secrets. I don't believe you want to buy a fucking motor car at all!'

He then dashed up the stairs. All of this depends upon Dixon's later memory for its accuracy, and must be treated with some caution. However, it may be reasonable not least because Dixon was writing to a brief for a magazine, to assume that Dixon and Gillow did not immediately strike up a friendship. It is very unlikely that Dixon was used to being spoken to like this, and he was quite capable of giving as good as he got. In any event, Dixon was determined to have the car, and after a night's sleep, he returned contritely to the showroom and asked if he could buy the car at the price agreed the day before, prior to the row.

Terms were agreed. This was the last day for entries for the TT that year, and Dixon had to have a car that day, and hand in the entry to the RAC. He had only a few hours left. The car was found, and now the hard work could begin.

CHAPTER TWO

1932 – THE MAKING
OF A RACER

Dixon had never driven a sports racing car before, and his first experience was in the traffic of London. The car was so low that he could touch the ground with his right hand from the driving seat. Dixon found visibility very restricted. The drive through London convinced him that he had made a mistake, and that there was something special about racing drivers. Dixon experienced a rare sinking feeling. Once clear of the

A charming photograph of Dixon the family man with daughter Jean at the wheel of his first Brooklands Riley Nine.

city and suburbs, heading back for Middlesbrough, Dixon began to feel the exhilaration of a sports racer. Where possible he drove at eighty miles per hour, almost flat out, and began to get the feeling of the brakes and steering. He was not impressed.

This was June. The car had to be ready, in Ulster, by 20th August. The first few weeks were spent testing the car on the public roads around Middlesbrough. Dixon later recalled that it was exciting, and that he did not have to resort to his insurance. In an interview he said:

> *I have no illusions about my entry. I know that I am up against the pick of the world's racing motorists, but if I can finish the course among the rest, I shall be satisfied. I have every confidence in my machine, and if I can get as much out of it as from the bikes, then I should make a fair show.*
>
> *I have been chafing at the bit for a long time and I simply want to get back into the game. I suppose the speed bug has bitten me pretty badly.*
>
> *I am looking forward to Ulster with a zest that I have not experienced in years.*

The decision was made to concentrate first on the brakes and steering, to which Dixon gave high priority. He had learnt this from his motorcycling days. Although he was a brilliant tuner of engines, as he had proved with his motorcycles, for the moment Dixon was prepared to rely on the engine as developed by the factory. There was some hope that the engine would be replaced before the race by one with a stronger crankshaft fitted. Whether this happened is not clear, and Dixon did not refer to it again.

Whilst testing, Dixon would make notes on the aluminium dashboard. He was a compulsive taker of notes, scribbling them on cigarette packets and odd letters, which he would sort out at the end of the day and meticulously record.

Even at this testing stage 'Dolly' Dixon did not know the purpose of the car. When it appeared in the drive of the family home in Linthorpe, Middlesbrough, Dixon admitted it was his and said that it 'would be nice to play around with it for a bit', but did not mention Ulster. He may have thought that his wife had suffered enough worry during his motorcycling days.

As the period of testing passed, Dixon became firmly convinced that the brakes and steering were not up to his standards. He did not directly criticise the car, and considered it to be among the first rank of current sports cars. It simply did not match his standards. What other racing drivers found acceptable was unacceptable to Dixon.

One of the first changes was to the sprung steering wheel. This was a common fitting to sports cars of the 1930s and was meant to absorb vibration from the rigidly fixed engine, which was commonplace. Dixon reasoned that since the Riley's engine was mounted on rubber, a sprung wheel was unnecessary. Dixon's view was that when in difficulty it was necessary for the driver to be able to brace himself against the wheel.

The road wheels were carefully balanced, and every steering joint greased. The steering was still unacceptable. Dixon thought of a novel way of testing it. Both front wheels were chocked off the ground and wooden braces fitted between one wheel and the chassis side member, front and back. Someone sat in the driving seat and turned the steering wheel as far as possible clockwise and anticlockwise, without using excessive force. Dixon meanwhile observed the results, which were illuminating. No single component in the steering was entirely to blame, but all were in part responsible.

Dixon had fitted racing steering arms, polished and lightened, and no doubt very attractive. These were discarded and much heavier and stronger arms fitted. They were less pretty, but more effective.

The next test was for front axle 'float'. This was not shown up by the wooden block test, and another test was devised. The front nearside wheel was rigidly fixed to the chassis side member with a bolted on bracket. This was allowed to float under stress. The steering wheel was again manipulated under Dixon's eye. There was 'float' everywhere.

The solution was to fit springs with less camber angle, and the fitting of spring shackles almost rigidly to the dumb irons. The rear shackles were made much heavier and adjusted tightly against the side faces of the springs, with only enough movement left for the necessary spring action.

This improved the handling, but Dixon knew it could be better. He had noticed that the front leaf springs did not react to various weakening and strengthening experiments. He concluded, rightly, that the chassis was flexing badly. Dixon took some time to come up with an experiment which would show this. Eventually, one occurred to him. The rear axle was clamped to the chassis, then the front of the car was lifted four or five inches off the ground, and a knife edge support was placed under the centre of the axle. As Dixon said, a lot of 'funny stuff' was shown, with the chassis twisting and flexing at many points. At first, no solution was clear, even to Dixon, with his instinctive engineering ability, but he later found a solution.

Dixon contemplated the further effect brought about by changing kingpin castor angles. Greater castor angles brought about more easily self-centring steering, but this threw extra weight on to the outer wheels on corners, straightening up the steering before its time. When reducing the castor angle to make this symptom disappear, Dixon reasoned it was important to make sure there was no play between the steering wheel and the road wheels. It was also important to ensure that the front axle could not twist in the forward direction under braking stresses, giving negative castor effect. Dixon was able to avoid this tendency by fitting road springs with more rigid front sections than rear. With this, and other modifications, Dixon was able to reduce the castor effect to a minimum. He now described the car as a delight to steer.

Attention was turned to the brakes, whilst Dixon still contemplated the twisting effect of the chassis. The brakes were far from satisfactory, and although Dixon had a reputation as a fearless rider, and later driver, he had a very real concern for his own safety. Dixon found it impossible to get accurate compensation, especially when wear took place in the linings. This caused the shoes to take up different positions. One problem was that the operating cable, which had to follow a course around eleven pulleys in an attempt to properly compensate, was too heavy. A cable with a much smaller section was substituted, with excellent results.

A further problem was that on high speed braking tests the rear wheels would lock up; a familiar problem. Dixon's response was to constantly adjust and experiment with the leverage governing the relationship between the front and rear braking. He eventually arrived at a ratio of twenty-five per cent to the rear, with seventy-five per cent to the front. Dixon noted that on braking, weight is thrown forwards, exacerbating the problem by lifting the weight from the rear. This was hardly a unique observation, but Dixon had at least identified the problem.

The braking was much improved. Dixon had satisfied himself at that stage by the polishing of the drums that the shoes had bedded in well, but he wanted further proof. He fixed a clock indicator to the hub. When the wheel was turned the indicator showed to what extent the linings were concentric with the hub. The result did not satisfy Dixon. He concluded that the polishing effect on the linings was caused by flexing of the shoes. This resulted in reduced braking efficiency, and a spongy feel to the brake pedal.

Dixon saw weight reduction as a major priority. He had, of course, seen the plans for the Riley TT cars, where there was very considerable weight reduction. There was a conflict between the need to reduce chassis flexing and weight reduction. Dixon came up with a solution which achieved both ends.

It has been described how the chassis was tested for flexing. Dixon spent many hours watching whilst the chassis, stripped of its body, was rocked on a knife edge. The person doing the rocking was probably Len Ainslie. Dixon resolved that the only solution was to replace the body with one which would add to the rigidity of the chassis. The then TT regulations were fairly flexible about modifications from the original, although the theory was that the cars were standard touring cars. Dixon's body for the car was to consist of three T section hoops, each 1.5 inches by 3/8 inch, with Duralumin panels of 18 gauge. One hoop was to be mounted at the point where the rear bonnet edge would be, the second positioned around the dashboard, and the rearmost at the rear of the seat.

Although Dixon's workshop was well equipped, having been recently fitted out for production of the four cylinder motorcycle, Dixon did not have the equipment to readily make the hoops, and considerable effort was involved.

The Duralumin used for the body panels was formed cold and unannealed, and although this was less difficult than forming the hoops, it was still a very considerable job, as Dixon was anxious to cut the material as little as possible. Once formed, the sheets were riveted every two inches to the hoops, with the lower edge set screwed to the outside of the chassis frame at three inch intervals. The overall effect pleased Dixon greatly, and gave the car the rigidity it, and Dixon, required. It had, of course, no doors, and had the TT regulations required doors (which would have been expected of a true tourer) Dixon's plans would have come to nothing. The concept of using the body to stiffen the chassis was advanced, and all-metal bodies were rare at the time.

Whilst the body was being built Dixon thought further about weight saving. His first saving was to remove a 20 pound support for the fuel tank. Dixon concluded that this was unnecessary. The tank was fitted between two cross members, and fastened down with metal straps. It gave Dixon great pleasure to lose 20 pounds so easily.

The car had two large six volt batteries, mounted in the tail. A starting handle could not be used during the race, but Dixon decided that if it was necessary to start the car more than three times in the race, the race was lost anyway. He replaced the two heavy batteries with the lightest twelve volt on the market. The battery was fixed to a wooden frame, mounted over the gearbox, This meant that the heavy metal frame from the tail could be discarded. The relocation of the battery meant that a considerable amount of heavy duty cable from the battery could be thrown away, again saving weight.

The differential casing and other components were chipped, ground and filed, with additional weight saving. The battery change alone saved 50 pounds, and the new body showed a saving of 40 pounds. Dennis May was later to claim that Dixon was not preoccupied with weight saving, and that he would load the tail of his cars with lead weights to improve the sprung/unsprung weight ratio. He reported that a young man who bought one of Dixon's cars found these weights in the tail, and removed them, thinking that Dixon had attempted to sabotage the car's performance. This seems unlikely, in view of the lengths to which Dixon described himself having gone to save unnecessary weight. He may have used some extra ballast, after the car had been lightened, to adjust its balance, and the most likely conclusion to be drawn is that the car May referred to was an exception, and had been weighted for a particular purpose. Or perhaps Dixon *had* attempted to sabotage the young man's performance!

Attention was again turned to the brakes. Despite his wish to save weight, Dixon discarded the lightened brake drums which had been fitted, because he thought they were liable to distortion. Heavier standard drums were fitted. As to the concentricity of the brake drums, Dixon concluded that the most he could do in the time available was to fit oversize linings. These were made concentric with a portable grinding machine, fixed to the hub. The grinding wheel was fed slowly with an eccentric arrangement. Spare sets of shoes were prepared in this way, each marked so as to match a particular back plate.

The engine arrived from the factory. It will be remembered that this was the factory's contribution to Dixon's entry.

There was no time to run the engine on the road, as the car was awaiting its body, and was not ready for the road. It was fitted to Dixon's Heenan and Froude dynamometer, and left running for several days. This tested the engine and ran it in at the same time. This first engine may have been given the benefits of some of Dixon's masterful tuning, but it was on later cars that his true abilities as a tuner were to be shown. He was fairly satisfied with the factory's product, and the engine ran in standard form.

Various other modifications were made. The car featured a hand throttle mounted on the steering wheel, which was to become a feature of Dixon's cars. This assisted in changing gear whilst double declutching. Louvres were cut in the bonnet by Dixon, using a tool he made himself.

It is not said that Dixon's degree of preparation was unique in contemporary motor racing. What was remarkable was that this was Dixon's first experience of preparing a racing car, and he clearly went to enormous lengths to arrive at clever, and in some instances, brilliant solutions. He and Ainslie worked incredibly hard, along with anyone else assisting.

Dixon had shown in his two wheel days an amazing capacity for work. He did not think of food or sleep, and worked obsessively. A contemporary press report related that out of 144 hours in the last days before leaving for Ulster, Dixon had slept for four, and it is doubtful if Ainslie was allowed to sleep for more. Dixon and Ainslie had lost 56 pounds of personal body weight between them during the weeks of preparation.

As Dixon left for Ulster in the early hours of Monday 15 August, he is reported to have said:

Well thank goodness that's over. Now I can get some rest!

In fact, as we shall see, there was to be little rest. The car was loaded with racing equipment and Dixon drove off for Stranraer to embark on the boat for Ulster. Ainslie had gone ahead. The crossing was no doubt an ordeal for Dixon, who had a fear of the sea.

CHAPTER THREE

THE 1932 ULSTER
TOURIST TROPHY RACE

Dixon's motor racing career lasted barely five years. In that time he had glorious victories, which he relished, and defeats which would have daunted a lesser man. Dixon always excited the crowd, and became the hero of the hundreds of thousands who supported motor racing in the 1930s. Whether he won or lost, the crowd was with Dixon as he drove

One of motor racing's best known (and loved) photographs. At the 1932 Ulster TT, Dixon and Ainslie ended up in a field of rhubarb after misjudging Quarry Corner. Neither was seriously hurt, and Fred can here be seen calmly switching off the engine in mid-flight.

with skill and panache at Ards, Brooklands and Donington. The crowd was never more with him than in his first race, the Royal Automobile Club's Tourist Trophy race of 1932. When Dixon arrived in Ulster he was an unknown in motor racing. He left a hero.

Dixon travelled through the darkness to Stranraer, where he had arranged to meet Ainslie. They crossed the Irish Sea to Larne, where the precious car was slowly swung from the hold of the ship, under the watchful eye of its creator, who thought it suspended from a sewing thread.

The car was taken to the garage of Jimmy Shaw, an old motorcycle racing friend, who had offered shelter for the car, and somewhere to work in the privacy Dixon craved. Dixon later recorded that the car had behaved magnificently on the long journey from Middlesbrough. He had at times been able to open it up to its limit, but had found that certain jobs needed doing.

Practice started on Wednesday 17 August. Tuesday night was spent dismantling, checking and checking again. It would have been sensible for Dixon and his riding mechanic to have a good rest, but this was not Dixon's way. After a few hours sleep, Dixon turned up for practice. This was his first experience of driving a racing car on a circuit, and Dixon must have been anxious at least not to make a fool of himself. His car, he later recorded, attracted an enthusiastic crowd, including the Riley works team and officials from the factory. It is not known whether Victor Riley was there, although presumably Dixon would have recorded his comments had he made any. Victor Gillow was there, and was said by Dixon to have been amazed by the transformation of his car.

Eventually Dixon and Ainslie set off. Sensibly, Dixon drove slowly for the first few laps. Despite his reputation as a daredevil, which was well earned, Dixon seems to have had a strong streak of good sense when necessary, and regard for personal safety. His cornering on those first few laps of thirteen and two thirds miles was described as 'beautiful but slow'. By the third lap, when he was presumably beginning to know the corners, Dixon's speed and confidence built up rapidly. After completing six laps, about eighty miles, Dixon pulled into the pits. He was astonished by the scenes of excitement which greeted him. He had broken the 1100cc record and the record for the 1500cc class, at eleven minutes three seconds. Dixon was only one minute slower than Sir Henry Birkin driving a 2.3-litre supercharged Alfa Romeo. This was an astonishing performance for a first attempt, demonstrating that Dixon had enormous innate skills as a driver.

The night was spent rebuilding the engine, and more sleep was lost. Dixon's performance must have made many rethink the likely result of the race, and on Thursday it was known that many drivers were going out to beat the records set by Dixon. Chris Staniland of the Riley works team managed eleven minutes dead, a speed of 74.51mph. Hamilton in a 750cc supercharged MG was only one second slower, and then improved on this at ten minutes fifty eight seconds. Victor Gillow, perhaps not forgetting the source of Dixon's car, or the scene at the showroom, must have tried very hard, and managed ten minutes fifty-one seconds. Shortly after this Gillow had a near miss avoiding someone else's accident. Dixon's performance had breathed new life into the race.

The car's steering still did not satisfy Dixon, now that he had tried it in racing conditions. He could not get the accuracy in cornering he had enjoyed on motorcycles. Dixon had brought with him from England a pair of ultra lightweight wheels. He took these on Wednesday afternoon to be fitted with tyres. His request was not well received, and the tyre company pointed out that these were 'Austin Seven' wheels, and that they would accept no responsibility if Dixon used them. Dixon insisted, and after a long argument he got his way. The wheels were fitted to the car, and Dixon drove back to Jimmy Shaw's garage, looking like a 'high class pram' as someone put it.

That night was spent working on the car, and after only a short sleep, Dixon was back on the track to test the tyres. It is probable that his riding mechanic that day was Jimmy Shaw. The steering was much improved, and Dixon paid the car the highest compliment he could. He said it was like a 'motorcycle on four wheels'. Dixon's explanation for the improvement brought about by the lightweight wheels was that they threw less 'gyroscopic convulsion' on the steering gear, this effect being magnified by much reduced castor action. Thursday was the last day of practice before the race on Saturday. On Friday there was the weigh in. We know that Dixon had been shown the plans for weight reduction in the works Rileys, and he must have been well satisfied to see that his car weighed in at less than the team cars. Unfortunately, by the time Dixon came to reminisce about this in 1945, he had forgotten the respective weights.

On the night before the race, final preparations were started. No doubt Dixon and Ainslie intended to have a rest, although Dixon's 'relaxation' could be hectic. They had lost a great deal of sleep in the preceding weeks. The cylinder head was removed for the last time. There was consternation when Dixon found distortion, creating a leak between two cylinders. A straight edge showed that the distortion was serious. No machine tool capable of correcting the problem was available, at least at that time of night in Ulster.

Dixon agonised over what to do. To leave the engine in that state was alien to him, and it is doubtful whether he ever thought of withdrawing. The only solution was to lap the head face down on a sheet of glass covered with emery paste. Dixon and Ainslie worked through the night, taking turns to correct the distortion in this laborious way. As light dawned over Belfast, the job was completed. There was only time for a brief sleep for the pair of them before the race began.

Dixon's car was numbered twenty. His reserve driver was Jimmy Shaw. Thirty-six cars entered, all British, except for two 2.3-litre supercharged Alfa Romeos, driven by Earl Howe and Sir Henry Birkin. The Alfa Romeos had a handicap of two minutes thirty seconds. The same Class (Class 4) also contained four unsupercharged Talbots.

Altogether there were nine Rileys, the four Nines entered by Victor Riley, Dixon's Nine, a Nine entered by Mrs 'Bill' Wisdom and driven by her husband Tommy, Gillow's Nine driven by himself, and two 1486cc Rileys entered by Victor Riley. One of these did not start. MG was heavily represented by nine 746cc cars, eight of which were supercharged. In addition to this impressive line up there were two Frazer Nashes, an Aston Martin, a Lea-Francis and three Crossleys. Thirty-five cars lined up for the start.

Dixon's class, class seven, for cars of 750cc to 1100cc, had a handicap of seven minutes six seconds. The handicapping system did not make for an impressive start. The smallest cars left first, and the largest last. The apparent leader was not necessarily the actual leader, and the true position could only be known by carefully watching the lap boards.

The weather was kind that year, a fact which pleased the drivers and spectators but not the handicappers, who had based their figures on wet conditions. Estimates of the number of spectators varied between 400,000 and 500,000.

There were many vantage points over the long circuit. The authorities, in an attempt to bolster the failing economy, had imposed a levy of half-a-crown (12.5p) on every spectator's car entering the course, and the crowd might otherwise have been larger.

Dixon arrived late at the start, although not too late to take his place on the grid. His state of anxiety and exhaustion can only be imagined. The Riley Nines left first, together with the Crossleys. They were followed by the Frazer Nashes and the Lea-Francis. After a pause the unsupercharged MGs left, followed by the Aston Martin, and the single 1.5 litre Riley. Next were the supercharged MGs in a swarm, and then the Alfa Romeos, superchargers screaming, tore off, closely followed by the Talbots, last to leave.

Whitcroft led the race after the first lap, closely followed by Eyston, both, of course, on works Riley Nines. Vernon Balls screamed into the pits with one of the Crossleys, with the remains of a shock absorber in his hand, which he threw on to the pit counter with instructions to repair it. Slackening off the other shock absorbers, he rejoined the race, but completed only five laps before succumbing to engine trouble.

The MGs were battling it out, but Rileys dominated the race, and Dixon moved into the lead. He had lived up to his earlier promise. As Dixon passed Comber Straight a marshal indicated to him that a car wished to pass him. He assumed that it would be one of the larger cars, but it was not, as Victor Gillow was on Dixon's tail. Dixon thought that Gillow had the advantage on the straights, having spent more time on his engine, but that he had the advantage on the corners. There was real competition between these two. Dixon was determined to pass Gillow before the pits, so as to prevent him taking the lead, and put his foot down. Perhaps both had memories still of the scene at the showroom.

They reached the railway crossing, which had a right bend, and which caused the car to jump. Dixon jumped, almost landing on Gillow. As Dixon later said, his brakes were of no use to him in the air! Try as he might, Dixon could not pass Gillow until Dundonald, where he regained the lead, passing the pits first. Pit signals indicated to Dixon that he was increasing his lead as the laps went by.

Dixon pulled into the pits for fuel shortly after 2.00pm, Ainslie unfastening the fuel filler as the car streaked in. This stop took sixty-two seconds. Dixon's pit managers, (perhaps including brother Frank) advised Dixon to slow down, which he did with devastating results. On lap twenty, whilst still in the lead, Dixon approached Quarry Corner too fast. The car hit an embankment and flew through the air, landing in a field of wild rhubarb.

The most famous of Dixon photographs, and probably the most famous TT photograph of all, shows Dixon smiling as the car sailed through the air. He even found time to switch off the ignition as the car sailed on, to prevent damage to the engine by over revving. Dixon was uninjured, having clung on to the steering wheel. Ainslie was less lucky, and cut his face, which required hospital treatment. The only damage to the car was a twisted wheel. Dixon's race was over.

It has been said that Dixon fell asleep at the wheel, and that this was the cause of the crash. It was also said that he was distracted by a misleading pit signal, and that this was the cause. Frank Dixon much later supported the sleep theory. The truth may be a combination of the two. We know that Dixon must have been mentally and physically exhausted. He had had weeks of work on the car, and no rest in Ulster. Dixon blamed the pit signal, but acknowledged that he was enormously tired.

The pit signal consisted of a board on a pole, divided in two by a horizontal line. The top square showed the position in the race held by Dixon, the lower showing how many minutes he was behind, or in front of the next car. If the top figure was, for instance, one, and the bottom figure, for instance, was one, then Dixon was one minute ahead of the next car. The signal Dixon got as he approached Quarry Corner for the final time was a two at the top, with a zero below. This must have been bewildering. It could only mean that at the timing line Dixon was neck and neck with another car, which Dixon thought would have to be another Riley Nine. That was just not the case. As Dixon's exhaustion-befuddled mind struggled with this, he suddenly realised that he was approaching Quarry Corner at full speed. The signal had absorbed his concentration for long enough to make it impossible to take the corner properly. Dixon had crashed before, on motorcycles, and his philosophy was to head for the softest patch, and hope for the best. He did not believe in swerving, or in savage braking. One lesson he claimed to have learnt from this episode was not to slow down when tired. Being at the limit keeps the adrenaline flowing. Slowing down leads to relaxation and danger.

The race was won by Cyril Whitcroft on a works Riley Nine, number seventeen. Eyston in the works Riley number sixteen was second, with Hall on a supercharged MG Midget third, and first in class. Staniland's Riley retired with engine trouble, and von der Becke was flagged off, having failed to complete enough laps in the available time. Edgar Maclure's Works 1.5-litre Riley was eighth overall, and first in class. The race was convincing proof of the excellence of sporting Rileys, which have rightly been called the 'forgotten champions'.

There is no doubt that victory would have been Dixon's if he had not crashed. Lady Houston, a great British patriot, and reputedly the richest woman in England, sent Dixon a cheque for £50 in recognition of his great effort. In a letter Victor Riley said:

> 'I am taking this, the first opportunity I have had, to write to you to express my sincere admiration for the way in which you prepared your car and the magnificent way in which you drove it, and my equally sincere sympathy that such a fine effort should have such an unhappy end.
>
> Despite all the papers say – and you will know more about the thing than I do – the fact that I was the official entrant of the team cars did not make the slightest difference to me. You deserved to win the race, and if you had had better luck no one would have more sincerely congratulated you than I should have done. I hope you will race the Riley on many future occasions ... I have a wonderful photograph of you 'going over the top'.
>
> The Mayor of Coventry (and we) want you at the reception and dinner he is giving on Wednesday next. Come and bring your mechanic too.

It is not recorded whether Dixon went to the Mayor's reception, although it would be surprising if Dixon missed a celebration. By the time the letter was received he was working on his entry for the Brooklands 500.

Dixon and his wife were guests of Middlesbrough and District Motor Club at its 'smoking concert' that year, where Dixon presented the prizes won by members in the season's trials. His exploits at Ulster meant that he was given an enormous reception at the Club, with which he had a long association. On the night, Dixon was presented by the Club with a sketch by Gordon Crosby of his leap into the rhubarb patch. Dixon later gave the drawing back to the Club, to hang in the Clubhouse.

CHAPTER FOUR

RED MONGREL AND THE 1932 BROOKLANDS 500

Dixon arrived back in Middlesbrough from Ulster on Tuesday 23 August. He was determined to continue racing, and was not discouraged by the result of the TT. If anything, he was more determined and had learned lessons for the future. The TT car was not suitable, he decided for the race he now had in mind, the Brooklands Racing Drivers'

Red Mongrel *was Dixon's brilliant unsupercharged 1100cc single-seater racing car built round a Riley Nine engine and special chassis. It lapped Brooklands at well over 110mph.*

Club 500. Why he made this decision is not clear, as two-seater sports cars did participate in the 500. Dixon had in mind a *monoposto* car, with a highly tuned version of the Nine engine he had used in the TT. Nothing was carried over from the TT car. Astonishingly, as the race was to be held on 24 September, Dixon had only thirty-two days to build a car from scratch. This would have daunted a works team. To those around Dixon in August 1932 it must have appeared an impossible task.

There was no time to make drawings of the car, and, as Dixon put it, a lot of chalk was used. Presumably the car was simply sketched out on the workshop floor. Again, Dixon knew that he needed the help of the factory, and he went again to Coventry, and found that help forthcoming. Victor Riley could not overlook Dixon's performance in the TT.

The car was to be narrow, as narrow as the standard Riley chassis at the dumbirons. It would have a torpedo-shaped body, and central steering. The differential would be locked for track work. The rear axle was narrower than the front.

When the Arrol-Aster company went into liquidation Dixon bought a number of chassis members, without thought then of going into motor racing. A suitable pair of Arrol-Aster side members was found. Quarter elliptic rear springs were manufactured by Jonas Woodhouse of Leeds. These were of sufficient strength to allow experimentation by removing leaves and were made long enough to ensure that there could be maximum deflection without unduly stressing the material. A standard Riley rear axle would be used in conjunction with the quarter-elliptics, which slotted in to the 'U' section chassis side members.

Dixon was impressed by the integral body he had constructed for the TT car, and decided to use the same principle again, gaining rigidity from the body and undertray. This meant that the cross membering of the chassis could be reduced to a minimum, reducing weight. There were only two cross members, with a steel tube passing between the dumb irons, with a bracing bolt passed through it. The stressed-skin body was much easier to apply to the single-seater, which had an overall width of only twenty-two inches, than it had been to the TT car. There was a strong undershield, bolted at three-inch intervals throughout its length to the frame girders.

Normal Riley front engine mountings were used and bolted rigidly to the chassis members. At the rear of the engine, to support the gearbox and engine, was a two inch by one inch spring steel bar bolted to the frame. To reduce unsprung weight on the rear axle only front-wheel brakes were used. The ball end of the nose of the torque tube was rearranged as a slide fit, because the axle would now have a new arc, brought about by the new springs. Following his practice with the TT car, Dixon mounted the thirty gallon fuel tank on the rear chassis members, holding it with a metal strap, again saving weight.

As can be seen from the dimensions of the car, the cockpit was tiny, and Dixon, although short, had a stocky build. This meant he had a problem with the steering wheel. A conventional steering wheel would not have allowed him to sit in the cockpit. Dixon reasoned that if he had to do a lot of wheel twirling at Brooklands he would probably end up 'in a bed or a coffin'. He devised an extraordinary 'wheel', with only one third of the circumference of the rim in place. Dixon described it as a handlebar arrangement, a concept which no doubt appealed to him. Seating was arranged by stretching lengths of coil spring across the frame, as used in motorcycle saddle construction. This passed over the propeller shaft, which was enclosed in a torque tube, as was the Riley custom, and which would, at worst, give Dixon a nasty bump if it rose as he went down. During testing Dixon had frequent contact with the torque tube.

The steering was modified with a transverse spindle, equal to the width of the chassis, positioned centrally over the gearbox. Bearings were provided by brackets. The drop arm was outside the car.

Dixon was very keen to have as clean a profile as possible, and every projection which could be was enclosed by the body. There was to be a standard Riley radiator, beneath a cowling, which raised problems of cooling and air flow. Dixon's view was that one of the problems of tuning a car running on alcohol fuel was to keep the engine sufficiently warm, and for this reason the air flow was restricted and carefully managed. The faithful Ainslie spent time counting the number of holes in the honeycomb radiator, and then the total area of the holes was calculated. Dixon decided it was possible to enclose the radiator if a small slot equivalent to the area of the holes in the radiator was left. In the event, as a contemporary photograph shows, this small aperture, so carefully calculated, was almost entirely blanked off for racing. Presumably Dixon had found that the engine was not running hot enough. There were no bonnet louvres, as Dixon wanted the air to pass over the length of the engine before exiting beneath the car.

It will be recalled that the TT car had a standard Riley engine, untouched by Dixon's skill as a tuner. This car was to be different, and Dixon turned his mind to the problem of increasing the output of the engine. The factory had provided a spare Nine TT engine, and Dixon decided to concentrate on the cylinder head and induction. Dixon did not approve of superchargers, and never used one on his Rileys. His view was that superchargers simply masked poor induction systems by ramming the mixture into the cylinders. The TT had convinced Dixon that the crankshaft was adequate for its purpose, although the two bearing crank of the Nine engine was a potential weakness.

We know that Dixon's experience as a tuner was gained in motorcycling days. In turning his mind to problems raised by the car racing engine, Dixon applied the principles he had learnt earlier. So far as induction was concerned, Dixon had learnt from twin-cylinder motorcycle engines that the best results were obtained when a carburettor was devoted to each cylinder, and he had no doubt that this would be the case with a car engine.

Dixon was not the first to use a single carburettor choke per cylinder on a racing car. Miller had used the same principle on Indianapolis cars some years earlier, and the Riley works Irish Grand Prix cars of 1931 had been fitted with four Amals. How much Dixon knew of this is impossible to say. To him it may have been unique.

Dixon believed that on a four-cylinder engine a single, or even a twin, carburettor set up starved certain cylinders, whilst over-feeding others. There were clear difficulties in controlling each of the four SU carburettors Dixon used, and to overcome this, and to avoid setting up each carburettor individually, the four SUs were mounted on a stiff plate. A four-cylinder throttle plate was made to ensure exactly simultaneous and uniform opening and closing of the throttle. A simple sliding plate was fitted to the bottom of the carburettors, to control their regulation perfectly evenly.

One float chamber fed two carburettors. The fuel flow passages were enlarged to prevent restriction. The single float chamber to two carburettor arrangement was not a total success, although as we shall see, records were broken by the car so equipped. Dixon felt that induction was uneven.

There was a problem with dashpot oscillation. This was cured by damping the dashpot pistons with a heavier than normal oil. Other adjustments were made, and the problem was solved.

Rubber sheeting was used in the engine bay to screen the intake from rapid air currents, and to direct air flow. Probably more importantly from Dixon's point of view, the sheeting prevented prying eyes from seeing the induction arrangements when the bonnet had to be opened. Dixon was obsessively secretive when it came to his vehicles. He did not like visitors to his workshop, and would hide his cars in other premises. His induction arrangements were always hidden by some device, usually part of a tyre cut to size. It was said that at Brooklands Dixon would padlock the bonnet of his car if he left it unattended. He hated anyone but his own mechanics in his premises at the circuit. On one occasion he found a character called Bill Rogers, a mechanic with the Austin team, sitting on the wheel of Dixon's car talking to his mechanics in Dixon's workshop at Brooklands. Dixon asked him what he wanted, abusively, and told him to go. Rogers was a quiet, genial man, but said to be a product of the toughest part of Birmingham. He had been known on one occasion to throw two large Irishmen out of his ferry cabin single-handed. Dixon became more unpleasant, turning as he could from a man of charm and good humour to an abusive bully. Luckily for Dixon, Bert Hadley, a works Austin team driver, who knew of Rogers' reputation, separated the pair. Dixon was a strong man, but no match for the agile Rogers.

It has even been said that Dixon did his final tuning in total secrecy, but this may be an exaggeration, another myth which has developed around Dixon. It is unlikely that Dixon would, or could, attempt to keep his secrets from the faithful Ainslie.

Dixon turned his attention to the ignition. He realised that there would be no time in the race to change the magneto if it became defective. He produced a quick clamping device to hold the magneto against this eventuality.

To avoid power loss all the starter ring gear teeth were removed from the flywheel. This converted the flywheel from an air brake into a smooth mass. Aluminium castings were made to cover the clutch springs and other drag inducing protrusions.

Another concern of Dixon's was to reduce the amount of time spent in the pits. It was inevitable that oil would be needed during the race. Like most engines of its era, the Nine engine burned oil at speed and was not renowned for its oil tightness. Dixon came up with a system which was to be a feature of his cars. He adopted the principle of the bird cage feed. A three gallon oil tank was mounted in the cockpit. From the bottom of this a large bore pipe went to the sump. This reached the level at which it was intended to maintain the sump oil. When the oil fell below a certain level, air passed up the vent pipe into the tank. The effect of this was to allow oil to flow up the pipe into the sump through the feed pipe. When the mouth of the vent pipe was submerged, the air supply was cut off, and the oil stopped flowing. It was elementary plumbing, but a brilliant concept for a racing car.

The engine was mounted on a dynamometer, and showed 68bhp at 6000rpm, the engine speed Dixon intended to use in the race. The engine ran smoothly and happily at this speed. The output of the standard Riley Nine engine has been variously quoted as 38bhp and 28bhp, at much more modest rev limits. In any event, this was a considerable achievement, especially when it is remembered that only the induction had been seriously modified. Whatever the myths about Dixon's tuning skills, the reality is that he achieved his aims by patient attention to detail.

Dixon ran the test he had frequently used on motorcycles. The engine was run in the dark with the exhaust manifold removed, exposing the ports. Dixon then observed the results. His aim was to see that all of the exhaust flames from the four cylinders were identical. He was pleased with the results, which were better than when he had run the same test with two carburettors. Dixon was satisfied that all of the cylinders were producing an equal amount of power.

One lesson Dixon had learnt from the development of the TT car was the need for sleep. Despite this, he was incapable of working in a conventional way. He slept by day and worked at night, to avoid interruptions. Despite the impossibly busy schedule he had set himself, Dixon does not appear to have worked himself into the exhausted state he had reached in the run up to Ulster.

Dixon was quoted in the contemporary press as saying:

Rileys (sic) could not believe that I intended to build another car for this race. As a matter of fact, from the first bolt to the last, it will have taken me only a month to build the car. I have not had a moment to myself since I came back from Ireland. But I have managed to get regular sleep, No chances this time if I can help it.

I work all night on the car because I am undisturbed, and sleep all day. At the last moment, however, everything seems to conspire to defeat the object and it looks as though I shall have to put in some overtime on the job.

Dixon had always been keen to work at night, often working through the night at home whilst the family slept, frequently attracting criticism from his wife for lining his bench with the best table cloth!

The car had a long tail, taking no stress. The bottom half of the bonnet added rigidity by being fixed, whilst the top was in one piece and hinged. Dixon was so concerned to get the most out of the car that he feathered the edges of the bonnet straps, which were compulsory under the regulations for the race. Quick acting releases were made for the bonnet straps to assist in the pits.

The car gained the name *Red Mongrel* from the coat of red paint which was hurriedly applied. There was no time to smooth the body out perfectly, and the red paint was designed to cover the faults. Mudguards were fitted to allow the car to be driven to Brooklands.

Dixon again found the sensation of driving a racing car on the road unnerving. He complained about visibility, although the car was open. The steering must have seemed strange with the unusual wheel arrangement. Despite all this he arrived safely at Brooklands.

Dixon had, of course, raced motorcycles at Brooklands frequently, and with success. It is astonishing that he failed to take into account its notoriously bumpy surface, and yet that is the only explanation of the events which occurred at Brooklands in September 1932. On arrival at the circuit Dixon was anxious to take the car out. He was completely unprepared for the way in which it behaved. At speeds over 100mph the car jumped around, throwing Dixon about in the cockpit. He realized that he could not stand 500 miles of that punishment, but had to content himself with extra padding, which proved to be inadequate.

In addition, the scrutineers were far from happy about *Red Mongrel's* steering arrangements. There was a real chance that they would not allow the car to start, and they insisted on a trial.

Extraordinarily, the scrutineers insisted that Dixon drive past them on the Finishing Straight. This pointless test satisfied them, despite the fact that Dixon, showing his usual disrespect for authority, drove the car towards the line of scrutineers and stewards, correcting at the last moment. Perhaps this display was to demonstrate that Dixon had control of the car.

Dixon found that in practice he could achieve a lap speed of 110mph. This gave him 6mph on handicap. He was still much troubled by the rear springing, but realised that nothing could be done. Dixon was pleased to find that his power checks were reflected in his performance.

Dixon's number for the race was 22. He was to drive alone, having entered no second driver. Sir Malcolm Campbell, Cyril Paul, Whitcroft and Cuthbert drove works Rileys. There was a rumour that Nuvolari and Borzacchini were to drive 2.3 Alfa Romeos, but the cars did not arrive. The sole entry in Class E was Count Czaykowski's 2-litre Bugatti. Class H consisted of ten MGs and two Austins. Also entered were two Maseratis, an Amilcar and a Salmson, a 'flat iron' Thomas Special, an Aston Martin, another Bugatti, an Invicta and a Speed Six Bentley. The Rileys were strongly fancied and Dixon's car created considerable interest. The story of the creation of *Red Mongrel* has taken time to tell. Dixon's part in the 500 takes little telling. Dixon was subjected again to the most enormous pounding as the car leapt around the notoriously bumpy surface of Brooklands. Dixon proved himself to be stronger than the car. Very soon after the start the tail began to break away. The tail was unstressed, but it could not take the enormous pounding it was receiving from the circuit. Dixon screamed into the pits and the tail was removed. He set off again, minus the tail, and behind the field. Because he was Dixon he ignored the personal discomfort and drove harder. The bumps seemed to get larger, and Dixon realised that the springing arrangements for high speed at Brooklands were very different from those required for the road. Very soon the axle had pounded a hole in the fuel tank, and the shock absorbers were fractured. Dixon was grateful for the mechanical excuse to retire, as he knew he could take no more of the punishment he was receiving.

The race was won by Horton in an MG. Cyril Paul was second in a Riley. Horton's 750cc car averaged 96.26mph. Paul's average was 99.61mph, but he was more heavily handicapped. Campbell had ignition trouble and was fifth. Tragically, Clive Dunfee's Bentley crashed and hit a tree, killing the driver.

Dixon had upset the Brooklands officials for the first, but not the last, time by screaming into the pits to remove his tail as the 3-litre cars were leaving the start. The day was not a good one for Dixon. He described later how he crawled off to a pub to drown his sorrows. Dixon usually spent his time after a race drinking and celebrating, but this was quite different. He must have been devastated by the result of his race. Clearly the car was not right for the circuit, despite its performance. Dixon had made a serious miscalculation over the car, overlooking an essential factor, the suspension. The time in which the car had been created had not allowed for its proper development, but Dixon should have remembered the Brooklands surface. Even this result did not detract from the achievement of creating a car from scratch in a month which was capable of at least taking part in a premier race like the 500.

Dixon may have been despondent on the day, but he had tremendous powers of recovery, and by the following day had decided what to do next. There is no doubt that he sought acknowledgement from the racing world which had earlier rejected him. He had had material help from the Riley company, and may have felt that he owed something in that direction. Also, the 500 had not been a glorious failure like the TT, but an ignominious defeat. Urgent action was necessary to recoup the position. The racing season was at an end, and Dixon's thoughts turned to record breaking. This would have publicity value, particularly as the motor show was about to take place. Thoughts of further failure do not appear to have entered the picture.

Dixon found that the International Class G record, for 1100cc cars, was 108.11mph, attained by George Eyston in 1931 on an unsupercharged Irish GP type Riley. If this record were to be beaten, two things were required. More power was needed, and the suspension had to be very much improved. Dixon found on experimenting that an upward movement in the rear axle of 4.5 inches made the ride acceptable. The front suspension was found to be much less important.

On 28 October 1932 Dixon was back at Brooklands with *Red Mongrel*. The Brooklands course was always open, and something was always happening, whether racing, testing or record breaking. The Brooklands officials had reduced the timekeeper's fees for that week, to encourage the use of the course. Dixon had arranged with the RAC for permits, booked the course, and secured timekeepers.

The legendary 'Ebbie' Ebblewhite, Brooklands' timekeeper of many years was in charge of timing. Dixon later recorded that 'Ebbie' asked him how far he was going, to which Dixon is said to have replied 'I don't know really, Ebbie, but I'll go until the thing busts.'

The compression ratio of the car had been increased to 13:1, and improved sparking plugs fitted. Time was spent checking the car, and arranging for refuelling and a supply of tyres. Dixon was going for more than the hour record.

As Dixon started the weather threatened rain, and it was not long in coming, but nothing was to prevent Dixon from doing something noteworthy that season. The 50 kilometre record was quickly taken, and then the 50 mile record. *Red Mongrel* was running well, and got better as it warmed up. Dixon believed that his engines were at their peak as they became more heat soaked. Shortly, the 100 kilometre record was Dixon's, and he prayed he would make the hour. Soon he saw his pit team in a state of excitement. He had taken the hour record at 111.09mph. Dixon went on to take the 200 kilometre record and then decided that he had had enough, again having regard for personal safety as the rain lashed down. He had achieved more than he had set out to do.

The International Class G records set by Dixon were:

50 kilometres – 109.18mph
50 miles – 110.37mph
100 kilometres – 110.78mph
One hour – 111.09mph
200 kilometres – 110.67mph

Dixon was a world record holder. 'Ebbie' was to be a privileged man that wet October day. The rules required that he confirm that the car was as claimed, which included measuring the capacity of the engine and its general specification. This meant that he saw the secrets of Dixon's carburettors and other improvements, a closely guarded secret.

The car had averaged 14mpg on alcohol fuel during the attempt, which was satisfactory to Dixon. He probably retired to consume some alcohol himself. No doubt all Weybridge knew of his success.

Dixon now had the winter in front of him. *Red Mongrel*'s future had to be decided. It was only suitable for track events, as road races, like the TT, required two seats. 'Ebbie' knew of the car's capabilities, and this would be reflected in future handicapping. Dixon decided to play about with the engine. The valve timing was improved, and the overlap increased. Dixon wanted new camshafts, but did not want to have them made for him, to preserve secrecy, and because he wanted to experiment with profiles. He had no cam grinder at his disposal, but made up a grinding machine by adapting one of his lathes.

Careful records were kept of the results obtained with different cams, carburettor settings and magneto settings. Dixon used his usual technique of testing with open ports in the dark, studying the flame. Even Dixon had to concede that his neighbours in Middlesbrough grew tired of the noise, probably very quickly. The result of all this was that bhp was raised from 70bhp at the time of the record attempt to 77bhp at 6000rpm. More was available, but at risk to the engine.

CHAPTER FIVE

1933 – A YEAR OF DISAPPOINTMENT

Dixon's first full season as a racing driver was 1933. Although he put in some tremendous performances, and deserved more success than he was to enjoy, it was a year of disappointment and mechanical failure. We know how much work and skill had gone into *Red Mongrel*, and Dixon was not disappointed by its performance, which was exceptional for an

Dixon winning the 1933 Mannin Beg race on the Isle of Man; one of only two finishers from fourteen starters.

unsupercharged 1100cc car. He was to be disappointed by its reliability. It may be that Dixon, always driving to the limit, simply asked too much of the car. By the end of the season Dixon had turned his attention to six-cylinder Rileys, which were to be his primary interest for the rest of his racing career. *Red Mongrel* was sold, with, as we shall see, tragic results, but that was in the future, and no doubt at the beginning of 1933 Dixon looked forward to the season with anticipation of success.

There had been floods at Brooklands over the winter which had undermined the bridge over the river Wey. This required repair, and work was not completed by 11 March, which was the date of the opening meeting. A restricted event took place on 11 March without the use of the Outer Circuit, consisting of 'Mountain' races and short sprints over the Finishing Straight. Dixon won a sprint in *Red Mongrel* at 76.96mph.

Dixon was at the historic inaugural meeting at Donington on 25 March 1933. There was considerable interest in road racing in Britain, although illegal in England and only found abroad and in Ulster and the Isle of Man. The opening of Donington Park was therefore a major event in British motor racing history. Donington was operated by the Derby and District Motor Club, and set in the grounds of Donington Hall, formerly the seat of the Earls of Huntingdon. By 1933 it was a hotel owned by J G Shields. He was approached in 1931 by the Derby and District Motor Club and persuaded to have a course for motorcycles constructed in the grounds. Shields no doubt thought that this would benefit the hotel. By 1933 a course suitable for racing cars had been constructed at a cost of £12,000. The course had originally been around the drives and farm tracks of the estate, and this was added to and improved. Dixon was a regular competitor at Donington, and his off course activities were as legendary as his track successes. The drivers tended to base themselves at Donington Hall, sleeping, eating and celebrating there. Fred Craner was circuit manager, and 'Mr. Donington' and he had to cope with Dixon's excesses, which was probably not easy, as he shared Dixon's volatility, as well as his short stature. He could be blunt and abrasive, and it is unlikely that these two saw eye to eye.

On one occasion in Donington's early history Dixon swept into the entrance to Donington Hall with his entourage to find that Craner, in an attempt to recall the glories of the Hall's past, had installed a footman in the entrance hall, complete with glorious silk breeches. As Dixon entered he told this magnificent figure to carry his bags, and received the frosty reply that that was not his function. He refused to reply to Dixon's request to know what his job was. Dixon was heard to say that he would have that lot off him. Two hours later, after he had celebrated his own arrival, Dixon was seen in the silken finery, which was far too large for him, and in a belligerent mood. The footman had disappeared, only to be found later locked in a cupboard. The two Freds, Dixon and Craner exchanged some colourful words over the incident, quite out of keeping with the atmosphere of elegance Craner had tried to create.

When the Austin team stayed at Donington they all tended to occupy one large room, barricaded in, on the basis that there is safety in numbers. One of the team, Bert Hadley, was later to recall that he woke one Sunday morning, having been successful in a long distance race the day before. He looked out at the grey dawn, and saw what he thought was a large number of outsize mushrooms on the lawns. As the light improved he saw that they were chamber pots of various sizes. He also saw Craner and a constable, complete with notebook and pencil. Apparently Dixon's party, ably assisted by Cyril Paul, had become so boisterous in the night that Craner had called the police. There were no charges, but Dixon, Paul, and perhaps others were ejected from the hotel.

Saturday March 25 was a perfect day, with what came to be called 'Donington weather'. Dixon was there with a Nine, probably the TT car. In the second heat of the class for unsupercharged cars up to 1500cc he led from the start, followed by Hutchison in a red Bugatti and Tucker's Frazer Nash. Dixon was very fast on Starkey's Corner, and had to drive all out to retain the lead, putting in a lap record of 59.3mph on lap three. He later increased this to 59.5mph. The frantic pace of the race sent cars off the track and into the woods, and this included Dixon, who was enthusiastically pushed back on the circuit. Hutchison had got past him, but when the Bugatti began to misfire, Dixon almost caught him, but came second, 22.8 seconds behind. Dixon was second, again to Hutchison, in the final. Casswell's Frazer Nash was third.

Dixon entered the International Trophy race in May, but was not successful. The race was to be run over the reverse of the usual Brooklands course, and the circuit included the Finishing Straight. The

Fork incorporated a series of artificial bends, which were an attempt at handicapping. There were four bends of increasing severity, intended to present progressively difficult corners for cars of greater capacity.

Dixon had changed *Red Mongrel*'s camshafts, and rear-wheel brakes had been fitted. With hindsight, Dixon regarded his decision to enter this event as a mistake. The cockpit had been opened up to allow more elbow room, and Dixon had fitted an orthodox steering wheel in place of the curious 1932 affair. The cockpit alterations affected the streamlining of the car, lowering its ultimate speed. The car was never put back into record breaking form, Dixon not having the time or inclination to do so.

Practice sessions for the race were reasonably satisfactory, and Dixon found he could cover the course 'as fast as the next man'. The handicapping system meant that a massed start was possible, always a more satisfying way of starting a race. By half way Dixon was among the leaders, content to stay with the pack, as long as no one got too far ahead. At this stage the engine began to sound unhappy, and Dixon roared into the pits. An examination showed that the cylinder head gasket had gone. This was quickly replaced, and Dixon rejoined the race. All was not well, and with the tachometer indicating 118mph, the engine again showed signs of distress. Dixon, never easy on an engine, kept his foot down. The car very shortly came to a halt and a cursory examination showed that part of the crankcase was missing.

Dixon's race was over. A later detailed examination of the engine showed that the gudgeon pin holes in the pistons had elongated as a result of using too small a pin in the Elektron (magnesium alloy) piston. The piston had contacted the cylinder head, causing the initial gasket problem, then the gudgeon pin broke under the hammering it was receiving.

The car was taken back to Middlesbrough. The remains of the engine were further examined, and much larger gudgeon pins were made up to work directly in the connecting rods. Pad ends of Duralumin were made up to allow the maximum bearing surface on the piston. Dixon was also not happy with the slight variation in the mixture strengths between cylinders, again demonstrating his preoccupation with induction. He diagnosed the fault as the sharing of a float chamber by two carburettors.

By clever redesign and 'wangling', Dixon was able to give each carburettor its own float chamber. These difficulties may explain his absence from the Donington meeting on 18 May.

Dixon was at the BARC Whit Monday meeting, where the main race of the day over seven laps was for the coveted Gold Star. *Red Mongrel* performed well in practice and Dixon was a favourite to win. Down the Railway Straight the car was touching 120mph, but again success was not to be Dixon's, as mechanical breakdown intervened. The cause was simple, and yet the results devastating. Suddenly the engine revs soared, and the valves were damaged beyond repair. The gear lever had jumped out of top gear at maximum revolutions, with results which were to be expected. The Gold Star was snatched from Dixon, but he professed not to be disappointed, as his real goal that year was the 500, and everything else was simply a testing ground for that. He was consoled by the information that he had set a lap record of 116mph, although some sources place it at 111.92mph, which may be more realistic. Charles Brackenbury won the race on a Riley, and so the race could be counted a success for the marque. Dixon had gained further experience, and the history of *Red Mongrel* can be seen as one of continual development and improvement. Dixon also took part in the Cobham Senior Long Handicap at the Whitsun meeting. He was unplaced, but almost caused the ultimate winner C J Turner to crash his Bentley as he passed Dixon's Riley going on to the Byfleet banking. Two of Turner's wheels were over the banking, creating a cloud of dust. Dixon had been lapping at 108.74mph, and was driving high on the banking, as he preferred to.

The one real victory of Dixon's year came on 13 July when he won the Isle of Man Tourist Trophy, the Mannin Beg, in the TT car. This was a historic event, as it was the first of the Mannin Beg and Mannin Moar series. Public roads could, of course, be closed for motor racing on the Isle of Man, where the motorcycle TT event had for so long taken place. It was also significant as Dixon's return to the Island where, as a competitor, he had been the hero of so many struggles on two wheels.

The race was held around the streets of Douglas, and was a gruelling series of tight corners and bends over a circuit of 4 miles, 1,056 yards. It was a challenging course, with solid stone walls and eleven acute corners, as well as several lesser bends.

Cars of up to 1500cc normally aspirated, or 1100cc supercharged took part in the Mannin Beg, whilst the Mannin Moar was for the larger cars. The regulations did not encourage worthwhile foreign competition, and it was said that they kept out the best of the British voiturettes. The supercharged 1500s, such as the Bugattis and the Delage, which would have added to the spectacle and prestige of the Beg, had to enter the Mannin Moar race. Riding mechanics had to be carried, which precluded single seaters from the race. Earl Howe said in an open letter to *The Motor* that the races would be 'second rate affairs' and the regulations were generally derided. 230 miles had to be covered, and there were 14 starters. Only two finished in the allotted time. All of this is bound to diminish Dixon's victory, but the fact is that he finished when so many did not and his unsupercharged car was very fast.

Rileys were not well represented, there being only Dixon's TT car and Victor Gillow's entry. MGs were heavily represented, with ten cars, all supercharged and with preselector gearboxes. The other competitors were T G Moore's Frazer Nash, and Sullivan on his Sullivan Special Morris Minor. Dixon was on the front line of the grid, having achieved the fastest lap in practice at 60mph, a time of 4 minutes 36 seconds. As the Lieutenant-Governor of the Island, Sir Claude Hill, entered the grandstand, the sound of the national anthem died away, and the cars were off.

Earlier threats of rain had been replaced by sunshine. There was a large crowd at every vantage point, and every doorstep was a grandstand. Kaye Don led at the end of the first lap in an MG Magnette, closely followed by Hamilton's Magnette. Dixon lay fourth, sandwiched between the howling pack of MGs. It must have been a thrilling sight as the cars snaked down the promenade at over 100mph. No doubt Dixon's spirited driving thrilled the crowd as usual.

By lap 10 Victor Gillow had retired with valve trouble, and Dixon was the sole representative of the Riley marque. The pace was very fast, Hamilton lapping at 58.93mph over the tight circuit in first place. Dixon lay fourth. Kaye Don had slipped to second. Cars were retiring with a mixture of mechanical problems, no doubt exacerbated by the demanding course. Dixon lost fourth place as a result of a skid at St Ninian's, probably brought on by over-enthusiasm, and then the car suffered universal joint trouble. This put Dixon well back in the field, and a lesser man might have given up. Dixon's response was to set off, after repairs, at a furious pace. Hamilton still led, and R A Yallop on a Magnette moved into second place when Don retired with engine trouble. Dixon was left to work his way up a diminishing field. Yallop, 8.5 minutes ahead of Dixon, came in to refuel, allowing Dixon to catch up a little, the pit stop taking 1 minute 15 seconds. To the spectators it seemed possible for Dixon to catch Yallop, but there must have seemed little chance of catching Hamilton, who had driven a superb race.

On the 33rd lap Yallop failed to appear at the grandstand and word reached the crowd that he had retired with ignition trouble. Dixon was now second. Could he be first? We shall never know whether Dixon could have caught Hamilton, because Hamilton suffered appalling luck when he had to retire with axle failure at Falcon Hill. Dixon continued to drive like a demon, ignoring pit signals to slow down, and the crowd cheered wildly as the man tipped to win swept past the grandstand in the lead.

Mannin Beg, 1933. Dixon in the TT Nine sandwiched between the supercharged K3 MG Magnettes of Hamilton (16) and Eyston (15).

There were now only three cars, Dixon's and two Magnettes, driven by Ford and Mansell. Dixon had just to nurse his car to the end to win, but this did not persuade him to slow down, and he lapped Mansell. Ford was second, and there were prospects of an exciting race for second place, until Ford had engine trouble. His mechanic worked feverishly on the car, and he set off again. Dixon swept to victory, ahead of Mansell, who was also an ex-motorcycle racer. Although Ford did not finish in time to qualify, at the request of the Lieutenant-Governor of the Island, he was awarded third place. Dixon's winning speed was 54.41mph. Mansell's was 51.4mph. Ford managed only 49.33mph.

Whether Dixon's natural elation at winning was tempered by the knowledge that his win was probably due to Hamilton's ill luck we cannot know. Dixon had fought to win where so many others had retired, and had carried on despite his own mechanical problems. No one can deny him the glory of his first victory on four wheels. Mansell, whose father was managing director of the Norton concern, had put up a tremendous performance in a car of only 746cc, averaging 51.4mph, against Dixon's average of 55.41.

Dixon's real ambition for 1933, and for every year of his motor racing career, was to win the BRDC 500. Unfortunately, Dixon's part in the 1933 500 takes little telling, and it was another disappointment for him, probably the greatest of the year.

Dixon entered two cars, the Ulster TT car, driven by Cyril Paul and Phillip Turner, and *Red Mongrel*, to be driven by himself and Chris Staniland. In the early stages Dixon drove a superb race, and lay second to Eyston on the MG 'Magic Midget' after 1.5 hours, averaging 107.91mph. Unfortunately, the race was to he marred by a tragedy, and that tragedy was to be Dixon's downfall.

In mid-afternoon Watson, driving Elwes's MG Midget, left the Byfleet Banking, after a refuelling stop, at 100mph. The car swerved and somersaulted, although the cause was not apparent. Watson was thrown from the car, and burning fuel spread across the track. Dixon was close behind, and witnessed the horrific crash, which cost Watson his life. It was not unnatural that Dixon lifted his foot from the accelerator quickly, causing the plugs to oil. It would have been wise to stop at the pits to deal with the oiled plugs, but Dixon pressed on. The solution he adopted was

to weaken the mixture in an attempt to cure the plug trouble. This made matters worse, and the cylinder head gasket blew. Dixon had to stop to change the gasket, and shortly after rejoining the race a piston melted. Dixon had to retire. The day was not entirely lost, as Paul and Turner brought the TT car into third place at 88.87mph. The race was won by Hall driving his supercharged 1087cc MG K3 Magnette at 106.53mph, with Martin second, driving a 1087cc MG L-type Magna at 92.24mph.

Dixon had a small success in the BARC Junior Mountain Handicap, coming third behind C A Richardson also driving a Riley. Dixon's car was driven to success in the women's Mountain Handicap by Rita Don, Kaye Don's sister. Dixon rode as riding mechanic. It was said that Dixon assisted by holding the hand throttle open if he thought Miss Don was closing it prematurely, and that he stuck pins in her to urge her on!

The remaining challenge of the season was the Ulster TT. Once again Dixon set off for Ulster, no doubt hoping to end the season with a convincing win in a major race. The race was held on 2nd September. Dixon said before leaving Middlesbrough:

'Every time I go to the track I discover some point about the car and its handling – each yielding another fraction of a mile an hour … I am looking forward to the Ulster race with confidence fostered by this experience. Moreover, I am more prepared for the race.'

In fact the race was Nuvolari's, but nothing can detract from Dixon's brilliant performance, which was very much appreciated by the crowd. Dixon's performance in 1932 meant that he was now favoured to win.

There were, as usual, five classes, based on engine size, which governed the handicapping system. Thirty-two cars entered, with twenty-five starting. Tragically, practice was marred by the death of Lewis's mechanic in a crash whilst driving Balmain's 746cc unsupercharged MG Midget.

Riley was well represented, with four cars entered by Victor Riley, two by Victor Gillow and one by Hector Dobbs, as well as Dixon's TT car. As usual, MG was well represented with five Magnettes entered and three Midgets. There was the Sullivan Special Morris Minor of 732cc, two Invictas of 4467cc making a first appearance, together with three Alfa Romeos of 2366cc and a Maserati of 2494cc. A lone Alvis made up the entries, but failed to start.

Nuvolari drove one of the 1087cc supercharged K3 MGs, this being his first drive on the MG, which had a preselector gearbox, of which Nuvolari had no experience. The workings were described to him with a mixture of a bit of Italian and a lot of signs. Nuvolari's win was remarkable, particularly as he managed to break several records in the process. Nuvolari's entry in the race changed its complexion, bringing an excitement it might otherwise have lacked.

The rules of the race were changed to bring the race up to 35 laps from 30, a total of 478 miles. The intention was to make the race a six hour event. The race was witnessed by a huge crowd, taking advantage of the many vantage points around the circuit. It was watched by Prime Minister Ramsay Macdonald, and Sir William Morris, owner of the MG Car Co Ltd.

Dixon's number was 16, and he was in the first group away as 'Ebbie' dropped the flag. Victor Gillow immediately assumed the lead, Dixon being slow off the mark. Nuvolari was in the next group to leave, the MGs being supercharged, with the Alfa Romeos next, and the large Invictas last. There were the usual mechanical failures early in the race, and only nine cars were to finish.

By 11.30 Dixon was fourth, with Hamilton in the lead, Crabtree second and Gillow third. Hamilton had broken the lap record, and the pace was very fast. The rivalry between Dixon and Gillow continued, and this led to Gillow driving wildly with spectacular results at Quarry Corner in the rain. Nuvolari, although not among the leaders, and probably still learning the characteristics of the car, was moving up the field, and broke Dixon's 1932 lap record by seven seconds, a terrific achievement in a strange car. By 12.30 Dixon was second to Hamilton, with Gillow third, and Nuvolari sixth. Nuvolari's progress must have been spectacular as he continued to break lap records. His position would have been higher but for a pit stop.

At 1.00pm Dixon was still second to Hamilton, with Gillow fourth to Rose Richards on an Alfa Romeo, Nuvolari having moved up to sixth place. It was then that the rivalry between Gillow and Dixon was to reach a peak, as Gillow fought to catch Dixon. In the attempt he made a serious mistake at Quarry Corner, hitting a telegraph post. Fortunately he and his riding mechanic were not hurt, but he was out of the race.

Hamilton continued to lead on handicap, with Dixon chasing him, almost two seconds slower on each lap. Nuvolari had stopped for tyres, but was fighting his way back. Dixon went in for tyres whilst still second. Dixon had devised a unique way of jacking up the car, using a pedestal with which he could easily lift the car whilst the tyres were changed. The pit stop took only 4 minutes 11 seconds, and then Dixon and his mechanic were off. Shortly after this the first sign of trouble with the exhaust system manifested itself, and Dixon had to stop at Ballystockart to wire up the exhaust pipe, thereby dropping to fourth place. This delay cost him 11 minutes, and he had to stop again within two hundred yards. By this time Nuvolari had taken the lead, with Hamilton second. Dixon, despite a further stop with exhaust trouble moved into third place. Nuvolari was to lead to the finish, and to win by a narrow margin over Hamilton.

Hamilton might well have won if he had not had a long stop with solenoid problems. A contemporary report recorded that Dixon could have come first or second without the exhaust trouble which cost him a place in the race. The same report commented that Dixon's driving was splendid, and contained none of the rashness for which he had previously been known. He came home in fourth place, which must have been disappointing, but worse was to follow, because it was announced that Dixon had been excluded from the honours because of the problem with the exhaust system, which meant that he had broken the rules of the race, which required the use of an exhaust system at all times. Dixon's mechanic had held the exhaust on with his bare hands for the later stages of the race, and on top of this, had been splashed with battery acid, destroying his trousers. One report suggested that Dixon had been excluded on the insistence of Sir William Morris, whilst another reported that Morris had given Dixon a cheque for the £100 he would otherwise have won. Both reports are unlikely to be true, and it may be preferable to believe the more generous version of Morris's involvement. In any event, Dixon was to leave Ulster again having been robbed of victory after driving a magnificent race.

Nuvolari swept to victory, followed by Hamilton, who had driven an exciting, if erratic race on his MG. Rose Richards on his Alfa Romeo finished third.

The last Donington meeting of the year was held on 7 October. It was not the usual Donington weather and it rained heavily. The second event of the day was for cars of up to 1100cc. Six cars entered. Good racing was expected between Hall on a MG K3 Magnette of 1087cc, Dixon's Riley Nine and R F Turner's supercharged 747cc Austin. Hall was in the lead on the first dash to the Hairpin Bend. Unfortunately, he had left sacking over the engine to keep it warm, and had forgotten to remove it. This led to rapid overheating, causing Hall to stop. Turner and Dixon were close behind, with Turner taking the lead, hotly pursued by Dixon. On the second lap Hall overtook to take the lead again. Dixon was frantically trying to pass Turner, but he maintained second place. Turner was fastest of the day on Hairpin Bend, and out-cornered Dixon on fast bends. The road was wet, and the Austin just slid around the bends in perfect control. On the last lap Dixon just managed to get past Turner into second place, and that was the finishing order. Hall's time was 11 minutes 15 seconds (58.28mph) and Dixon's 11 minutes 24 seconds (57.25mph). Turner's speed was 57.18mph. It was clearly a close race. Nine cars were entered for the under 1500cc race, including Dixon's. Eccles on a Frazer Nash, Appleton on a Bugatti and Dixon were on the front row of the grid. Dixon's Riley blew its head gasket on the second lap, and the race was won by Eccles.

Meanwhile, Dixon was very much a celebrity in his own country, where of course he had his family and business. He had very close links with Middlesbrough and District Motor Club, and was to be its president. He helped the Club raise funds to buy its premises, lending the Club £4000 himself, a measure of his wealth and business success. The Club is one of the oldest motor clubs in the country, and began with enthusiasts meeting, mainly on motorcycles, on a roundabout in the town in the early days of motor sport. The Club still thrives, and many of Dixon's trophies were displayed there, as well as the Gordon Crosby sketch referred to earlier.

On 13 December 1933, at the Club's premises in Clarendon Road, Middlesbrough, a complimentary dinner was held for Dixon. The President of the Club, John Gjiers, proposed 'The King' and a toast to Dixon was proposed by William Ryan. The programme specifically mentions the Mannin Beg victory, and Dixon's 'outstanding performance in competitive motorcycling'. Victor Riley was to attend, but could not, it was said, through illness. He sent a lengthy message of congratulation to Dixon. The toast was responded to by Dixon's great friend and rival, Cyril Paul. The mayor of Middlesbrough, Councillor Cooper, attended having, he said, turned down ten other invitations to do so. The Mannin Beg trophy was passed around, filled with punch, and no doubt Dixon made the most of his night.

A press report appeared of Dixon speaking to the Saltburn branch of Rotary in December, and he then slips from view until the beginning of the 1934 season. He related his early tribulations in trying to get started in motor racing, and again suggested that financial considerations were important in his decision to take up the sport. It is doubtful, despite Morris's cheque, that Dixon saw any profit in the 1933 season. He may have been looking to the long term.

CHAPTER SIX

1934 – Triumph & Disaster

Although Dixon had demonstrated enormous skills as a driver and engineer and a huge capacity for work, the level of success he deserved eluded him. He had always excited the crowd, with his spirited and dramatic driving style, and had often started favourite to win. He had shown he could challenge the best, and was certainly capable of becoming a winner.

For 1934 Dixon prepared two sensationally successful six-cylinder Rileys for racing, with a choice of engine from 1485cc to 2-litres. For the 1934 Mannin Beg race, the smaller engine was fitted to both cars, driven by Dixon (ret.) and Paul (3rd).

At the end of the 1933 season Dixon purchased from the Riley company two six-cylinder chassis. He still entered fours in races, but usually to be driven by others as part of his team, although occasionally competing in them himself.

On what basis Dixon acquired the Sixes is not clear. He was not a works entrant, but had in the past received help from the factory, and he may have obtained the Sixes on reasonable terms. This would have been a sensible arrangement for Victor Riley, as Dixon's ability must have been apparent to him, and his exploits and popularity with enthusiasts could only benefit the company.

The Riley historian David Styles has rightly said that Dixon turned his cars into giant-eaters. It was common for enthusiasts to refer to a car as *Dixonised* after it had received treatment from Dixon. This encapsulated the way in which Dixon uniquely improved the cars on which he worked, reflecting the very real difference between Dixon's cars and the standard Riley product.

The six-cylinder cars were the Tourist Trophy Sixes numbered 4/102 and 4/104. The difference between the Dixon cars and the factory team cars was that in 1934 the works cars were MPHs, and thereafter TT Sprites. Following his experience with the TT car and *Red Mongrel*, Dixon lightened the chassis of the cars and improved their handling. The engines were bored out to 63.5mm, bringing the cubic capacity to 1808cc, although engines of various sizes were prepared to qualify in different races. The factory had improved the crankshaft and connecting rods, but this was not enough for Dixon, and he made further improvements. His cars were significantly faster than the works cars.

Following his belief in the ultimate importance of induction efficiency, Dixon chose again to have one carburettor choke per cylinder, although reverting again to shared float chambers, probably due to lack of space. The chosen carburettor was the Amal, although Dixon usually used SUs. They were carefully screened from prying eyes. We have seen that Dixon was not the first to adopt this system of induction, having been preceded by Miller and Riley themselves, but again he Dixonised the system by inventing a new method of throttle control. This consisted of a single sliding plate, with holes of the same diameter as the inlet ports. This was mounted between the carburettor bodies and the inlet ports, and operated on roller bearings. It was a considerable improvement on the more usual butterfly-throttle valve, and was to reappear when mechanical fuel injection was developed for cars in the 1950s. Dixon did not patent the system.

In appearance the Sixes had a strong resemblance to *Red Mongrel*, with similar methods of construction, comprising a long tail and no bonnet louvres; the body aiding the stiffness of the chassis. As with *Red Mongrel*, the flywheel was lightened. The cars had standard Riley Silent Third gearboxes.

There were again changes at Brooklands. A new stand, the Cobham stand, had been erected and the old wooden hangars at Byfleet Banking demolished.

March 3rd saw the opening meeting of the season. Frost had delayed the finishing of repairs to the concrete, and the full circuit was not available. Two-mile Sprint Handicaps from Railway Straight to Fork and half-mile scratch sprints down the Finishing Straight to Fork were held.

Despite the development of the Sixes, Dixon chose to enter a Nine for the day's events. It was early in the season, and perhaps the Sixes were not ready, although this seems unlikely, given Dixon's obsessive work rate, and he may have simply decided that the nature of the day's racing was better suited to the smaller cars.

Dixon came third in a Mountain Handicap, behind Rayson's Brooklands Riley fitted with a supercharger from a Mercedes-Benz. It no doubt screamed wonderfully. Eccles's 2.3-litre Bugatti came second. A good opening result for Dixon against stiff opposition.

The last race of the day was the Walton Senior Mountain Handicap. Dixon came second, breaking the Glass G lap record previously held by Straight's MG K3 Magnette, the new record being 71.15mph, 0.48mph better than Straight's time The race was won by Rayson, again on the Supercharged Brooklands Riley, at 63.82mph. Shapling's Type 43 Bugatti was third. Another good result for Dixon.

There is no record of Dixon being at the opening meeting of Donington in April, but he was back at Brooklands for the Easter meeting, again racing two Nines. He excelled in the Ripley Lightning Short Handicap, providing exciting racing by lapping at 113.91mph, to win at 104.83mph, a tremendous performance for an unsupercharged Nine. Horton was second on a MG Midget, with Fotheringham's 2.3-litre Bugatti third. Ashby's Riley broke a shock absorber at speed on the banking, snaking alarmingly among the many fast cars.

For the Ripley Senior Long Handicap Dixon was handicapped 10 seconds, following his earlier success. Despite this, Dixon drove to win at 107.49mph, with fastest lap of 115.82mph. Mattock's MG, with six Amal carburettors, was second, with Dobbs on Dixon's other Nine third. A superb result for Dixon and his team.

There was a varied field of eight cars for the Ripley Lightning Long Handicap, including Cobb's massive Napier Railton. Despite his efforts, Cobb could not catch the leaders. Dixon was handicapped fifteen seconds, but drove a challenging race, with a lap of 114.94mph, to come second to Waddington on his Austin Six.

The 1934 Mannin Beg and Moar races were held in April, despite reports of heavy financial losses in 1933. Dixon entered the two new Sixes in the Beg, one driven by Cyril Paul, fitted with engines of 1485cc to qualify on engine capacity. The race was over a 3.7 mile course, shorter than previously, but still around the houses. Three Rileys were entered by the factory, and there was the usual huge opposition from MG, with an entry of eleven supercharged K3 Magnettes. Excitement was caused by an announcement that Humphrey Cook would drive one of the new ERAs in the Beg, a supercharged 1100.

Unfortunately, the car was not ready in time. Raymond Mays was to drive a 1500cc ERA in the Moar, but, although Mays practised, the car was withdrawn because the spring rates were not suitable.

There was an unfortunate incident in practice when Kaye Don crashed a K3 MG whilst testing the car on the public roads after official practice had finished. His riding mechanic, Frank Tyler was killed. Don was subsequently convicted of manslaughter and served a four-month prison sentence. This caused a lot of concern among competitors.

Dixon might easily have won the race, but whilst leading with a massive advantage of 2 minutes, 24 seconds, he ran out of fuel. This might be viewed as a disastrous error of judgement, but the reality was that the car had sprung a leak in its reserve tank, an explanation proved by the fact that Cyril Paul finished in third place without difficulty, both cars having a twenty-one-gallon fuel tank, with a six-gallon reserve tank.

The race was better than that of 1933, but it has been said that the absence of the supercharged 1500s and lack of foreign competition gave the race limited appeal.

Dixon, assisted by brother Frank among others, set about changing the engine of one car to qualify for the Mannin Moar race. An engine of 1807cc was fitted. The fuel tank was suspended on rubber, to avoid further threats of leaks. The Beg had been held on Wednesday, with the Moar on Friday. Practice on the Thursday resulted in a smashed differential, which had to be repaired, using parts from various cars. As usual, Dixon worked furiously into the night, and the car was ready by 7am. Dixon retired to bed, leaving instructions that he was to be woken at 8.30am, or 8.15am if the car showed signs of trouble. He was woken by Frank with the news that the oil pressure was not satisfactory. This was rectified, and the car tested again. This showed a broken cylinder head gasket. Most men would have retired then, but Dixon set about changing

Dixon, having run out of fuel in the 1934 Mannin Beg while massively in the lead, manages a brave smile in congratulating Cyril Paul on his third place in the second Dixon Riley.

the gasket. The race was to begin at 10 am., and Dixon was at the start with only 20 minutes to spare, again to begin a race in a state of exhaustion.

By lap ten Dixon was in third place, beating the track record with a speed of 76.56mph on the seventh lap. After 21 laps he was second, and might well have contemplated victory if a big end had not failed, putting him out of the race, but only after he had sent for tools and taken off the sump to see if there was any hope of repair. The race was won by the Hon. Brian Lewis, driving a Scuderia Ferrari Alfa Romeo.

It was later reported that Mussolini sought an explanation as to why Dixon, in a car with half of the capacity of the Alfa Romeos, had come so close to winning. It has not been possible to corroborate this story, and it may be a myth. It was further reported that at the end of the season Dixon and Lewis were approached by Ferrari to drive for his Scuderia. Again, this is not corroborated, and certainly Dixon did not take up any such offer, although the financial and other gains would have been substantial. The report may not be true, but alternatively, Dixon may have preferred to stay in Middlesbrough and to develop his own cars than to work for the difficult Enzo Ferrari.

Dixon is reported as taking part in the *Daily Dispatch* 1000 guineas race on Ainsdale Sands, organised by the Southport Motor Racing Club. The race was won by P Stephenson driving a supercharged Austin, having led from the start. Dixon went direct to the sands from the Isle of Man races, arriving five minutes before the race started. He was said to have commented 'It was a great rush and I had to change into racing kit in my car on the way here', a considerable feat in a racing car. Dixon finished fourth, but might have tasted victory had he not been held up for two laps at the Birkdale end with engine cooling problems. He was 6 minutes 5 seconds behind the winner.

The first long distance race of the year at Brooklands was the Junior Car Club's International Trophy, on 28 April. This was the second race of the series. In the foreword to the programme, Lord Nuffield commented that 'No light task is before the man and machine that will prove supreme in this great contest'. The race again used the system of handicapping used in the first International, a system based on increasingly more difficult artificial corners for cars of larger engine capacity. Although the system allowed the drama of a mass start, it was not popular among the competitors, who feared oiled plugs would result.

Dixon's two new Sixes were entered, fitted with 1633cc engines; Dixon driving one, and Cyril Paul the other. There was a splendid entry for the race. The group for the largest cars contained Earl Howe's Type 51 Bugatti, T E Rose Richard's 2.3-litre Bugatti, Whitney Straight's 3-litre Maserati, Buddy Fetherstonhaugh's 2.5-litre Maserati, the Hon Brian Lewis's 2.5-litre Maserati, with Grant and Munday sharing a 2.3-litre Alfa Romeo. The middle of the three groups contained no fewer than thirteen 1087cc supercharged K3 MG Magnettes together with Rayson's Riley Nine and Lace's low chassis Invicta. The third group contained Dixon's two cars, three 747cc supercharged MGs, five 2-litre Bugattis, Dobbs' Riley Nine and Fotheringham's Le Mans Singer of 1930cc.

Campbell was recovering from illness and Mathieson was seeking a cure for diphtheria by cruising in the West Indies. The new Austin was not ready in time to qualify, and Appleton's Appleton-Riley Special was too slow, depleting the still impressive line up for the start.

It was a showery morning, but the sun struggled out for the start. The cars were marked with a flash of colour on their tails to show which channel they were to use on the artificial bends at the Fork. After twenty laps Dixon was second, and after thirty laps he was in the lead, and won a special prize of £10. His average speed was 88.16mph. Unfortunately, Dixon had to retire with oil feed problems. He never liked the Riley plunger oil pump, thinking it vulnerable to the effects of oil surge, even with effective baffles fitted. Dixon much preferred a gear driven pump, with the oil coming from a small supplementary sump beneath the main one. The artificial corners may have exacerbated the problems.

Paul spun his car at Members Bridge corner, and after stalling, push-started the car, finishing fourth and winning a group prize. The winner was Straight by 4 seconds, with the Hon. Brian Lewis second and Rose Richards third. The team prize was won by the Bugattis of Earl Howe, Rose Richards and Eason Scott. The race was a success for the organisers, if not for Dixon.

Dixon was interested in land speed records. In 1934 he bought Kaye Don's *Silver Bullet* car, with the intention of going for the world speed record. This will be dealt with in a later chapter.

June 17th saw Dixon competing for the first time in the Le Mans twenty-four hour race, sharing a works Riley with Cyril Paul. The factory entered three MPH cars, KV 9477, KV 9478 and KV 9763. KV 9763 did not run in the race, but Dixon and Paul drove one of the other cars, numbered 28. The factory also entered two Imps, driven by Edgar Maclure and Newsome. A sixth car was prepared for Dorothy Champney (later to be Mrs Victor Riley) and Kay Petre. The ladies' car was red, whilst the others were painted blue, an unusual choice, given that blue is the French racing colour.

As usual, the race started at 4pm on Saturday, in magnificent weather. Alfa Romeo led from the start, but as night fell Dixon was sixth, and by early morning he was duelling with the much larger Alfas for second place. By 11am on Sunday, Dixon was second, with Sebilleau third. Later the order was reversed, and Dixon finished third. All six Rileys finished, a good result for the company, against the powerful continental teams, with their larger engined cars and huge resources.

In July, Dixon's attention turned from France to Brooklands and the British Empire Trophy Race over 100 laps. Dixon led for a large part of the race in car number 35, but had to retire with transmission trouble. Pat Fairfield drove one of Dixon's Nines, probably *Red Mongrel*, without success. Dixon was not to share in the £1000 prize money donated by Lord Nuffield. Tragically, John Hawkesworth crashed, suffering a fractured skull, from which he later died.

July 7th saw the third meeting of the year at Donington. It was Dixon's first trip to Donington that year. The weather was magnificent, and Donington's shady trees were very welcome.

Dixon drove through the heat and dazzling sunshine to win the second heat of the 25-mile handicap race. Hill was first off in his MG, with a two minute handicap. Perry and Dunfee had a one minute start on supercharged MGs. Dixon drove a bored out Six, and had 45 seconds over Eccles's 2.3-litre Bugatti. Hill retained the lead on the first lap, with Turner's Austin second. He had problems with oiled plugs. Dixon was third on lap two, ten yards behind Hill, and by lap three he had a lead of half a mile. Eccles was second on the fourth lap, but half a mile behind Dixon. Dixon's laps were almost as fast as the solo motorcycles, his best being 2 minutes 15.2 seconds, or 68.5mph. His total time gave him a comfortable lead over Everitt, who had won the first heat, and he was an easy winner.

The fifth race of the day was a five-lap race for cars up to 1500cc. Paul had driven a Dixon 1486cc Riley in the previous race and handed the car over to Dixon, who made the running from the start. He was described as being lurid on Starkeys. He controlled the car despite the difficulty (as others saw it) of a two thirds steering wheel. Dixon finished a convincing mile ahead of Everitt on the supercharged 746cc MG.

The sixth race of the day was for unsupercharged cars up to 3000cc. Dixon turned his car right round at Starkeys on the first lap and retired. Paul had a convincing win in Dixon's 1486cc Riley.

The last heat of the day was not run until 7.30pm. There was criticism of the way in which the meeting had been organised. Eccles was in a twin cam Bugatti, Boyd on a Maserati. Dixon drove fast and hard, and was second on the second lap. He did not reappear after the second lap, and an ambulance set off for him. He had crashed at Starkeys. The cause was then a mystery. It was suggested that the lowering sun blinded Dixon, but eyewitnesses were reported to have said that the propeller shaft broke, or that the brakes failed. Another contemporary report said that an experimental component in the final drive failed, and Dixon was later to confirm this, without specifying the nature of the component. He said this caused the brakes to fail. Pat Ferguson, who will feature in this story, was closely associated with Dixon at a later stage. He shared Dixon's home for a time, drove racing cars for him, and had the opportunity of discussing with him at great length the earlier exploits. He is firmly of the view, because Dixon told him so, that the propeller shaft broke, probably as a result of force reversal on deceleration. Dixon would not have wished to make this public, which is why the press reports are so speculative. Dixon probably floated the rumour of the experimental component in the final drive because he would not want it known that a standard component had failed.

In any event, the car came fast down the hill, and careered into the bumpy grass, crossed the other branch of Starkeys hairpin, and crashed into the sand bank which had been, fortunately, erected to protect the crowd. The car caught fire. Dixon's injuries were serious, and included broken ribs, head injuries and a punctured lung. He was taken immediately to Derby Royal Infirmary, and was said to be in great danger for several days, lapsing into unconsciousness at intervals.

Dixon had had many spills during his motorcycling days, but nothing as bad as this. It might have been thought that his motor racing days were over. The doctors said they were. Dixon had lost all his teeth, his nose was broken and his appearance permanently altered. Dolly Dixon took her husband a diet of oysters, cream and fruit into hospital, and on this diet Dixon slowly improved, showing dogged perseverance. Whilst he recuperated, his remaining cars were not idle. Cyril Paul drove one at Donington in August, and was the victor in a 25-mile handicap, coming second in another race.

Despite his injuries, Dixon still had his sights on the remaining races of the season. The next major race was the Ulster TT on 2 September. It was thought unlikely that Dixon would be fit to drive then, if ever again, but he did not give up. It was said that he escaped from hospital to practise. This was probably an invention of the press, who loved to glamorise Dixon, but Cyril Paul reported in August, at the Donington meeting, that Dixon intended to enter three cars in the Ulster race, with Brackenbury as reserve driver.

As promised, Dixon arrived in Ulster with his cars, a Six and two Nines, and took part in practice. One of his wrists was badly swollen, which must have made steering difficult, and he still had a vicious scar on his face. He said:

'My ribs are healed and there is every possibility I might drive. I feel fit again, although my wrist is still affected. The only thing I am worried about is my ability to stand up to the physical strain of the long race over the 478-mile course. I shall be better able to do that after one or two practice spins … I do not intend to take any risks. This crash at Donington put me in hospital for the first time in the twenty-two years I have been racing, and I hope it will be the last time I shall have to go to hospital.'

Dixon was given a tremendous reception, his fellow drivers being amazed at his recovery after what they knew was a serious crash. Despite medical advice that he should take a long sea voyage, Dixon's only sea voyage was from Stranraer to Larne on the way to Belfast.

Dixon and Charles Brackenbury at the 1934 Ulster TT, for which Fred entered two Nines and a 1485cc Six. Paul retired in a Nine, and Fairfield came third in class in the second Dixon Nine. Dixon and Brackenbury did not start.

The rules for the 1934 race were changed. It was felt that the entries were straying too far from the concept of a touring car. Superchargers were not allowed, as the public and manufacturers had shown no inclination to accept superchargers for production vehicles. Full touring trim had to be carried, including hood, wings and lamps.

Nuvolari did not race because of a controversy over his bonus. Hamilton had been killed in Switzerland driving for Whitney Straight. The stars of the TT were missing. The question was whether Dixon would race.

Riley was represented by Dixon's two Nines and his 1485cc Six, with three Riley Nines and a 1485cc Six entered by Victor Riley. The rest of the field consisted of six MG NE Magnettes of 1271cc, three Lagondas, three locally entered V8 Fords, a Bentley, two Invictas, two Talbots, four Frazer Nashes, three Aston Martins, four Singers and a MG Magna.

The race had been won only once by an unsupercharged car (Cyril Whitcroft in 1932). Public opinion supported the ban on superchargers, now that it was apparent that they would only be used for pure racing cars. Participants were probably less happy. They certainly resented the compulsory wings, as they prevented an easy check on tyre wear.

Dixon did not race. Neither, it seems, did Brackenbury take his place. The Six simply did not start. Cyril Paul retired on lap twenty-one, the cause unknown, and Fairfield, on Dixon's other Riley, finished third in his class. The race was won by George Eyston in an MG Magnette, with E R Hall second on a Bentley and Fotheringham third, driving a 1495cc Aston Martin.

Dixon must have been disappointed to miss the race in which he had driven with so much promise in 1932, and from which he had been disqualified the year before for a technical infringement.

Again, Dixon showed a serious side to his swashbuckling personality, with an ability to appreciate risk, and a wish to avoid unnecessary danger. No doubt he would have driven if he possibly could, and the decision was probably a wise one. He had still the prospect of the 500 to come.

The BRDC International 500 was held, as usual, in September, on the 22nd. Dixon entered *Red Mongrel*, driven by Cyril Paul, and the TT Nine, to be driven by Dixon's pupil, Pat Fairfield, who had 'apprenticed' himself to Dixon to learn the art of motor racing. Dixon drove one of his Sixes, numbered 33, fitted with a 1985cc engine. John Cobb entered his massive Napier-Railton, which was to prove totally unsuitable in the conditions which prevailed, although it started a favourite. Class H had five MG Midgets, all supercharged, and three Austins. Class G consisted of four Rileys, the Appleton Special, Cuthbert's supercharged Riley Nine, and ten supercharged MG Magnettes. One was driven by Hall, the 1933 winner. There were three Aston Martins, one blown, a Riley and a Frazer Nash in Class F. Dixon was in Class E, along with Hindmarsh's Singer and a 2-litre Bugatti. Black drove a 2.3-litre Scuderia Ferrari Alfa Romeo, and Seaman a Maserati in Class D. Class C consisted of a Bentley, Bertram's 4.9-litre Bugatti, and the straight-eight ex-Scuderia Ferrari Duesenberg entered by Whitney Straight and Count Trossi. The only entrant in Class B was Walter Hassan's red Barnato-Hassan Special, driven by Earl Howe and Dudley Froy. Class A consisted, of course, of the Napier-Railton.

The race started at noon, in the wet. George Eyston took the lead in his MG Magnette, with the mighty Napier Railton thundering behind him. A Victor Riley-entered 1486cc Riley took up fourth place, driven by von der Becke. The rain grew worse, plumes rising from the tyres. The conditions were too much for John Cobb and the Napier Railton and Dixon was lapping at a much greater speed, although no doubt also affected by the weather. Dixon moved into second place, then first, ahead of Eyston.

Eyston came in to change tyres, and to allow his reserve driver Walter Handley to take over. On leaving the pits, Handley tried to catch Dixon, and crashed into a barrier. He stepped out unhurt, but the car was out of the race.

Fairfield moved up into second place, behind his mentor, with von der Becke third, the first three places therefore being taken by Rileys. The race might have finished in that order, but in the wet Fairfield was involved in two dramatic skids, in one describing four complete circles, and in the second hitting a barrier on the Railway Straight. Fairfield emerged with only bruises, but his race was over. Cyril Paul retired with engine trouble, leaving only Dixon to represent his team. By 4.00pm Dixon still held the lead, contenting himself with a narrow margin over the von der Becke/Maclure car, no doubt taking care in the wet.

Wisdom's Magnette was in third place after Fairfield's dramatic exit from the race, which continued in this order for some laps, until Dixon was seen limping into the pits with a flat front tyre. Maclure took the lead. Dixon's pit staff worked furiously to fix the car, and he streaked off into the rain. It seemed he could not catch Maclure, unless Maclure had trouble, with which he then obliged by means of a blocked fuel line. Maclure limped across the line second, behind Dixon, who had now won his first classic race. He had achieved his ambition. Eyewitnesses said there was a tear in Dixon's eye after his victory. His motor racing career so far had been directed at a win in the 500. He had won £250, the Wakefield Trophy, the BARC Cup, and the Colegrave Trophy.

It is remarkable that Dixon drove to victory single-handed, so soon after his crash. It was by no means unknown for 500 entrants to drive alone, and Hall had won single-handed in 1933, but it was more usual to have a second driver. In 1934 the Magnettes which came third and fourth had two drivers each. G F Manby-Colegrave drove into fifth place single handed, and Dobbs gained sixth place on a 1087cc Riley single-handed. Anyone who has driven a 1930s sports car will have some appreciation of the effort involved in driving 500 miles under racing conditions, especially in the wet. That Dixon had pulled off this feat so soon after his Donington accident, and after his disappointing withdrawal from the Ulster race, was remarkable.

Dixon had ended the 1934 season on the highest note he could. In November he was the guest of honour at a dinner given for him by his friends at the RAC, in Pall Mall, London. His friends included Riley dealers, who must have benefited from his exploits. Dixon was presented with a cheque for £125 by the dealers. Victor Riley was in the chair and, it was said, exploded any myth that there was any conflict between Dixon and the Riley company. Whether there had earlier been any conflict is difficult to say, and none appears in the contemporary press reports. The fact that Victor Riley found it necessary to dispel the story suggests it had some basis. Conflict may have arisen because Dixon felt he was not getting enough support from the company whose products he had done so much to promote. Dixon cannot have been easy to work with. In any event, he seems to have ended the racing year on good terms with the company, and the fact that he continued to use Riley-based cars suggests that any rift was not a serious one.

Dixon won the BRDC Track Star with 18 points.

CHAPTER SEVEN

1935 – DISASTER, SUCCESS AND DRAMA

O n Sunday 10 February 1935 a two-seater plane took off from Newton House, near Bedale, North Yorkshire. The pilot was Herbert Barker, and his passenger was Dixon. Dixon had, it was reported, a real fear that after his accident at Donington he had lost his nerve for racing, although

Dixon checks the contact breaker gap on the Six in the Isle of Man. Note the stressed skin bodywork of this masterpiece of the tuner's art. The six carburettors are covered from prying eyes by a rag …

the success he had in the 1934 season does not support this. He took the strange decision to counteract the reports by doing something he was afraid of doing, and Dixon was known to be afraid of boats and of flying.

Shortly after take off, as the plane flew over the outskirts of Middlesbrough, a short distance by air from Bedale, the engine stalled. Barker struggled to land the plane safely on the Middlesbrough golf course, then at Linthorpe, but he was not to succeed, and the plane crashed on the course. Dixon was dragged from the wreckage, again seriously injured, with among other things, a suspected fractured skull. This was only months after the Donington accident, and it now seemed unlikely that Dixon would race again. For eleven days he was unconscious. His brother Frank was later to say that this accident altered Dixon's personality, coarsening him. For many days Dixon lay desperately ill in Middlesbrough General Hospital. He slowly recovered, and by March could sit in a chair. He had again to resort to a diet of oysters, fruit and cream.

In April 1935 George Brough launched his Brough Superior car after many admirers of his motorcycles had put pressure on him to produce a car. The car was based on a Hudson engine and chassis, imported from the USA. It had initially a straight eight-cylinder side-valve engine of 4168cc and a single plate clutch connected the engine to the three speed gearbox. Dixon is credited with a considerable part in the development of the car, and is said to have developed the suspension in particular. The basic Hudson was extensively modified, with 12-volt electrics, a Serck radiator, hydraulic jacks and a central lubrication system. Atcherleys of Birmingham made the body, which was finished with burr walnut where appropriate. The car was expensive at £695, but was effortless and luxurious, with a maximum speed of 90mph. It could be fitted with a Shorrock supercharger to special order. The Earl of March, an enthusiast for fast cars, took an interest in the Brough Superior.

In June 1936 a six-cylinder model appeared, again with the engine by Hudson, since the eight-cylinder Hudson engine had been claimed exclusively by Railton. The hood could be easily and quickly lowered to fit flush with the bodywork and Brough described it as a dual purpose car. When supercharged the car was known as the Alpine Grand Sports, and had a 0–60mph time of nine seconds and a top speed of at least 110mph. How much Dixon had to do with the development of these cars is difficult to establish, but it may well be that he was responsible for making the car suitable for British conditions, and this may explain his involvement in the suspension development, although this was primarily Hudson in design. That Dixon was involved must be accepted from the number of sources which credit him with it, and it would be natural for Brough to call upon Dixon, whom he had known for many years, and who had proved himself to be one of the most able development engineers of his day.

Dixon missed the opening meeting at Brooklands on 16 March. He was at the Easter meeting. The weather was good. The final race of the day was the 10 lap British Mountain Handicap. Dixon drove splendidly, lapping at 76.31mph, then two laps at 76.86mph, winning by 12 clear seconds from the scratch Bugatti 3.3-litre Type 59 Grand Prix car of Eccles. Dixon's average was 74.68mph. Dobbs's Riley was third. There then followed a remarkable and inexplicable event. Dixon failed to stop at the end of the race, and continued for a further three laps, until a distraught official walked into the centre of the track, waving a stop sign. He was summoned before the Stewards, and Dixon's explanation was that he had not seen the finishing flag, and that he was afraid to stop because of the cars behind. The Stewards accepted this explanation up to a point, but said that his carrying on for three laps after the race finished would have to be recorded. In fact, Dixon got off lightly. Other drivers had been fined and disqualified from racing for similar offences. It was later said by Dennis May in one of his articles *'Is it true what they say about Dixon?'* that Dixon had not stopped because the flying accident had affected his eye muscles, and that he could only see by willing himself to look straight ahead. It is extraordinary to think that Dixon would have raced in this condition. We know that Dixon, daredevil that he was, had a strong sense of self-preservation, and it is hard to accept that even he would race with defective eyesight. It is more probable that Dixon was simply overcome by the joy of winning, and was showing off to the crowd, who could not get enough of his driving. The escapade was probably nothing more than Dixon being Dixon, defying authority, and thoroughly enjoying himself.

The first meeting of the year at Donington was on 13 April, but Dixon did not take part. The next big event was the races on the Isle of Man, the

F.W. Dixon. "Riley". 2nd in Mannin Beg. 1935

Dixon came second in the 1935 Mannin Beg to his pupil Fairfield (1100cc ERA). The other eleven starters retired.

Mannin Beg and Mannin Moar. These were held again despite the financial losses of previous years. The course, which was found in practice to be excessively bumpy, had a new 180 degree corner on the sea front. The restrictions of previous years continued. Most of the thirteen starters were MGs, but the most interesting were the ERAs. Raymond Mays drove a works entry, and the South African Pat Fairfield drove a white 1100cc ERA. Dixon was beaten in the Beg by Fairfield. Only Dixon and Fairfield finished, every other competitor retiring with mechanical failure, a result which attracted particular criticism from the press, which commented adversely on the state of preparation of the cars. Dixon won a prize of £50. Fairfield, who won £100, had been Dixon's pupil. He came from a family which had become wealthy from fruit growing in South Africa, and it was said that he had given Dixon £1000 to teach him to drive, having seen Dixon in action. This was a vast sum of money for the time, and the story may not be entirely true, but Dixon had given Fairfield tuition, and his driving style was said to be reminiscent of Dixon's. Tragically, Fairfield was killed at Le Mans in 1937 when driving a works BMW 328.

This was to be Dixon's last race around the houses of Douglas. In the following year the two races were replaced by a single race over part of the motorcycle TT course. Dixon practised, but did not race, withdrawing because he said the course was too dangerous. It was said that this was at the request of his wife. Dixon was no coward, and the course must have been very dangerous.

1935 was Silver Jubilee year for King George V and Queen Mary and 6 May was made Jubilee Day. The Junior Car Club by some means managed to make Jubilee Day the day on which it held its International Trophy Race at Brooklands. The weather was perfect. Dixon was there and came second to a promising newcomer, Luis Fontes, driving a green Alfa Romeo numbered 13! Fontes' winning speed was 86.96mph, and Dixon's speed was 85.76mph. Dixon seems to have driven a steady rather than spectacular race, although it was clearly close for first place. Elsie Wisdom brought a Riley home fifth.

1935 was the year of Dixon's parents' Golden Wedding. The celebrations included a splendid dinner (Fred seated third from end on left).

11 May saw a happy family event for Dixon. A party was held for Dixon's parents to celebrate their Golden Wedding. Dixon loved a party.

On Whit Monday, 10 June, Dixon was in action at Brooklands. The event is not memorable for any success Dixon may have had, but marked another round in his constant battle with authority. Dixon found himself again before the Stewards, the Earl of Cottenham, Sir Algernon Guinness and Colonel F Lindsay Lloyd, to answer a complaint of baulking another competitor in the Gold Star Handicap. There had been a field of sixteen for the seven-lap race, with one non-starter. Brackenbury won in Martin's 2.3-litre Bugatti, which lapped at 138.34mph. There were numerous instances of baulking, and Dixon was before the Stewards for allegedly baulking Oliver Bertram in the huge Barnato-Hassan Special. Bertram made no complaint. Dixon had been lapping fast, high on the banking, where he preferred to be. He was told not to enter again if he could not comply with the rules. Dixon appears to have answered this solemn tribunal in his usual robust way, pointing out the absurdity, as he saw it, of expecting him to slow down and look behind at 125mph in a 1350lb (610kg) car. Characteristically he said that if he was expected to comply with such a rule, then he was not interested in BARC races. It is difficult to imagine that Dixon found it easy to answer to men like these, whose background and attitude was so different from his. They were the sort of wealthy amateurs Dixon had fought against to get into racing, and it was clear that he had little time for them.

Dixon later wrote to the Committee of the BARC, and although his letter is not available, the reply was published in the press. We can deduce the tone and content of Dixon's letter from the reply. He seems to have objected to the medical examination which was insisted upon after his plane crash, although this does not seem an unreasonable requirement. The incident of the previous April is referred to, and it is significant that Dixon was reminded that he had been before the Stewards on three occasions between 5 June 1933 and June 1935. This was bound to be viewed with disfavour. Dixon received little comfort from the attitude of the Committee, which supported the Stewards.

This unfortunate incident did not daunt Dixon, and he continued the season with a second appearance at Le Mans, driving for the Riley team, again sharing a car with Cyril Paul. Fifty-eight cars entered and started.

Lagonda challenged Alfa Romeo, which had had a string of wins. Early in the race Dixon had trouble with the car and lost ground. Rejoining the race he drove with his familiar verve and skill, and made up for lost time as he drove into the night. In the early hours he pulled into the pits, and for some unexplained reason the car was enveloped in flames. The flames were quickly put out, but the race was over for Dixon, and the result of the race was disappointing for the Riley team after its successes in 1934, with von der Becke coming fourth overall and second in the 1500 class, and third in the Rudge-Whitworth Cup. The race was again a convincing win for Alfa Romeo.

Despite his battles with the Stewards, Dixon was still very much a favourite of the crowd which attended Brooklands, presumably because he always provided a great spectacle, and 6 July saw Dixon there for the BRDC British Empire Trophy Race. The race was a remarkable victory for

Dixon fitted 2-litre engines to his cars for the 1935 British Empire Trophy over 240 miles at Brooklands. Dixon was the overall winner, and Paul third in the second Dixon Riley.

the Riley marque, its cars coming first, second and third. Dixon, driving a Six, as usual now, with a two-litre engine, numbered 31, had a convincing win, with Edgar Maclure coming second, and Paul third, driving Dixon's other Six. The other member of the Dixon team was Hector Dobbs.

The course was over the Brooklands track running clockwise, the reverse of the original Locke-King concept. Artificial corners were placed on the Railway Straight, at Paddock and at the Fork, this being designed to add interest to the race. The system was again unpopular with competitors, particularly because of the tendency of the slow corners to cause plug oiling. The race was run over 240 miles, 80 laps of the circuit, and by quarter distance Paul, on car number 32 led, with Dixon second and T A W Thorpe third in a Frazer Nash. We do not know what orders Dixon had given his team members, but no doubt he was determined to win, and by the halfway stage Dixon was in the lead, with Paul second and Prince zu Leiningen third on an ERA, Thorpe having retired. Dixon maintained the lead, averaging 75.9mph at the three quarter stage.

Maclure in another Riley moved up into second place. Only fifteen of the original thirty-three cars finished within the time. Dixon won by 2 minutes 10 seconds, a convincing win from Maclure, second. Paul came in 3 minutes 40 seconds after Maclure, with Dobbs, driving the only other Riley in the race, eighth. The Dixon team carried off the team prize. This was a remarkable day for Dixon and his team, and for Riley. The race was described as unspectacular, probably because of the artificial corners, but Dixon had won convincingly, and his driving was no doubt anything but unspectacular.

July saw the Nuffield Trophy meeting at Donington, run in magnificent weather. The Nuffield Trophy was due to start at 4.00pm. The distance was increased from 40 laps to 60, a total of 150 miles. It was hoped that this would lead to pit stops to refuel, but although there were few pit stops to take on fuel, there were plenty of stops for other causes. There were three scratch cars entered, all 1.5-litre supercharged, although the ERA of Seaman did not race because of a run big end in practice. Dixon drove a Riley four of 1486cc. He seemed to take his time, and then lost two minutes in the pits whilst he adjusted his shock absorbers. At 23 laps the leader was Sir John Samuel in a Q-type 750cc MG Midget. Dixon was

The pre-race drivers' briefing at Brooklands demonstrates that several competitors were not averse to doubling up as grease-monkeys. The pensive Dixon – centre stage – has as usual been working up till the last minute.

described as 'rather wild' on Starkeys, on one occasion nearly baulking Fairfield, and later swinging right around in front of Maclure.

This was nothing compared to the driving of Jucker in a Frazer Nash, whose exploits were such that the stewards flagged him off. At seven laps from the end Fairfield had a lap lead over Maclure in the Brooklands Nine, although he caused alarm by calling into the pits briefly to check that he had enough fuel. Fairfield won in 2 hours 25 minutes 10 seconds, 63.67mph. Maclure was second, 1 minute 13 seconds behind, with Briault third and Dixon fourth at an average speed of 61.47mph.

Dixon's history in the Ulster TT has been described at length, and his record in the race until 1935 was an unfortunate one. Despite his tremendous efforts and superb driving, he had so far failed to win. All that was to change in 1935.

The race was held on 7 September, under the same rules as the year before, that is, to encourage cars which were real tourers. There was a good entry of 38 cars. Dixon did not drive a Six, but instead a 1496cc four. The most likely explanation is that he did not have a Six which would qualify under the regulations. Although entered by Dixon, the car was probably a works car, and was identical in capacity to the Victor Riley-entered cars. Riley entered three cars, for Paul, von der Becke, and Maclure. Aston Martin was well represented with seven cars. This year there were only five MGs. Three Northern Irish entries of German Adler cars with front wheel drive were entered. Fiat was represented by three cars, and Singer by four. The large capacity cars consisted of a Lagonda, Railton, Bugatti and Bentley. A Marendaz Special at last took part in the race, having been entered twice before without competing. The weather was probably the best which had been seen in the series. As usual, the cars left at intervals, starting at 11.00am. The 1271cc NE Magnette MGs left first, followed by the Rileys and Aston Martins. The crowd was deprived of the drama of a mass start, and it was not easy to tell who was leading without looking at the scoreboard. However, Dixon drove with such ferocity and pace that it was apparent that he had a good position.

After three laps Dixon had passed the MGs which had left first, and after eight laps the order was Dixon, Paul and von der Becke, all, of course, on Rileys. By 12.30am Lewis's Bugatti had moved into second place, with Earl Howe, also driving a Bugatti, third. The race saw several lap records made and broken, some by Dixon. By 1.00pm Dixon had slipped to second place behind Hindmarsh's Lagonda, with Hall's Bentley taking up third place. Dixon drove at a terrific pace to regain the lead, assisted by a pit stop made by Hindmarsh. Hall then lay second. He was to make up his starting time deficit, and to take the lead from Dixon on distance, but still trailed by his credit laps under the handicapping system.

Shortly after the halfway point, Dixon made a fuel stop, which was carried out so quickly that he made up 45 seconds on Hall, who had also made a pit stop. Dixon retained the lead on handicap. The Singer team was withdrawn when the steering failed on three of the four-car entry, with dramatic results, but no real injury.

Dixon was under real pressure from Hall and on consecutive laps broke the class record. The race featured some spectacular accidents, in one of which Dixon hit a wooden post at Dundonald Bridge, but continued, still in the lead. With four laps left, Dixon led by 4 minutes 38 seconds, and was clearly set to win. This meant that he could ease up a little. The race ended with Dixon 1 minute 13 seconds ahead of Hall after a great duel.

The statistics show what a tremendous performance Dixon had given. His average speed of 76.9mph was the highest speed at which the race had been won in an unsupercharged car, and it was the second highest speed ever at which it had been won, the fastest time being Nuvolari's in 1933 in a supercharged MG K3 Magnette.

Paul was sixth overall, and von der Becke ninth. The day was a great one for Dixon and for Riley. Dixon received £300 for his win and a Trophy, the prize money again being donated by Sir William Morris. We can assume that even if the car was a works car that it had been 'Dixonised' and was superbly tuned. Dixon had laid to rest the ghost of the TT.

The season was far from over. Dixon had his greatest challenge still to come, the Brooklands 500, held on 21 September. The race was the first in which women were allowed to compete, and Mrs Gwenda Stewart and Kay Petre took up the challenge.

Dixon entered a Nine, driven by Alan Hess and E K Rayson and two Sixes, one which he shared with Handley, of 1986cc and a second driven by Cyril Paul and Charles Brackenbury of 1808cc. This was a formidable team, and must have represented a huge investment of time, effort and money by Dixon. He was out to win, and to take the team prize.

Victor Riley entered a team of two cars, driven by Fairfield and Percy Maclure and von der Becke and Edgar Maclure, both of 1986cc. There was a large international entry, with a strong Alfa Romeo challenge. Bugatti, Alvis, Bentley, Duesenberg and Maserati were all represented in the large capacity classes. Billy Cotton (Snr) drove a Riley Nine, and Dobbs entered a further Riley of 1808cc. There was also the massive Barnato-Hassan Special and Cobb's mighty Napier-Railton.

There was a threat of rain, but it soon cleared. Dixon started a favourite, and his chances of winning a team prize must have seemed high. Cobb's mighty machine was last to go.

The race was a disappointment for Dixon and his followers. His car went enormously well, lapping at times at over 130mph, faster than the Napier-Railton, and would have won if it had not first had problems with tyres, and then a wrecked engine. Whilst driven by Handley the Six holed its crankcase, and was out of the race. This followed several pit stops by Dixon's cars, and it may be that Handley pushed the Six just too hard in an attempt to catch up. Dixon's second Six retired whilst driven by Brackenbury with a loose floor-pan and seat. Brackenbury narrowly missed a very unpleasant accident! It was a measure of the effort, skill and sheer excitement provided by Dixon and his team that *The Field* Team Trophy was awarded to Dixon's team, despite its failure to finish. It was

probably too much to hope that Dixon could do it again, but once more he had thrilled the crowd by a tremendous effort.

Dixon's season was drawing to a close in a unique way. On 28 September he drove at Shelsley Walsh hill climb. It may be that hill climbing was not Dixon's forte, and he did not do well in the competition, although he drove with his usual verve. It was said that he 'did not seem quite at home' driving a two-litre. He managed a time of 45.6 seconds on his first run, with von der Becke attaining the same time precisely on a works two-litre Riley. After the lunch break Dixon drove slowly up the hill in the Tourist Trophy winning car, before competition began again, with most competitors improving on the times obtained on their first run. On his second run Dixon managed to reduce his time by three fifths of a second, but von der Becke beat him by managing fastest time of the day for an unsupercharged car, 44.2 seconds. Von der Becke took the Midlands Automobile Club Cup for the fastest unsupercharged racing car. He was also class winner in the 1500cc sports class. Raymond Mays took fastest time of the day on a two-litre ERA at 39.6 seconds.

October 5th saw the final event of the year at Donington, which staged the Donington Grand Prix, a 300 mile race. It would have been very much to Dixon's taste; a great challenge. As the cars battled it out at Donington, Dixon however had very much more on his mind. He was occupying a cell in Durham Prison.

Dixon was no stranger to the law. No doubt he regarded it as he regarded all authority. As early as 1922 Dixon was fined the sum of £1.00 for driving a car with no licence. More importantly, he appeared at court in Tottenham on 18 December 1924 and was convicted of dangerous driving and of failing to provide information leading to the arrest of a car driver. In January 1934 Dixon was convicted of the not very serious offence of unlawfully using trade plates and employing an unlicensed driver, presumably in connection with his business. In Middlesbrough on 4 May 1934 Dixon was convicted of the offence of being drunk in charge of a motor car. The charges he faced on 3 October 1935 were the most serious of all.

It may be too easy to see Dixon simply as a man with a strong personality, with a streak of lawlessness and irresponsibility, and certainly many remember him as a person fond of drinking to excess, and whose fun was often obtained from reckless activities. These were all features of his character which a harsh critic might claim were proved by his appearance before the court in October 1935.

It has been possible to piece together what was said by the witnesses, as gleaned from the depositions in the committal proceedings which led to Dixon's appearance at the Quarter Sessions, and from press reports of the trial. The reader must make up his own mind, but as will be seen, the jury may have had a certain amount of sympathy for Dixon.

Four witnesses gave evidence that at about 10pm on 11 September 1935 they were standing talking at the junction of Albert Street and Bridge Street, Middlesbrough. A car, described as a sports saloon, registered number AWK 712 appeared. One witness described how the car came 'right head on for us'. It was described as swerving from left to right, with the brakes being applied when the car was about one foot from the kerb. These witnesses reported this to two police officers in the area, and one, PC Edward Wykes, was to describe how he saw the car in Albert Street cross the junction with Bridge Street on the wrong side of the road.

Some of the witnesses had taken the number of the car, and this was to prove fatal to Dixon's defence, as very shortly after this the same car was seen by two officers in nearby Clarendon Road. The officers were Superintendent Richard Mansfield and Inspector Clark. They were cycling in Clarendon Road, ironically then the home of the Middlesbrough and District Motor Club and were to describe how, as they reached the vicinity of the Club, a car appeared. Its lights were 'brilliant' and there was a 'violent roar' from the engine. The brakes were applied violently, and the car swerved, driving thirteen feet along the pavement.

The driver of the car was quickly found to be Dixon, who was almost certainly known to the officers, if for no other reason than that he was a local celebrity. There were three other occupants of the vehicle, who got out.

The Superintendent asked Dixon what he meant by driving in that manner, and said that he noticed in the light of the gas lamps that Dixon's eyes were heavy. Dixon was reported to have said: 'You have no right to interfere with my driving, the law's all wrong, but I am going to have it altered.' The officer claimed he could smell drink, and told Dixon he was taking him into custody because he was incapable of driving. Dixon is alleged to have said: 'You're not' and then to have said: 'You will not take me, I'll show you some tricks.' The officers then took hold of Dixon, and Mansfield alleged that Dixon put his leg around his, and threw him to the ground. Mansfield apparently kept hold, and Dixon's sturdy frame fell on top of him. It was alleged that Dixon tried the same action on Inspector Clark, and that again Mansfield was thrown to the ground. The officers then managed to get the 'grips' on Dixon. They instructed a passing cyclist to call for the police van, into which Dixon was placed, having refused to walk it was alleged, still struggling.

Mansfield was to say that in the van Dixon again said: 'The law is all wrong. I am going to have it altered', and more seriously, that Dixon said 'Do you want squaring, because I will square you', to which the officers appear to have taken considerable offence.

Dixon was taken before a station sergeant, whose opinion it was that Dixon was unfit to drive a motor vehicle. A police surgeon gave evidence that he attended and examined Dixon. His evidence is worth considering, because he was to say that in his view 'Dixon had had more to drink than was wise when in charge of a car' and that it was 'possible' that when arrested Dixon 'might' have been incapable of being in charge of a car. He expressed the opinion that he had the impression that Dixon might be a person who would recover quickly from the effects of alcohol. Questioned by the Stipendiary Magistrate at the committal proceedings, he said that half an hour before the examination Dixon would be affected by alcohol such as to affect his power to control a vehicle. Taken as whole, the Doctor's evidence suggests that he was not entirely convinced of Dixon's unfitness.

Dixon was charged with the offences alleged in Clarendon Road. By this time Dr Wynn Williams, Dixon's own physician, had arrived, together with Dixon's brother Frank. Doctor William's evidence was later to be important at the trial. The police had found a wine bottle in Dixon's pocket, which became an exhibit at the trial. Frank suggested, very practically, that Dixon should mark the bottle. Dixon commented that he had only drunk a quarter or a third of the bottle.

By 13 September the police had brought together the allegations arising in Albert Street, and Dixon was further charged with these offences in the presence of Frank, who it seems was always there in a crisis. Dixon was asked if he was the driver of the car in Albert Street. His reply cannot have helped his defence much, because he said, it was alleged, that he did not know who had been driving, and that he did not know where he had been.

At his trial before Mr Recorder Joshua Scholefield KC, the indictment faced by Dixon alleged driving a motor recklessly in Albert Street, driving in a manner dangerous to the public in Albert Street, driving under the influence of drink in Clarendon Road, reckless driving, driving at a dangerous speed and driving in a manner dangerous to the public, all in Clarendon Road and assaulting Richard William Mansfield, a police officer, in Clarendon Road.

The licensee of the Criterion Hotel gave evidence for the prosecution that Dixon had been in his hotel for about an hour on the night of 11 September, leaving at about 10.00pm and driving away in a sports saloon. One William Hedley Young, a stevedore, known to his friends as 'Captain' Young, gave evidence for the defence that he had left Dixon that night after being in his company, and that Dixon was sober. He further gave evidence (as it will be seen, to some possible effect) that the car was not driven at an excessive speed in Clarendon Road, and denied (to no good effect) that the car was stopped in Albert Street at a dangerous distance from the men on the corner.

A defence witness, Joseph Goragon, a grocer, confirmed Dixon's presence in the Criterion, and said he was in conversation with Dixon, who he said was perfectly sober. By coincidence an ambulance man who had attended the scene of Dixon's plane crash was in the Criterion and gave evidence that on recognising Dixon he had introduced himself, and that when he left at 9.55pm Dixon was sober.

Another witness gave the somewhat surprising evidence that he had seen the car in Clarendon Road, but that it did not appear to have been driven improperly. This witness gave evidence that the officers kicked Dixon's legs away, and denied that Dixon had thrown the officers to the ground. He had been so anxious to give evidence to the court that he had tried four times to contact Dixon, who had been away, and had eventually answered an advertisement for witnesses. The struggle did not arise until the police van arrived. Finally, Dr Williams gave evidence that in his opinion Dixon was perfectly sober when he saw him, having asked him to say 'hippopotamus', which he did without difficulty!

On 4 October the jury found Dixon guilty of the two offences in Albert Street, and of the offences in Clarendon Road, with the exception of driving with excess alcohol and driving at a dangerous speed. Significantly, they added a rider to the conviction for assault upon the officer that the offence was committed under 'great provocation'.

Dixon was sentenced to a total of three months' hard labour, and was disqualified from driving for six months. The rules governing motor racing did not allow the holding of a competition licence without a licence to drive on the road, and this included entering a car for someone else to drive. Dixon was prevented from driving in competition, or from entering a car, for six months, but because of the time of year, this had no practical effect. However, a later conviction, as we shall see, was to bring about the end of Dixon's motor racing career.

The time spent in Durham Prison was not wasted. Dixon was released in late December, and was, it was reported, met by his wife, his daughter Jean and the ever-present Frank. Dixon had kept a book of drawings and ideas recorded whilst in custody. One of his patents, which showed the beginnings of his ideas on four-wheel drive and a land speed record car was applied for on 18 November 1935, whilst Dixon was in prison. It is probable that this was just coincidence, and that most of the work had been done beforehand. On his release, Dixon talked enthusiastically about his plans for the new racing season, to begin the following spring.

Dixon had been thinking further about his plans for *Silver Bullet* (of which more later). He had also found time to think about the system of traffic lights introduced by Hore-Belisha, and had concluded that it was unnecessary to have a light on each corner, when a single set of lights in the middle of the junction would suffice, which would form a 'circus' around which the traffic could travel.

It is impossible to say whether Dixon suffered shame or remorse as a result of his sentence. He was to produce a greetings card for his friends, it was said drawn by himself, which illustrated anything but remorse. Whilst in prison Dixon was elected President of the Middlesbrough and District Motor Club, a position he would hold until 1937. It would seem his peers did not condemn him, and he may have been seen as a victim of

Dixon's 1935 Christmas card bore the inscription: Oh yes, 1935 is out – so am I! I believe I am going to have a Happy New Year, and I wish you and yours the same, and all the best for 36!

draconian motoring laws introduced to persecute the driver. Dixon was a popular figure, and he may have gained nothing but sympathy for his fate.

Against this must be weighed the announcement by Dixon in early 1936 of his intention to leave the Middlesbrough area to live in the south, a surprising decision for a man with roots and a business in the north. What he felt we can only speculate upon, but Dixon seems to have survived his imprisonment with his energies and enthusiasm intact.

CHAPTER EIGHT

LATE TRIUMPHS

The *Evening Gazette*, Middlesbrough's local paper, for 7 January 1936 announced that Dixon intended to leave the north to live in Reigate, Surrey. Dixon's new address was Ardverness, Wray Common Road, Reigate, Surrey. The house had been the home of the Colman family, the mustard manufacturers. When the announcement was made by Frank

Park Garage, Middlesbrough, managed by Dixon's brother Frank, continued in business after Fred migrated south to Reigate in 1936.

Dixon, Fred was in Coventry, probably at the Riley factory. He intended, it was said, to take his cars with him, and to continue his work. Park Garage in Linthorpe Road, Middlesbrough was to continue to be owned by Dixon, and managed by Frank. Whether the decision to leave Middlesbrough was linked to Dixon's conviction and imprisonment has already been speculated upon. Frank said that Dixon had been considering the move for some time. He may have been attracted to Surrey by its proximity to Brooklands. Dixon seems to have had in mind the production of a car to challenge the World Land Speed Record held by Sir Malcolm Campbell, and, as we shall see, spoke of a revolutionary car. As we will also see, the plans came to nothing.

The press reports must be viewed with suspicion, as must the reports in the press of Dixon's plans for the future. It is very unlikely that Dixon had the resources to produce a record breaking car.

By 1936 Dixon was well established as a motor dealer in Middlesbrough, operating his sales and repairs business from the Park Garage premises. Frank Dixon, who favoured a distinctive short haircut and brown suits, had been Fred's long time manager, but not partner. Frank was to survive into old age, dying in 1989. Fred kept an office at Park Garage, but rarely used it. He was frequently away racing or on other business, and the running of the garage was left to Frank and their loyal secretary, Miss Lynas, a resident of Stockton. The foreman of the garage was Norman Settle, and he had responsibility for the repair and stores side of the business. Occasionally he would attend race meetings to help out the racing staff.

Dixon had agencies for Wolseley and Rover cars and was distributor for MG, Riley and possibly Singer. He held an agency for Brough Superior cars, but not the motorcycles, and the variety of work at the garage must have been enormous.

Norman Settle was assisted by Gillie Allinson, senior mechanic. Little is known of him, except that his brother had a well-known garage on the A66 at Brough and that he served in the REME during World War II.

The other mechanics were Charlie Micklewright, Frank Keeler, an Ariel Red Hunter enthusiast, Bob Grierson, an ex-Ford employee at Dagenham, Cecil Bradley, Ron Temperton and Sam Monkley, apprentices, the Swiss Jack Ragenbass, machinist and turner, who was brilliant at making anything not otherwise available, Keith Hutchinson and K Cockerill, who left after a dispute over pay.

The sales staff consisted of Bryan Roberts, who also assisted Frank. Joe Freek was employed to wash and clean cars and to collect them from the manufacturers.

The garage was well equipped. A Douglas twin-cylinder engine was converted in 1936 to supply piped compressed air and suitable tools were obtained to work from this. There was a facility for pressure washing cars with the use of a vessel containing 48 gallons of water, which was then sealed and air pressure applied. This was enough for one car.

Wal Handley was a frequent visitor. George Brough also visited, mainly to show off his Brough Superior Car. He turned up once in a Brough fitted with a Hudson Straight Six with a supercharger forcing mixture through an enormous SU carburettor. The car was much tested on the A19, then a single carriageway road. Brough wanted to advertise that his six-cylinder car was faster than the Railton with its eight but it is not known if this claim was ever used.

Park Garage was a Mecca for local Riley owners who wanted more performance from their vehicles. Cylinder heads were machined, with much time spent lapping on a surface plate. Solid copper cylinder head gaskets were fitted, together with twin SU carburettors which would produce an extra five mph. Machining, polishing and lightening of the crown wheel and pinion was common. Clearly none of these cars saw the full Dixon treatment, about which we know Dixon was intensely secretive. It was not only Rileys which appeared for this treatment. Other cars were tuned, including on one occasion a Bugatti, but this merited attention from the racing shop.

In 1936 the mechanics were paid £1 14s (£1.70) per day and a fuel pump attendant 7s 6d (37.5p), with overtime on Saturday morning, for which the staff, who were not well paid even by the standards of the day, were grateful, paid at 1/- (5p) per hour for four hours. Labour charges were proportionately low and a typical decoke (routine in those days) would cost about £1.00.

Racing activities were kept separate from the garage, probably in premises near Park Garage, in Simpson Street or Stonehouse Street, Middlesbrough. Walter Maidens was in charge, assisted by an apprentice called Walker. There the racing Rileys were worked upon, stored and polished. *Silver Bullet* was kept there.

Dixon's own Riley 1.5-litre was attended to by the racing shop. It is thought to have been a Kestrel, but with a similar engine to the racing Rileys and carried the number AWK 712. Dixon was probably driving this car on the ill-fated night out in Middlesbrough which led to his imprisonment.

The British Empire Trophy Race was held at Donington in 1936, having been moved from Brooklands. Dixon drove a 2-litre car, together with von der Becke and Dobbs. Percy Maclure drove a Nine. Arthur Dobson was equipped with a single offset seat 1.5-litre car. Von der Becke's car was fitted with independent front suspension, the first Riley so equipped.

Dixon shared his car with Handley, holding a good position at 3.00pm, when he handed over to Handley. Handley's driving was more spirited than cautious, and he rocketed out of the pits across the path of an Alfa Romeo driven by Staniland. A collision was avoided, and Handley managed to stay ahead for two laps, to the delight of the crowd. Then Staniland appeared at the pits alone. Handley had turned over at the Old Hairpin. The car was beyond repair, and Dixon was therefore out of the race, which he might have won. No Rileys were to finish the race, which was won by Seaman on a 2.6-litre Alfa Romeo. Fairfield was second on a 1.5-litre ERA, with Everett's Alfa Romeo third. Handley's face was cut, and he went to hospital, where back injuries were discovered. The change to Donington, a road track, was judged a success.

The Junior Car Club held its 100 lap 250 mile International Trophy Race at Brooklands. It was to be a dramatic race, with an excellent entry. The large capacity group consisted of a 2.9-litre monoposto P3 Alfa Romeo, Eccles' 3.3-litre Bugatti and Dobson's 2.9-litre Maserati. The next group consisted of a 2.3-litre Bugatti and a 2.6-litre Maserati. Group three contained an Alta, the Maserati-Derby, eleven 1.5-litre ERAs, a twin blower Frazer Nash, an eight-valve Maserati, another Maserati, and a 2-litre Riley, driven by Clifford and Dobbs. The next group contained Lord Avebury's Alta and an Amilcar, the Appleton-Riley Special, a 1090cc ERA, an MG, the Roy Eccles Rapier Special, the von der Becke/Mrs Wilson 1.5-litre Riley, and three Rileys driven by Maclure, Dobson and Dixon. The smallest capacity group consisted of three works Austins, Abecassis' Austin, seven blown 747cc MGs and Maclure's 1089cc Riley.

There was the excitement of a massed start. Staniland's blue Alfa Romeo, high on the banking, led on the first lap, followed by Mays' ERA, with Dixon third. Cyril Paul led on the next lap, but Dixon was slowing with a broken halfshaft. The race was won by Bira by one second on the blown ERA at 91mph, with Mays averaging 90.99mph. It was one of the closest finishes ever, but a disappointment for Dixon, who must have been a potential winner.

Dixon's calendar does not appear to have been so packed as in previous years. He may have been involved in other projects, or in his move to Reigate. It was said that Dixon would not race in BARC meetings, as he

Dixon at the wheel of his Six in the Isle of Man, 1936.

felt that the handicap system made it virtually impossible for a driver to win again having won once.

Dixon's next outing was the TT, held again over the Ards circuit. The race had an impressive entry. The over 3000cc class was represented by no fewer than sixteen cars, and consisted of three Lagondas, three Talbots, Hall's Bentley, eight Delahayes and a Bugatti entered and driven by Embiricos. Three six-cylinder 1970cc Frazer Nash-BMWs were entered by H J Aldington, the genius behind the marque. Bira was to drive one to seventh place, with Fane's BMW coming third, and first in class. Aldington drove himself, and came ninth.

There were two four-cylinder Speed Model Aston Martins entered, together with one 1495cc Aston. Riley was well represented. Victor Riley had entered three cars, for von der Becke, Paul and Maclure, all 1496cc fours. Dixon's reserve driver was C J P Dodson, and the car was again a 1496cc four, with the works team's spare engine being hurriedly fitted during practice. A C Dobson entered a further 1496cc four, but was not to finish. The Riley marque was further represented by two Nines, entered and driven by Baird and Chambers. Finally, there were four Balilla Fiats of 995cc, and two 927cc Singers. MG was totally unrepresented.

The race had every prospect of being an exciting one. It was to end in tragedy, and to be the last TT which the authorities would allow over the Ards circuit.

The 1936 TT represented a major step forward for women, as it was the first year in which they were allowed to enter the race. Only Elsie Wisdom actually took part, and was flagged off after 28 laps in her Fiat. There were seven female reserve drivers.

The weather was wet, rain pouring down on the crowd, estimated to be in the region of half a million people. All the Talbots withdrew before practice. The Delahayes were said to be the fastest cars ever to race over the Ards circuit.

As usual, the handicap system meant that the start was uninspiring, with the small cars leaving first. It was said that some of the foreign drivers had a light-hearted approach to the race, not appreciating its difficulties. Dixon, of course, knew every inch of the track, and it is very unlikely that he approached the race with anything other than seriousness and determination.

There was early drama when Embiricos' Bugatti and Mongin's Delahaye touched on the turn preceding The Moat. Both cars left the road and were badly damaged, although the drivers were only slightly injured. Seaman and Fane raised the two-litre record, as the rain continued to fall. Several cars, including Dobson's Riley, were involved in spectacular skids. At the end of the first hour Hall's Bentley led on handicap.

Dixon drove with his usual skill and wild panache. He was challenging the larger cars, and after one and half hours was ahead of the field. At the two hour stage Dixon led from Lewis's Lagonda at 76.78mph. Hall was third in the Bentley, with Clarke's Delahaye fourth. The Frazer Nash-BMWs were highly competitive, and Fane put the two-litre record up to 78.93mph. After a very brief pit stop, Dixon handed over the car to Dodson. The rain had continued, and Dixon had driven through it so well that he handed over to Dodson a commanding lead. Why Dixon handed over to the relief driver is not clear. In previous years he had driven the race alone. It may have been simply a sporting gesture, or it may be that Dixon did not feel capable of completing the race unaided. Most teams had a relief driver, but it was not expected that the relief driver would necessarily drive.

The Delahaye team had specifically entered two drivers for two of its cars, whereas Dodson was listed as a reserve driver. At the three hour stage the Dixon/Dodson car was well in the lead on handicap, with Hall's Bentley now in second place, Lewis's Lagonda third and the Martin/Brunet Delahaye fourth. Hall on the Bentley had a tremendous task to catch up with the flying Riley driven by Dodson, such was his pace. The rain stopped and the track slowly dried out. It was at about this time that the tragedy occurred which was to bring to an end TT racing over the Ards circuit. Chambers, driving a Riley Nine, which by an unhappy coincidence was powered by the engine from *Red Mongrel* which Dixon had sold to Chambers, went out of control as it came fast under the bridge at Newtonards. It was said that the steering gear had broken, and certainly something happened at the front end. The car skidded violently into the crowd, which was protected only by a rope, after hitting a lamp post. Two spectators were killed on the spot, with six succumbing later in hospital. Fifteen were injured. Chambers escaped relatively unscathed. This was too much for the authorities, and the race was the last over that course. The likelihood is that the rest of *Red Mongrel* was scrapped.

Despite all of this, the race went on, with the large cars providing all the spectacle as they attempted to catch Dodson, who had set a lap record of 79.13mph. This was a tremendous speed for a 1.5-litre car, but the record was broken almost immediately by Hall on the much larger Bentley. Records continued to fall. There were various mechanical catastrophes. Dobson's Riley broke a halfshaft, an almost unheard-of event for a Riley, and Lewis's Lagonda ran out of oil for no apparent reason, thereafter limping through the race, having crawled back to the pits for replenishment. At the fourth hour the Dixon/Dodson Riley led, Dodson driving faster than ever, putting up a lap at 80.35mph, which was again a magnificent performance for a car of the Riley's capacity. Hall's Bentley seemed to have little chance of catching the Riley, and its chances would be diminished if it had to stop for fuel.

The spectators speculated upon this, and Mrs Hall in the pits cannot have been confident that the car would complete the circuit without refuelling, as she had the churns and apparatus ready. The car was to finish without refuelling, but Hall still could not match Dodson's car, which, of course, had stopped. Dixon no doubt fretted in the pits. The race was won if Dodson could keep the Riley going and put up a lap at 85.35mph, the fastest of the race, and the fastest in the race's then history. At eleven minutes past five Dodson brought the Riley over the line to win, at an average speed of 77.62mph. Hall, who had driven a remarkable race, was second, with Fane's Frazer Nash-BMW third, a very good result for the car's debut (and finale) in the series. The Frazer Nash-BMW team won the team prize. There were eighteen retirements from the race, including three Rileys, with four cars flagged off and fifteen finishers. Rileys came first, sixth, tenth, Dixon had won his second TT. No doubt the thrill of winning was to some extent blunted by the fact that it was Dodson who actually flashed over the finishing line and took the chequered flag. Dixon had done the initial work which made the win possible. Although it was probably a works car, and certainly had a works engine, Dixon had no doubt prepared it for the race, despite the late engine change. Every competitor must have felt overshadowed by the tragedy which had accompanied the race, although tragedy has never been far away from motor racing. What had been a very popular and successful series of races had come to an end.

Dixon was again in action in September, for the BRDC 500 at Brooklands. He entered a team of cars, including a 2-litre Riley to be driven by himself and Charles Martin, a 1.5-litre to be driven by Wisdom and Daybell, and another 2-litre to be driven by H G Dobbs and Arthur

Dixon on the Members' Banking at Brooklands on 19 September 1936, where with Charlie Martin as co-driver, he won the BRDC 500 in his 2-litre unsupercharged Riley.

Dobson. Dixon had driven to victory alone in 1934, but on this occasion decided to share a car. The team entry must again have represented a large investment of time and money. There were eighteen starters, on what was described as a typical autumn day, with a slight haze. Dixon was very much a favourite to win. Hall, who had done so well in the TT recently, failed to start, because the Bentley was not ready. The eight-litre Barnato-Hassan Special, with Bentley engine, was entered, driven by Bertram and R K Marker. There was an official Riley team, including Cyril Paul and von der Becke on an independently front-suspended 2-litre works car. Another significant entry was the Pacey-Hassan Special.

The race, as usual, started unspectacularly in stages, according to handicap. Dixon set off in the third group, hub-to-hub with Fairfield's Riley, then forged ahead. Paul's Riley took the lead on handicap, at an average speed of 118mph, a very good time for an unsupercharged 2-litre. The enormous Barnato-Hassan Special was last off.

There were mechanical troubles almost immediately. Dobbs had to go in for new plugs. The pace of the race increased as the cars warmed up, and the Barnato-Hassan Special began to circulate at over 127mph. Cyril Paul set a good speed, closely followed by Dixon. On the twenty-fifth lap Dixon passed Paul, and took the lead. Fairfield's Riley was third, giving Riley a dominating position in the race. By the fifty-first lap Dixon was well in the lead, 4 minutes 22 seconds ahead of his handicap and averaging 123.28mph – it will be remembered – on a 2-litre car without a supercharger. Dixon came in to refuel, change tyres, and hand over to Martin. Again, Dixon was an anxious spectator. The stop lasted two minutes and although Martin roared off, the Barnato-Hassan had taken the lead. Dixon had slipped to 3 minutes 22 seconds ahead of handicap, but Martin pulled this back to 5 minutes 22 seconds. The Barnato-Hassan came into the pits, and after taking four minutes to refuel and to change tyres, was again behind Martin, who was putting up a performance of which Dixon could not complain. Marker drove, and set off to catch Martin. Very shortly after, there was a depressing noise from the engine, and the huge car retired with a broken connecting rod. The greatest rival to Dixon and Martin had gone.

Martin increased his lead over handicap to 7 minutes 32 seconds, and then came in to hand over to Dixon, having given him a very good position in the race. The tank was filled and the rear tyres changed. Such was the lead left to him by Martin that Dixon could reduce his lap times, so as to nurse the car. Only mechanical failure could realistically threaten Dixon's position. At 155 laps the race was led by Dixon, with Wisdom and Daybell's car second, Hamilton's Alfa Romeo third and the Pacey-Hassan Special fourth. Although he had slowed down, Dixon was still the fastest car on the track, on speed as well as handicap. The Wisdom/Daybell Riley slowed down, firing on four or five cylinders, and throwing out blue smoke. The Alfa Romeo also suffered problems and the Pacey-Hassan Special moved into second place, where it was to remain. Dixon raised anxiety levels by coming in to refill the radiator. He feared gasket trouble. This stop cost him twenty seconds, but he still had an unassailable lead. At 175 laps Dixon was touring round at 117mph, with Baker-Carr on the

Dixon and his frequent collaborator Cyril Paul, outside Robin Jackson's shed at Brooklands.

Pacey-Hassan behind him by eight minutes. Dixon came in to win the 500, his second, a superb achievement, although it must be said that Martin contributed very much to this success.

The Pacey-Hassan was second, with Lord Howe and the Hon. Brian Lewis on a 4.5-litre Lagonda third. Fourth place was taken by Hamilton and the Marquis de Belleroche on an Alfa Romeo. Dixon was also to win the team prize, as Wisdom and Daybell came sixth, and Dobbs and Dobson eighth. The season was drawing to a close, and Dixon does not seem to have raced in any other important event in 1936. His mind may have been more on the move to Reigate, which seems to have been very much involved with his proposed land speed record attempt.

The successes of the year were recorded in the Middlesbrough and District Motor Club's Journal, a Club of which Dixon was still President. The Club's journal agreed with a correspondent who had referred to the 'little encouragement' Dixon had received from Teesside. There were no doubt those who would feel his departure very much, and certainly Teesside lost one of its most colourful and gifted characters, and one of its most talented engineers. The Club journal was to say: 'In our club there is not, and never will be, anyone quite like him. We are proud of him both as a President and a good fellow, and in congratulating him on his latest achievements, we wish him ever-increasing success in the future, for if ever success was deserved, he deserves it.'

The move to Reigate was made in October 1936. Also in October Dixon made it possible for Mrs Elsie Wisdom to take the women's lap record at Brooklands at a speed of 126.37mph. The car provided by Dixon was the 500-winning Six. Mrs Wisdom had previously set the record at 121.37mph, the record then being taken by Kay Petre on a Bugatti. Dixon stayed in the pits, and watched, no doubt anxiously. In practice a tyre burst at 130mph, and a lump of rubber struck Mrs Wisdom on the elbow. The tyres were changed. Mrs Wisdom was to praise Dixon's car, pointing out that the speed was the fastest recorded for an unsupercharged two-litre, nominally rated at 16hp. She gave Dixon all of the credit for her success, as he had prepared the car. In November the TT car was shipped to South Africa, to a new owner. Why Dixon decided to sell the car is not clear. No doubt it realised a good price, and Dixon may have needed the money for his new ventures.

CHAPTER NINE

1937, THE FINAL YEAR

T he year 1936 marked the virtual end of 'The Riley Years'. Dixon moved to his new home, Ardverness, Wray Common Road, Reigate, Surrey in October 1936. Sir Malcolm Campbell was a near neighbour, living at Little Gatton, Gatton Road, a house built by the novelist Sax Rohmer.

Fred Dixon's new premises were substantial, and gave him scope to continue his interest in developing cars, particularly a record-breaking car. He also became involved in a cleaning and laundry business, which presumably assisted his finances.

It was, as we have seen, a prerequisite of having a competition licence that the holder also held a licence to drive on the public roads. In June 1937 Dixon was convicted of a further offence of dangerous driving, fined, and more seriously, was disqualified from driving for two years.

The 1935 disqualification was for only six months, and fell at the end of the season, allowing Dixon to drive and enter cars from the beginning of the 1936 season. This new disqualification stretched into the 1939 season. Dixon could not compete himself, nor enter a team of cars. He was effectively disbarred from active participation in motor racing for two years. This, of course, ended as motor racing ceased on the outbreak of war in 1939. Dixon's motor racing career as a driver was at an end by June 1937.

Again, Dixon had transgressed the motoring law in a serious way. The case was heard at Surrey Quarter Sessions on 8 June 1937. It was alleged by the prosecution that Dixon was the driver of a car which, whilst on the wrong side of the road, forced a taxi and another car off the road, causing them to mount the grass verge. Both the taxi driver and the other motorist took the number of the offending car, and reported the matter to

In 1936 Dixon bought this substantial property at Reigate from the Colman's Mustard family.

the police, who wrote to Dixon, sending him a form requiring him to state who was the driver of the car. Dixon apparently replied that the driver was Alfred E Coomber, but later wrote to the police and stated that he had made a mistake, and that the driver of the car was Frederick William Dixon. Dixon made a statement to the police that he was on the road in

A Dixon Riley Six leads a single-seater Frazer Nash and an Austin 750 at Brooklands.

question at the time concerned, but that he was not involved in any accident.

Clearly the jury did not believe Dixon, and he was convicted. When asked by his counsel how many cars he had, Dixon said 'Down here I have about half-a-dozen'.

Dixon appealed against the decision to the Court of Appeal, where the case was heard by the Lord Chief Justice, who said the conviction was right and that Dixon was lucky not to have gone to prison. Dixon said at the time that he would appeal to the House of Lords if necessary. He seems to have given up the idea, and it was probably only Dixon hyperbole. Matters remained there and Dixon remained disqualified.

1937 was not all gloom. It was reported that Dixon had been taken on at a salary of £5000 to manage the Riley works team. There is little evidence that Dixon was anything more than a consultant, and he had described himself as a racing car consultant for some time. The report shows that Dixon had not lost all contact with racing, and with the Riley company. However, it is unlikely that the Riley company would have spent a lot of money on racing in 1937, as it was in serious financial difficulty, and would be taken over by Lord Nuffield in 1938.

May 1st saw the inaugural meeting of the Campbell circuit at Brooklands. Dixon was still eligible to drive, but did not do so, although one of the Sixes was driven by Charles Dodson. Carrying No. 2, the car was the only Riley in the race, which may reflect the financial position of the Riley company. The car retired with engine trouble after completing only eleven laps.

Dixon had left the scene by the time of the British Empire Trophy Race at Donington, and did not take part in the 500, where he had so magnificently distinguished himself in the past. The days of the 'Dixonised' Rileys, driven by Dixon, were over. Dodson drove one of Dixon's cars in the BRDC 500, reduced to 500 kilometres. Handicapping was by credit laps, not time, and clearly the race had been devalued. Dodson achieved a class win.

PART THREE
THE END OF
AN ERA

Dixon closely examines components which a contemporary newspaper reported were for the experimental engine for the Dart, *Dixon's conceptual World Land Speed Record breaking car.*

CHAPTER ONE

RECORD BREAKER
AND INVENTOR

Earlier chapters have related how Dixon broke many records in the course of his career, and how he was involved successfully in record breaking attempts at Brooklands and elsewhere. Dixon was interested in record breaking, which was very much more a preoccupation in the 1920s

Standing by the Silver Bullet *LSR contender, Dixon is interviewed on film in his Simpson Street workshop.*

and 1930s than now. Many well known, even household names, such as Campbell, John Cobb and Kaye Don were involved, and there was great rivalry in Europe and between Great Britain and the USA.

In April 1934 John Cobb organised an attempt on the world 24-hour record, and invited Dixon, Cyril Paul and Charles Brackenbury to join him. The attempt was made at Montlhéry using Cobb's massive Napier-Railton, and was to begin on 16 April. It was apparent from the start that tyres were to be a major factor in the attempt. Enormous stresses were placed on the tyres as the huge car swept from Montlhéry's banking on to the straight. It was significant that the attempt was not made at Brooklands, and this was a trend which had started in the 1920s in response to the increasingly bumpy track at Brooklands. The party flew to France, which must have been an ordeal for Dixon, who hated flying.

The sun shone as Cobb set off on the attempt at 12.15pm. He was to drive for the first hour and fifty minutes, it having been agreed that each driver would take a spell of about one and three quarters of an hour, after which the tyres would be changed and the driver replaced.

At the first halt it was found that the tyres had stood up well to the stresses, with only a slight puncture on the offside rear tyre to show what had been endured. Cyril Paul took the next spell of driving, and drove for forty minutes, and then drove into the pits as his seat-belt did not hold him firmly enough to counteract the battering he was receiving from the circuit. He was bandaged and attended to by a doctor, who was present throughout the attempt, and drove again later.

Dixon took over and returned to the pits after half an hour with no tread on the offside front tyre. This wheel was to be a source of trouble throughout the attempt, because of the immense strain imposed upon it as the car left the banking, which twisted the wheel.

Brackenbury followed Dixon, and the prearranged schedule worked smoothly. After six hours the team picked up the six-hour record by the narrow margin of 0.077kph. Brackenbury was driving at the time, and had been given the 'go faster' signal so that the record could be achieved.

As dusk fell the track was marked out by red lights. The Napier-Railton had a bar fitted holding three powerful headlights. As darkness fell, clearly the risks increased, but the high speeds were maintained. To achieve an average of 122mph, with stops, meant travelling at up to 130mph, whatever the lighting conditions.

Cyril Paul withdrew from the team in too much pain to continue, leaving three drivers. Soon after midnight the twelve-hour record fell. At about this time the track began to break up, and attempts to repair it were unsuccessful.

The car was refuelled. A wind which had arisen now fell and conditions were perfect. Unfortunately, it was not to last, and in the small hours of 17 April the weather broke, with rain streaming down on the track and on the car and its exposed driver. The big car skidded wildly as it came from the banking on to the straight. Despite this there was a barely perceptible reduction in average speed.

Daylight broke, but the rain continued, soaking the exhausted driver. Dixon was at the wheel when the end came. It was 7.35am, with barely four hours to go before the attempt would end, probably in victory. Dixon drove with his usual skill and courage as the car skidded on every turn. Suddenly the car skidded wildly as it came off the western banking, and in front of the stand went out of control. Dixon may have established a record for the longest skid ever, over half a kilometre. The car weighed over two tons with fuel and driver, and at the speed at which it was travelling, on the wet surface with that weight, there was nothing Dixon could do but hope. He could not even adopt his usual tactic of heading for the softest spot. The car ended up hanging precariously over the edge of the banking. The attempt was over, but it is unlikely that the team blamed Dixon. The accident was almost inevitable in the conditions which prevailed. That Dixon was unharmed must have seemed a miracle.

Although the 24-hour record was not taken, world records were. The 100 kilometres record was achieved at 122.82mph, the six hours at 123.01mph, the twelve hours at 121.19mph, the 3000 kilometres at 120.17mph and the 2000 miles at 120.71mph. Also taken was the Class A record (over 8-litres) for 1000 miles and 2000 kilometres.

On 5 June 1934 Dixon purchased *Silver Bullet* from Jack Field for an unknown sum. This was the car built by Sunbeam for Kaye Don to make an attempt on the world land speed record. Don made his attempt at Daytona in 1930, and it was a complete failure. The car had two V12

supercharged Sunbeam-Coatalen aero-engines in tandem, totalling more
than 47 litres, which gave 940hp each, nothing like the 2000hp each
which was claimed. It weighed over four and a half tons, it was said, and
was 32 feet long. *Silver Bullet* was part of a long line of monster record
breaking cars, beginning with Parry Thomas' 'Babs', and continuing with
Segrave's 1000hp Sunbeam, Campbell's *Bluebird*, Segrave's *Golden Arrow*
and the American *Triplex Special*.

   Silver Bullet was an impressive sight, with its enormous bonnet housing
the two huge engines. The silver-painted car was long and sleek, with a
shapely blanked off nose and after fairings on the wheels. The rear
sported rectangular stabilizing fins with a horizontal air brake. The
engines were especially developed for the car, and were development
projects for Coatalen's Sunbeam aero-engine line. Each engine was cast
in aluminium, with Nitralloy steel cylinder liners. The cylinder blocks
were angled at 50 degrees, and each cylinder had four valves, operated
by twin overhead camshafts. The crankshaft and big ends ran in
roller bearings.

   Cooling was by ice, contained in a chest where the radiator would
otherwise have been. There was no direct shaft coupling between the
engines, and coupling was achieved by drop gears and a secondary shaft.
A three-speed gearbox was fitted, taking the drive through twin propeller
shafts arranged to run at each side of the driver, allowing him to sit low in
the car. The four-wheel brakes were hydraulically activated, and for the
first time in a land speed record car, were water cooled. Suspension was
by semi-elliptic leaf springs and the frame was immensely strong. There
was no attempt at weight-saving, and weight was deemed to be a
necessity to keep the car on the ground.

   The *Silver Bullet* was rushed to Daytona to make the attempt whilst the
sand condition was favourable. It was untested and under-developed,
although the engines had been run and their output measured. Don was
plagued by blowbacks caused by the excessively long induction pipes,
which shattered the 17,000rpm centrifugal superchargers, feeding Amal
carburettors, to give a boost of about 7psi.

   The sand at Daytona Beach was bumpy in March 1930 when Don made
his attempt. The highest speed he could achieve was 186.046mph, as
against the current world record achieved by Segrave in March 1929 with

The 1930 Sunbeam Silver Bullet *was built for Kaye Don, but was a total failure. Dixon achieved nothing with the project, either, and abandoned it.*

Golden Arrow of 231.446mph. Morale suffered because of the constant failures, and there was friction between Coatalen and Don. Don was accused of cowardice by the wilder American newspaper pundits, and the project ended in ignominy, with the whole team returning home with 'their bulldog tail between their legs' as one American paper put it. Don claimed that he would modify the car and return to Daytona to make another attempt on the record, but he never did. It was cluttering up Don's garage, and in 1934 he was pleased to sell it to Field for a modest sum, although it had cost him £20,000.

Field arranged for Charles Cooper, John Cooper's father, and Carlo Querico to work on the car, but they failed to resolve its problems. Field said that when the superchargers blew, which was frequently, 'it was like shrapnel bursting', which must have been terrifying as the superchargers were almost in the cockpit. Several hundred kilos of ice had to be available at each attempt to cool the beast, and Field was injured when on one occasion the car burst into flames. In 1934 Field made an attempt at Southport on the British speed record, held by Campbell at 217mph. Don's problems manifested themselves again, and Field was unsuccessful. He was pleased to sell the car almost immediately to Dixon, it is said for £10, who is then alleged to have said 'It won't beat me!' Unfortunately it did. Dixon intended to remove the superchargers, which he never liked, and to fit twenty-four carburettors, though how effective this might have been is open to question. A harsh critic might say it bordered on the eccentric. There was a suggestion that testing might be done on Saltburn sands. The huge machine was taken to Middlesbrough and stripped down.

The car was described by the press as the 'Fred Karno' car. Dixon may well have lacked the means to develop the *Silver Bullet*, which was probably fundamentally flawed anyway, and the car disappeared from view when Dixon disposed of it. Its fate is not known, but it has been suggested that it was destroyed in the War, or more probably, that it was scrapped. There was a sighting of the car in a garage at Reigate, and it may have gone to Coley's scrapyard. It was a brave effort, and might have succeeded if properly funded, but there was little sponsorship in the depressed 1930s. If the car had potential, Dixon was the man to find it.

Dixon's experience with *Silver Bullet* set in train a whole new concept in his mind as to how a record breaking car should be designed. *Silver Bullet* was a typical record breaking car, huge and heavy and designed to shatter records by brute force. Dixon's thoughts turned to a different idea. He envisaged a car relatively light in weight, with an aerodynamic shape, and with a single highly efficient engine. His concept was of a two stroke engine with swashplates in place of a crankshaft, operated by axially arranged pistons. The volume of the engine is not known, but one of Dixon's then employees recollects that it was to be 1500cc with nine cylinders, but there was speculation that the capacity was to be as much as ten or twelve litres. The only 'light-weight' world land speed record car seen before that date was the American Frank Lockhart's 3-litre 16-cylinder Miller-engined Stutz Black Hawk of 1928.

Dixon applied for a patent for the engine on 1 June 1937, using his Reigate address. The drawings show an engine of six cylinders, but clearly the concept allowed for varying numbers of cylinders, depending on the size of the engine and the scope for deploying cylinders within what was effectively a barrel shaped cylinder-block. The cubic capacity is not shown, and again, the capacity of the engine was variable in relation to the power sought. The patent shows that there was to be an eccentric vane supercharger, forcing the mixture through cylinder wall ports, opening and closing as the pistons moved. The pistons were horizontally

A beautifully-restored 'Dixonised' Riley Nine showing the characteristic use of individual SU carburettors on each cylinder.

opposed, forming the combustion chamber as they moved together. A single shaft, parallel to the pistons, was driven by a swashplate at each end, rigidly connected to the shaft and in turn connected to the pistons by connecting rods via a ball and socket arrangement.

Cooling was by water. Preferably there would be two spark plugs per cylinder, firing alternately, to reduce the stress upon the plugs.

Dixon claimed in his patent that the engine would be 'an improved internal combustion engine which would be efficient, light in weight for the horsepower obtainable, relatively simple in construction and mechanical arrangement and such that multi-cylinder engines of high power output can be obtained, the advantage of light weight per horsepower increasing rapidly with the size of the engine.'

Castings for the engine arrived at the Middlesbrough racing shop in 1936 and were machined by Dixon's skilled Swiss machinist, Jack Ragenbass. It is not known if the engine was ever built, or if it survives, but in 1949 an 'ex-Dixon two-stroke test engine' was in the possession of John Treen.

The car would have a single backbone chassis with four-wheel drive and steering. There would be transmission brakes only. Dixon's ideas in this area will be explored later. In 1937 he patented his ideas on this subject. The car would have been revolutionary and had it been successful in taking the world record, which then stood at over 300mph, it would have been a remarkable achievement. Dixon may have been underfunded, but did build a scale model of the car, which he intended to call the *Dart*, to reflect its shape.

The body was long and tapering and the driver sat in a glass canopied cockpit at the front. The engine was to have produced 2000bhp, of which, said Dixon, 700bhp would be sufficient for the attempt. Why Dixon envisaged an engine with such an excess of power is unexplained. He estimated the speed at 350mph, and the weight at 1250 kilos, against the usual three tons or more for cars of this type.

Press reports about the car first appeared at about the time of Dixon's imprisonment, and continued until 1937, before quietly disappearing as Dixon turned his attention to other projects. However, Dixon's thinking in this area gave rise to novel ideas which he developed later, as we shall see. The project was a victim of lack of funding, but was a brave attempt to change the mould of thought about record breaking cars away from mighty multi-engined monsters.

CHAPTER TWO

INVENTOR AND ENGINEER
FOUR-WHEEL DRIVE

There is a direct, if convoluted, coincidence of events between Dixon's dislike of the cumbersome monsters of established land speed record breaking, an authoritarian Ulster millionaire, a brilliant but thwarted racing driver, a misogynous Ulster engineer, Colditz, Peter Sellers, and the

The Dixon-Rolt 4WD 'Crab' vehicle driven on trade plates by John Treen with its creator as passenger.

bleak landscape of the Falklands during Britain's futile war against the Argentinians. The purpose of this chapter is to tease out that unlikely combination.

Dixon's short and unhappy ownership of *Silver Bullet* has been described. He hated the crude concept then of the record breaking car, where sheer power and weight obscured innovative and subtle engineering.

After disposing of the monster, Dixon turned his creative, if at times disorganised, thoughts to a new concept in vehicles for attempts on the world speed record. The result was the *Dart*, described in the last chapter. This car was far removed from the behemoth Bullet and its ilk.

Dixon designed the car before the war and had built a scale model. At this time Dixon was preparing racing cars for Tony Rolt, and in particular, Dixon modified ERA R5B for Rolt to drive in the 1939 season. After the war, from 1947, Dixon worked for Rolt in developing Rolt's Alfa-Aitken. The car had begun life as the surviving Alfa Romeo Bimotore, with, as the name suggests, two engines. It was later developed further into a single engined 'blown' racer with the original twin superchargers. Dixon, who of course disliked superchargers, modified the car again by removing them and substituting 8 SU carburettors and an increase to 3.4 litres to make an unblown Formula One car. He undoubtedly made many more changes and improvements.

Rolt and Dixon were friends and colleagues for many years thereafter, until Dixon's death. It has been said that Rolt might have been a World Champion had not the Second World War intervened. He was a brilliant and daring driver. Rolt agreed to fund the development of a prototype of the *Dart* as a racing car, not as a potential record breaker. Originally it was intended to fit an ERA engine, but eventually Dixon's enthusiasm for the six-cylinder Riley engine prevailed. Meanwhile Dixon-Rolt Developments Ltd, formed with capital of £50 sterling, developed the concept of the strange and unique 'Crab' before 1939.

Rolt had a distinguished and heroic war, although his fighting in the field ended in 1940 at Calais when the 1st Battalion the Rifle Brigade was captured en masse. Thereafter he harassed the Germans by his constant attempts at escape, which led him eventually to Colditz Castle, the supposedly escape-proof fortress. Rolt was the author of a plan to allow two prisoners to escape from Colditz in a glider. He was to be one of the escapees. The glider was almost ready for flight when the Castle was liberated by the US Army in April 1945. Tony Rolt died in February 2008 at the age of 89. The plot takes another twist, when Tony Rolt and Pat Ferguson met up in Colditz. Rolt, assisted by Pat, harassed his captors by his repeated escape attempts.

After the war Dixon and Rolt teamed up again. The intention was to build the 'Crab' as a potential commercial proposition. The 'Crab' was the first four-wheel-drive, four-wheel-steer vehicle. It was a bold attempt, but hopelessly flawed. The technology of the day was not up to the demands of the concept.

Dixon's ideas in this area can be traced back to the patent he applied for on 18 November 1935, which in turn, as has been described, followed on from his ideas on record-breaking vehicles, with the complete specification being lodged on 9 November 1936. Dixon had, it will be recalled, been imprisoned on 4 October 1935. It may be that his time in Durham Prison gave him time to complete his application. In any event,

The restored 'Crab', showing swing-axle independent suspension, six-cylinder Riley engine and gearbox.

the patent describes a vehicle with a single central girder, with each of the wheels separately attached by an axle connected by a universal joint. The concept can be seen in the illustration to the patent. As the patent said, this allowed each wheel to be independently suspended, driven, and steered. The vehicle could have two- or four-wheel drive, two- or four-wheel steering, or could have a single wheel at one end, again independently fitted to the chassis. It could be wider at one end than at the other.

Dixon had in mind that the wheels would not be individually braked. There would be a central brake on the propeller shaft, which would normally be housed within the central beam, which would allow the braking effort to be equally applied, preventing, Dixon thought, the front wheels locking up. Was this the first intimation of an ABS system? The arrangement also allowed, Dixon said, water cooling of the brakes!

The patent also was said to prescribe a cure for an effect which Dixon called 'breezing', a phenomenon which was also described as 'transverse tyre scrub'. The idea contained in the patent was that the point of contact between the tyre and the road was kept virtually constant in relation to the chassis.

This patent was augmented by a patent of addition filed on 17 June 1953 by Harry Ferguson Research Limited. The modification was that, instead of the single central beam of the original concept, there were now longitudinal beams arranged in various patterns as shown in the drawings illustrating the patent. The wheels and axles were to be fitted in accordance with the original patent as independent swing axles. What this patent represented in terms of an improvement over the original concept is unclear. The idea of a single central beam with the propeller shaft running through it had a striking elegance. Dixon had little, or no, control over the project by then. The patent may have resulted from the development of an altogether different vehicle, which we will come to.

The 'Crab' was built around a tubular frame, in accordance with the original concept. It had the independently suspended and attached wheels and axles of the original idea. It had a complex and curious gearbox and final drive arrangement, with each wheel separately suspended, powered and steered. There was a differential on each axle

The performance of the 'Crab' fell far short of expectations, and much further development work by Ferguson and McCandless was neccessary to realise its 4WD potential.

and one on the driveshaft. There was a complex arrangement of universal joints.

The car was however, virtually impossible to steer. There was loads of understeer, and the effect of the complex final drive arrangment was to make it impossible to apply further lock once the drive system had locked itself. The wheels were steered by pivoting on the swing axles. Its name symbolised its prime fault; it spent as much time going sideways as forwards!

Rex McCandless, the Ulster motor cycle engineer who later became involved in the development of four-wheel-drive vehicles in association with Harry Ferguson, the Ulster tractor manufacture, described the 'Crab' as daft. His view was that Dixon was a:

... sound engineer ... but without a clue when designing from scratch.

Despite that opinion of the Crab, McCandless and Dixon were firm friends from 1945,when they first met at the Lisburn 100 Road Race. It has been said that Dixon had a huge influence on McCandless. In contrast to his opinion referred to above of Dixon's abilities, McCandless also said that:

Quite simply, in my opinion, he was the finest person in the world at understanding carburettors, and was a brilliant engineer.

He described Dixon's home in Reigate as 'magnificent'. Although by the time they met McCandless had a successful business in Northern Ireland manufacturing earth moving equipment, he agreed to work with (not for) Dixon at Reigate. Money was sent to him from the Irish business, and he said that he needed plenty, because whenever Dixon bought him a drink he had to buy one back!

There is a story that one of the first fruits of their collaboration was in relation to Ernest (Ernie) Lyons' entry in the 1946 Manx Grand Prix. However Ernest believes that may not be the case.

Lyons was an Ulster farmer and motorcycle racer at the highest level. He first met Dixon in June 1946 when he was competing in the Northern Ireland v Brands Hatch combined grass meeting. His mount was a Triumph Tiger 100. Lyons had fitted a pair of high compression pistons from a Dixon Riley, supplied to Ernest by Rex McCandless.

The machine was untested when it arrived at Brands Hatch, mainly through gearbox problems, and Ernest was horrified to find that it would only run on full throttle. His new found friend Dixon, advised him after all other remedies had failed to throw away the throttle needle. It worked. Ernest had by then missed the match races, but in later races set lap and race records.

The true story of the Manx Grand Prix is that so far as Ernest is aware, Dixon, Rex McCandless and Fred Clarke, the brilliant Triumph rider, designer and tuner, only did a minimal amount of work to the machine, changing a mudguard, the fuel tank and doing the usual pre-race checks. The Triumph Ernest raced at the Isle of Man was built by Clarke. Clarke's boss, Edward Turner, had given him permission to build him a mount for the Manx race, but had told him to build it only from standard parts. Turner then left for a lengthy trip to the USA. In his absence Clarke built the bike with the aluminium barrel and head of a light-weight generator engine which Triumph had been supplying to the Royal Air Force.

The machine was raced first at the Ulster Grand Prix. It did not perform brilliantly, but Ernest saw it as a trial run for the Manx and did not want to show the bike's true potential then. The problem was that by the end of the race it had used all its sparking plugs. Rex McCandless subsequently found that low fuel level in the carburettors was the problem, as it had caused overheating.

When Ernest and the Triumph arrived in the Isle of Man, Fred Clarke took over. Ernest, Dixon, McCandless and Clarke took the machine to Craig-na-Baa for a final carburettor check. Ernest thought that he had seen a fleck of aluminium on one plug but was reassured by McCandless. He was cautious, and arranged to weigh in the next day, the day of the race. Ernest is convinced that the rumour that the two Freds and McCandless had spent the night working on the machine is untrue. However, he had been banished from the workshop, and who can know

A production version of the 500cc Triumph Grand Prix used by Ernie Lyons to win the 1946 Manx GP.

what the trio of enthusiasts had been up to? In any event, Ernest won
the race.

Turner was very angry when he found out about the non standard
engine, but was mollified by Ernest's victory. However, Ernest and Clarke
abandoned Triumph because of its unenthusiastic attitude to racing.

Dixon had no more devoted disciple in the postwar years than John Treen, who had worked
with him at Reigate. This is Treen's own highly modified Brooklands Nine in the Goodwood
paddock; his wife at the wheel.

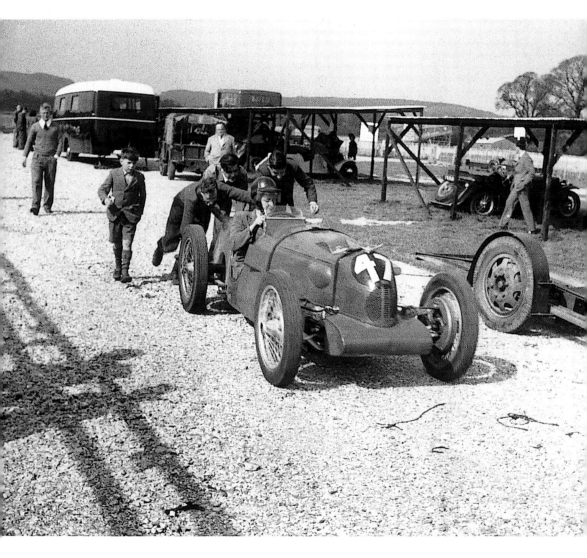

It was two years later before the Triumph Grand Prix racer was announced, a production version of Ernest's Grand Prix machine. Only 150 were issued and they were not a success. It was unreliable and the unpopular sprung hub, as well as the lapse of time since its success on the Island, all contributed to its failure. It is now a sought-after classic, however.

Later, John Treen built a small series of Treen-Riley tubular framed cars with modified Nine engines, of which several survive. This is his original Brooklands-based Nine under construction at Amberley in 1949.

Ernest was a great admirer of Dixon. He regarded him as a genius, and described him as 'the great F W Dixon'. He was, in his opinion, the person who taught McCandless much of what he knew.

The Norton team was so upset by Ernest's success that it gave McCandless a conultancy which lasted for many years. McCandless was the creator of the Norton Featherbed motorcycle frame, which allowed Norton to fend off racing competition from Moto Guzzi, Gilera and MV Agusta after the war. He was an engineer in the Dixon pragmatic mould, but probably more theoretically gifted. He had left school at thirteen with only a rudimentary education. He was difficult, abrasive and bad tempered, but his ill nature was leavened by his sense of humour, integrity and warmth. He later went on to develop autogyros, another brave lost cause.

Pat Ferguson was recruited by Rolt to help build the 'Crab' and it was mainly his work which led to the 'Crab' eventually being assembled. Pat Ferguson, (no relation to the tractor maker) was later to become Peter Sellers' team racing driver.

At the height of his fame in the Sixties, Sellers, a car enthusiast, decided to form his own racing team. The Lotus was the obvious choice of car in the Swinging Sixties and Sellers gave Pat £14,000 to purchase a Lotus Elan and trailer for the car. Pat recalls being sent by Sellers to the Norfolk factory to pick up a road version of the Lotus Elan as a present for Britt Eckland, then his wife, on her birthday. Sellers often wondered why she never drove the car, but they split up without Sellers ever knowing that she could not drive!

After the war, Pat went to live at Dixon's home in Reigate, where there were facilities to work on the car. By then Dixon had been deprived of his licence by the courts. Pat would often drive Dixon to London in the late evening, when Dixon would drink in clubs with his friends and then drive him home at about 3am. Dixon would retire until midday, leaving Pat to make progress on the car. Dixon's direct contribution to the assembly of the 'Crab' was limited, it seems. He was there to supervise.

Not only did Pat drive Dixon on the road, he also drove him to race meetings and raced for him. He drove, while Dixon tuned the cars and enjoyed himself. Pat would take the racing car back to the Surrey base on a trailer behind whatever was available. Dixon would urge him to drive faster and faster, however marginal the brakes on the tow vehicle were. Pat remembers Dixon with affection. He could be hard and critical on others, but he treated the young Pat Ferguson with kindness and respect.

So the initial team was formed. Rolt was the backer, Dixon the supervising engineer, and Pat Ferguson the assembling engineer. As the work went on, in 1951, a new and ultimately destructive player entered the scene.

Despite his dislike of supercharging, Dixon created for Tony Rolt the ERA-Delage, with two-stage blown E-type ERA engine in an ex-Chula Delage chassis. Here, Fred makes adjustments to the unpainted car on its first test outing at Goodwood in 1951.

Harry Ferguson became a millionaire through the development and manufacture of small, lightweight tractors with a unique method, invented by Ferguson, of attaching implements directly to the machine. He was a demonic figure, from the same mould as Henry Ford. Ironically, Ferguson successfully sued Ford in a huge patent action in the United States, which Ford was obliged to settle for over $9,000,000. It was said that no one worked *with* Ferguson. People worked *for* him. He crushed all opposition and ruthlessly pursued his own goals. These were by no means all financial. Ferguson had a passionate hatred of communism. It is said that he developed his revolutionary tractor so that a cheap and effective means of working the land could be provided to those who, without a means of making a living, might have turned to communism.

Ferguson had a soft spot for Dixon. He had been involved in pre-war racing at Brooklands and in Ulster, and there came to know Dixon. He thought Dixon had been underrated by the racing establishment and shabbily treated. Whatever the truth of that, perhaps he recognised another hard-driving self-made man of his own type.

Ferguson could see that a practical four-wheel-drive vehicle would fit in well with his tractor business. It would be a revolutionary new product, further assisting the working of the land and the defeat of world communism. The concept was far from Dixon's idea for a revolutionary high speed car. It seems unlikely that Dixon would be much interested in machines for agriculture.

So the story moved on. Ferguson became excited by the idea of four-wheel drive and wanted to be part of it. Unfortunately, Ferguson could be part of nothing. He had to dominate the whole project. McCandless and Ferguson met whilst McCandless was visiting Dixon at Reigate. Ferguson wanted to involve McCandless, and he too moved into the Surrey development premises.

It is clear from McCandless' description of the 'Crab' above that he had no faith in the machine. He said it was ... *much too complicated, too heavy, and therefore expensive to make and maintain*.

The four-wheel steering arrangement was rapidly dropped. It was obviously not going to work. Even now, the few cars with four-wheel steering have limited rear-wheel steering. The 'Crab' had equal steering at each wheel.

Dixon and Harry Ferguson, one the hard drinking hedonist, the other the austere teetotal authoritarian, were bound to fall out. A taste of Ferguson's traits can be had from his eccentric paternalism, which became an increasing part of his personality. He disapproved of double breasted jackets; his staff were forbidden to wear them. He insisted that all staff at all times kept a notebook in a particular pocket, which he would inspect at will. It may be that Dixon was losing interest. He had not set out to build a super tractor. His life had been speed. He was outclassed in ruthlessness and ambition by Ferguson. It proved to be an impossible partnership.

The end seems to have come when Dixon was a guest at Ferguson's home. By then development had been moved to Coventry. Dixon-Rolt Developments was now dead. Ferguson had formed Harry Ferguson Research Limited. Dixon was a mere adjunct to the project.

At Ferguson's home on this final occasion, Dixon demanded gin, by then his favourite drink. Ferguson regarded a small glass of sweet wine as an excessive indulgence, but reluctantly found Dixon a part-bottle of gin. Dixon consumed that and then fell from his chair. He got up and demanded a further supply. Ferguson refused. Dixon ran through the house demanding drink from the servants, with threats and abuse. They complained to Ferguson, who told Dixon to leave the house. That was the end of Dixon's involvement in the four-wheel-drive development.

How do we now get to the Falklands? Ferguson, in conjunction with McCandless, had moved away from the agricultural aspect of four-wheel drive. McCandless had conceived a military version of the four-wheel-drive vehicles they were developing. He had already developed, through his company Bell and McCandless, and without Ferguson's involvement, a four-wheel-drive 500cc racing car, fitted with a 500cc double knocker Norton engine, which dominated Irish motor racing in the Fifties. Two were built. In one event one of the cars gave a hard time to a C-type Jaguar. This racetrack development gave McCandless enormous insight in to the steering and suspension of four-wheel-drive vehicles.

His idea was for a light four-wheel-drive military vehicle which would 'out Jeep the Jeep'. The vehicle was built by 1951 and christened the 'Mule'. It was a superb technical success. It had a backbone chassis, a rear mounted Norton Dominator engine giving 28bhp, an open body, conventional controls (at Ferguson's insistence), and lightweight Avon tyres. It was fitted with Citröen 2CV driveshafts and inboard brakes. Its great advantage over the opposition was that it weighed only 360kg.

In comparative tests before the Chief of the Imperial General Staff, Sir William Slim, and Churchill's favourite scientist, Lord Cherwell, it far out-performed the Jeep and the Land Rover. It was much more tractable, much faster over poor terrain, much more manoeuvrable and so light that if it did get stuck its occupants could jump out and lift it out of the mire. It was an obvious winner.

The 'Mule' never went in to production because Ferguson's insatiable ego took charge. He wanted McCandless to work for him as an employee, not as a collaborator. He offered him £5000 per year and a house in England to work for him. McCandless, the no-nonsense Ulsterman, saw the trap of working under Ferguson's thumb, but not the other trap the brilliant if unscrupulous Ferguson had set for him. He fell out with Ferguson as he developed the second prototype under a barrage of memos and letters from Ferguson, and returned to his Ulster business. Ferguson had continually intervened over technical matters of which he knew little. Only then did Ferguson point out to McCandless that he had no patents in the 'Mule'. Although out-manoeuvred, McCandless did keep the second prototype, but Ferguson kept the first. No one in British industry, knowing how Ferguson had defeated the mighty Henry Ford in the courts, would take Ferguson on and develop the vehicle for production. McCandless made many attempts, with no backing, to prove ownership of the 'Mule' and its concepts. Ferguson thwarted his every effort and said that the idea was Dixon's in any event. There can be little doubt that Dixon would, if called upon to do so on behalf of his friend, have refuted that suggestion. The whole dispute came to a fruitless end when Ferguson took his own life in 1960.

McCandless remained a friend to the end of Dixon's life, and was with him the day before he died. Their collaboration was one of two hugely gifted and courageous individuals.

McCandless died in June 1992. He had lived long enough to see the fighting in the Falklands and to bitterly regret that his 'Mule' was not there in the field.

POSTSCRIPT

Dixon's life after his involvement with Ferguson must have been lived in much greater privacy than at any time since he was a young man. His death was announced on 4 November 1956, probably from a heart attack. Dixon had only recently returned from a holiday in Majorca.

Dixon had been for many years overly fond of a drink. It seems to have assumed an ever greater part of his life as he grew older, and is probably connected to his relatively early death. In July 1953 Dixon became the proprietor of the Bath Club in Worthing, Sussex. Whether that then became his home is unclear.

In October 1951 Dixon advertised that he had to 'clear his Riley stocks'. It must have been that his interests had moved on by then.

Dixon would have been hugely disappointed to have been so abruptly removed from the four-wheel-drive project. How distant was his original idea of a revolutionary record-breaking car from the vehicle produced after Ferguson's involvement? Dixon's original idea fell into oblivion. It may have been hopelessly impractical. Record breaking cars are still monsters.

The Ferguson company became a major player in the development of four-wheel drive and was acquired by General Motors. Tony Rolt and his son continued to be involved in the development of four-wheel-drive vehicles on a consulting basis. Ferguson's son-in-law Tony Sheldon created a private collection of Ferguson vehicles at his home on the Isle of Wight. The author had the great thrill of seeing Pat Ferguson reunited with the 'Crab', which he was largely responsible for having assembled over forty years previously, at Tony Sheldon's home in 1994.

Dixon has not fallen into obscurity. He is still remembered. Not infrequently his name is mentioned in contemporary motor racing and

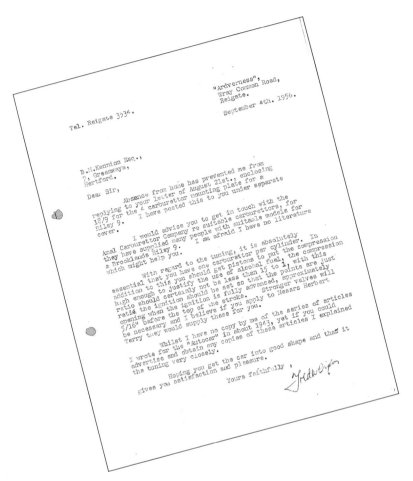

Only a few weeks before his untimely death, Dixon continues to spread the gospel.

other historic car publications. He is extensively referred to in many standard works of his period. A glance at the bibliography to this book will confirm that.

I hope that the telling of this tale will keep the Dixon legend alive and perhaps introduce him to a wider audience. Dixon is remembered by those who knew him with affection and respect, although he was no doubt in many ways a difficult man. Not all his contemporaries admired his drinking and mad exploits even if few could doubt his ability, drive and courage on and off the track.

In February 1997 on the instructions of his daughter, Christies of London sold many of Dixon's trophies and other memorabilia, including his scrapbooks. The sale raised over £50,000. Dixon's BARC 130mph badge went for £5000 and the scrapbooks for about £3000 each. Walter Denny's son remembered his father's exploits by buying some of the material. The success of the sale illustrates an abiding interest in Dixon.

Sadly, Dixon's only child died in South Africa, her adopted home, in February 1998. She is survived by her daughter – Dixon's granddaughter – whom he never came to know. It was with great pleasure that I was able to speak to her by telephone. Her pride in, and affection for her grandfather was obvious and for his biographer, warming. In a sunny land far away a lady with a smile in her voice remembers the man and his exploits.

In any event, Dixon will always be remembered I hope, as I described him in the introduction, as a great hero, a man of exceptional ability, and

The Dixon family collection of memorabilia, auctioned by Christie's in February 1997.

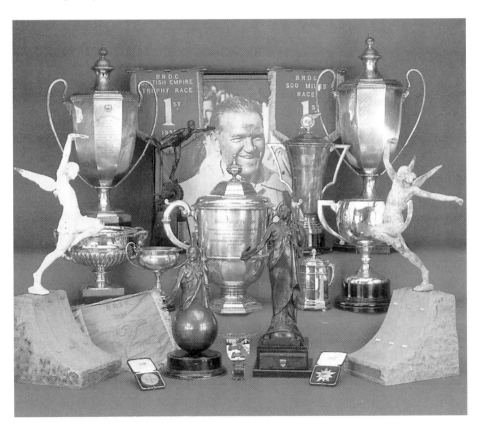

an inspiration to all who love those great days of motor racing of which he was an essential part.

Fred Dixon, we salute you for your achievements and for what you dared to dream!

David Mason
Darlington
2008

PATENTS GRANTED TO
F W DIXON

either as sole inventor, or in association with others
Compiled by Robert Elliott

Fred Dixon was granted fourteen patents in the course of his career, and while patents do not necessarily demonstrate the technical competence of their owner they often provide insights into their ability as a 'conceptual' engineer, and the attitude adopted towards the chosen technology. This is very much the case with Dixon.

His first patent was taken out while he still lived in the North East of England. Then follows a group dated from 1924 to 1931, which reflect his work as a development engineer with Douglas Motors. Only one – that for the 'Banking Sidecar' – predates his move to HRD. The rest are dated after his return to Douglas. After he left Douglas, there seems to have been a lapse in his inventiveness, and no patents were applied for until 1937, when he was in business for himself in Reigate.

Of the patents here listed, only three, the 'Banking Sidecar' (No. 217,754), the independent suspension 4-wheel drive (No. 467,891), and the multi-cylinder two-stroke engine (No. 496,725) can be considered really innovative. The rest claim minor 'incremental' improvements, mainly in motorcycles. We must not forget, though, that during the Twenties and Thirties, such incremental improvements were tremendously important to makers and riders of motorcycles alike. It is no coincidence that the objective of all Dixon's inventions from 1924–31 was not so much to improve performance (this could be done by clever tuning) as to make the bikes more robust, less costly, and (greatly significant for both the 'racers' and day-to-day motorcyclists of the period) to give greater reliability and easier access to the mechanisms for maintenance. This clearly arises from Dixon's hard-earned experience in motorcycle racing.

Spec. No.	Date Granted	Title	Applicant(s)
192,619	18 Feb 1922	Improvements relating to Sparking Plugs	F W Dixon & W Danby

(A method of cleaning dirty plugs by placing them in an adapter in the cylinder of a (presumably clean) engine – or alternatively in the hot exhaust stream!)

| 217,754 | 26 June 1924 | Improvements in sidecars for use with motorcycles | F W Dixon & Douglas Mtrs |

(This is the patent for the famous 'Banking Sidecar')

Extract from the Banking Sidecar patent specification of 1924.

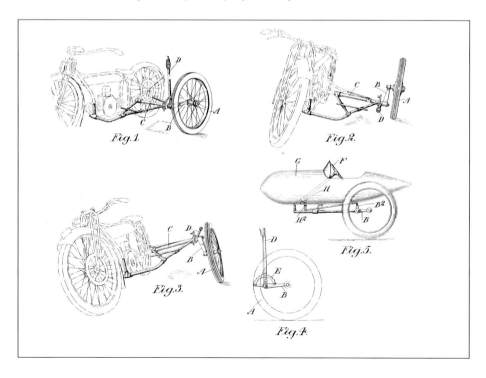

309,764	18 Apr 1929	Valve Mechanisms for Internal Combustion Engines and Means for lubricating the same	F W Dixon & Douglas Mtrs
312,489	30 May 1929	Internal combustion Engine Construction	F W Dixon & Douglas Mtrs

(An engine with horizontally opposed twin cylinders has a vertically divided crank chamber, with all the mechanism accessible via a single cover plate)

312,490	30 May 1929	Motorcycle Frame	F W Dixon & Douglas Mtrs

(Tubular frame parts are replaced in some sections of the frame by L-section members. This enables bolts to replace brazing, which lowers costs and makes for a more robust frame)

319,960	3 Oct 1929	Crankshafts for Fluid Pressure Engines	F W Dixon & Douglas Mtrs

(Easier crankshaft balancing, and the balance weights less likely to shift out of place)

320,791	24 Oct 1929	Lubrication Systems	F W Dixon & Douglas Mtrs
349,190	28 May 1931	Clutches	F W Dixon & Douglas Mtrs
350,524	8 Jun 1931	Speedometer Drive	F W Dixon & Douglas Mtrs

(A completely enclosed speedometer drive, fitted to the front wheel of a motorcycle with self contained lubrication)

467,891	18 Jun 1937	Chassis for Motor Driven Vehicles	F W Dixon
496,725	1 Dec 1938	Improvements in Two-stroke Cycle Internal Combustion Engines with Swashplate Driving Gear	F W Dixon

(Again, a rather deceptive title. The term 'two-stroke cycle' is used in its strictly technical sense to distinguish it from the four-stroke engine. This design is for a multi-cylinder, watercooled 2-stroke engine. The cylinders – the drawings show six – lie parallel with the driveshaft, and each contains two opposed pistons. Such an engine would have a relatively small vertical cross-section for its total capacity. This would aid streamlining, and is probably the design that Dixon intended for the *Dart* car with which he proposed to tackle the World Land Speed Record. At that time (and even today!) the development problems with a design like this would have been enormous.)

521,474	23 May 1940	Improvements in or relating to Variable Drive Transmitting Mechanism	F W Dixon

(A 'quiet and smooth' gear change mechanism)

556,145	22 Sep 1943	Improvements in or relating to Grub Screws Adapted to be Rotated by some Form of Key	F W Dixon

(This was intended to supersede the now familiar Allen key system, which uses a hexagonal socket and key. By the end of the war, cold-forging technology had advanced sufficiently to make the Allen key a far superior economic proposition.)

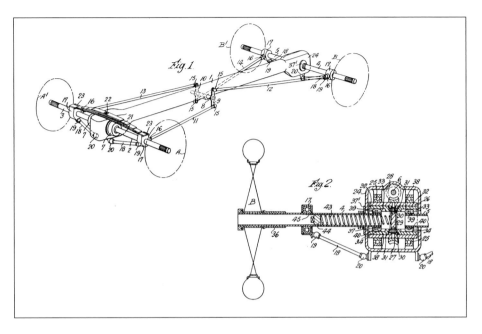

Extract from the 1935–37 provisional patent specification of the Dixon chassis, providing independent 4-wheel suspension, 2- or 4-wheel drive and 2- or 4-wheel steering.

692,874	17 Jun 1953	Improvements in or relating to Motor Driven Vehicles	Harry Ferguson Research Limited

(F W Dixon is named as inventor, and this specification is a Patent of Addition to No. 467,891, which must have been fairly close to its expiry date by this time. This patent is one of the very few which includes in its preamble the rather archaic phrase '… for which we pray that a patent may be granted to us …')

COMPETITION RESULTS

This Appendix lists Dixon's results in all of the races in which it is known he competed. It may not be complete, especially in the early years where records have not survived. Dixon's record breaking attempts are also included.

PART ONE

Two Wheels and Three

SALTBURN (Sand Racing)

(I am indebted to Martyn Flower for compiling the Saltburn results)

9 July 1921

(The first of the series at Saltburn)

Traders' 4-mile sidecar race

for machines up to 1000cc   1st on Harley-Davidson

Traders' flying kilo

for machines up to 1000cc

(John Gjiers Cup)   1st on Harley-Davidson.

20-mile Yorks Championship

for machines up to 1000cc   1st on Harley-Davidson

Traders' 4-mile sidecar race

for machines up to 1000cc   1st on Harley-Davidson

1 July 1922

Traders' 4-mile sidecars
unlimited

1st on Harley-Davidson
(Fred's brother Frank came
second on a Harley-Davidson)

Traders' flying kilo
unlimited

2nd on Harley-Davidson

Traders' 6-mile unlimited

1st on Harley-Davidson

Traders' 1-mile standing start

2nd (Frank Dixon came third)

26 July 1924

4-mile sidecar race
for machines up to 600cc

1st on Douglas (Langman was
second and Wood third)

Flying kilo
for machines up to 500cc
for machines up to 750cc

3rd on Douglas
2nd on Douglas (The same
machine as in 500cc race)

for machines up to 1000cc

1st on Harley-Davidson
(Frank Dixon was third on a
Harley-Davidson)

20-mile Yorkshire Championship
for machines up to 1000cc

1st on Harley-Davidson

20 miles
for machines up to 500cc

6th on Douglas Six

6 miles
for machines up to 750cc
for machines up to 1000cc

1st on Douglas
1st on Harley-Davidson

1 mile

for machines up to 750cc   2nd on Douglas

July 1925

1-mile standing start

for machines up to 1000cc solo   2nd on Douglas
for machines up to 350cc   3rd on Douglas
for machines up to 500cc   3rd on Douglas
for machines up to 750cc   1st on Douglas

Flying kilo

for machines up to 350cc   1st on Douglas
for machines up to 750cc   1st on Douglas
for machines up to 1000cc   1st on Douglas

50-mile handicap   3rd on Douglas

20-mile Yorkshire Championship

for machines up to 350cc   1st on Douglas
for machines up to 500cc   2nd on Douglas

4 miles

for machines up to 350cc   1st on Douglas
for machines up to 500cc   2nd on Douglas

24th July 1927

1 mile

for machines up to 500cc   1st on HRD-JAP
for machines up to 750cc   2nd on HRD-JAP
for machines up to 1000cc   2nd (mount unknown)

20-mile Yorkshire Championship

for machines up to 500cc   Retired on HRD-JAP
50 Mile Handicap for all classes   1st on HRD-JAP
10 Mile Club Handicap   1st on HRD-JAP

ISLE OF MAN TOURIST TROPHY

1912

Senior   Retired on Cleveland

1920

Senior   12th on Indian

1921

Senior   2nd on Indian

1922

Senior   Retired on Indian

1923

Senior   3rd on Indian
Sidecar   1st on Douglas

1924

Senior   3rd on Douglas
Sidecar   Retired on Douglas

1925

Junior   Retired on Douglas
Senior   Retired on Douglas
Sidecar   Retired on Douglas

1926

Junior   4th on Douglas
Senior   Retired on Douglas

1927

Junior   1st on HRD – JAP
Senior   6th on HRD – JAP

1928

Junior	18th on Douglas
Senior	Retired on Douglas

BROOKLANDS 1921

2 July

BMCRC 500	2nd on Harley-Davidson a 68.86mph
New Class E (1000cc Solo)	record for 200 miles at 74.31mph

BROOKLANDS 1922

17 June

Ealing and District MCC

200 mile sidecar races	Retired on Harley-Davidson

22 July

Essex Motor Club

Solo race	Unplaced on Harley-Davidson
3 Lap Passenger Machine Handicap	1st on Harley-Davidson

BROOKLANDS 1923

7 April

BMCRC Solo Handicap	1st on Harley-Davidson
1000cc Solo Scratch race	1st on Harley-Davidson
Passenger Handicap	1st on Harley-Davidson

26 May

BMCRC Three Lap Solo Handicap	Failed to start on Harley-Davidson
1000cc Passenger Handicap	3rd on Harley-Davidson combination
500cc Scratch Race	2nd on Harley-Davidson

BMCRC 200 Mile races

1000cc race	2nd on Harley-Davidson

28 July

BMCRC

Three-wheel handicap	1st on Harley-Davidson combination
1000cc Scratch race	Retired on Harley-Davidson
1000cc Handicap	2nd on Harley-Davidson

25 August

Ealing and District MCC	3rd on Harley-Davidson

29 September

Essex, West Kent and Wallington Clubs Meeting: match race between E P Dowey's Leyland car and Dixon's Harley-Davidson – 2nd despite severe handicapping

20 October

BMCRC

1000cc sidecar race	2nd on Harley-Davidson
1000cc solo championship	1st on Harley-Davidson

ROAD RACING 1923

June

French Grand Prix	3rd on Douglas

21 July

Spanish Twelve-Hour Race	Retired on Douglas

BROOKLANDS 1924

22 March

BMCRC

1000cc scratch race	Retired on Harley-Davidson
Experts' Handicap	2nd on Harley-Davidson
1000cc Handicap	3rd on Harley-Davidson

19 April

BMCRC

1000cc Scratch Race	Retired on Harley-Davidson
3-Lap Experts' Handicap	Retired on Harley-Davidson

7 June

BMCRC

5-lap Solo Scratch Race	Failed to start

August

Ealing and District MCC

200-mile sidecar races	Retired on Harley-Davidson

11 October

BMCRC Championship Meeting

Sidecar championship	Retired on Douglas
1000cc Sidecar Championship	Unplaced; machine not known

BROOKLANDS 1925

21 March

BMCRC Meeting

Rode in four races on Douglas	Unplaced in any event

11 April

BMCRC Meeting

Rode in four races	Unplaced in three; 3rd in three lap handicap

23 May

Ealing and District MCC

200-mile Sidecar Races	Result unknown

15 August

BMCRC 200-mile Solo Races	Retired on Douglas

10 October

BMCRC Championship Meeting

Class F (600cc with sidecar)	2nd on Douglas
750cc race	3rd on Douglas (same machine as Class F race)
1000cc race	Unplaced on Douglas (same machine as 600cc and 750cc race)
350cc Solo	Unplaced on Douglas
1000cc Sidecar	Unplaced on Douglas
350cc Sidecar	Unplaced on Douglas
500cc Solo	Unplaced on Douglas

24 October

BMCRC 3-lap 500cc Solo Handicap	Unplaced
500cc Solo Scratch Handicap	Unplaced
Unlimited passenger Handicap	1st

BROOKLANDS 1926

20 March

BMCRC Meeting

3-lap 500cc Scratch	Unplaced
3-lap Handicap Race, classes C, D and E	Unplaced
3-lap Experts' Handicap	Result unknown
Passenger Handicap	Unplaced on Douglas

10 April

BMCRC

5-lap Scratch Race 1000cc	Unplaced on Douglas
3-lap Handicap	Retired on Douglas after a spectacular crash

10 July

BMCRC Meeting

10-lap Scratch Race for Solo Machines up to 500cc	Result unknown

9 October

BMCRC Meeting Members' Grand Prix Races

350cc Solo Race	6th (mount not known)
600cc Sidecar Race	1st on Douglas

BROOKLANDS 1927

August

BMCRC

Hutchinson Hundred	Retired on Brough Superior after a crash on the first lap

(I am grateful to Dr Joe Bayley for his help in compiling Dixon's Brooklands results)

MISCELLANEOUS

1919

Scottish Speed Championship	No result recorded

1920

Scottish Speed Championship	Won solo and sidecar events
Middlesbrough and District Motor Club Gjiers' Cup	200 mile trial in Lakeland – 1st

1921

York Motor Club hill climb	FTD and record time
Otley Speed Trial	1st in solo and sidecar event
Horton Scar	FTD in sidecar event

July 1923

Belgian Grand Prix	1st on Indian

30 July 1924

French Grand Prix	2nd on HRD-JAP
French Grand Prix	2nd in 500cc Class on Indian

July 1927

Swiss Grand Prix	2nd on HRD-JAP

RECORD BREAKING

(Unless otherwise stated these are world records)

2 July 1921

Brooklands

200 miles

16 May 1923

Brooklands
Class G (1000cc with sidecar)
Flying start 5 miles – 85.87mph
Standing start 10 miles – 82.27mph

9 September 1923

Motocycle Club de France Records Meeting – Bois de Boulogne
1000cc solo Harley-Davidson flying kilometre – (speed unknown)
1000cc with sidecar flying kilometre – 143.76kph

25 March 1924

Brooklands
Class G
Standing start kilometre – 64.41mph
Standing start mile – 50.9mph
(British and World Records)

14 October 1925

Brooklands
Class F (600cc with sidecars) on Douglas
Flying start 5 miles – 85.138mph
Standing start 10 miles – 83.9mph
Flying start 5 kilometre – 137kph
Standing start 10 miles – 83.9mph
Standing start 10 kilometres – 133.84kph
50 kilometre – 135.184kph

27 October 1925

Brooklands
Class F on Douglas
1 hour – 74.07mph
several records up to 200 miles

31 October 1925

Brooklands
Class C (Solo machines up to 500cc) on 499cc Douglas
50 kilometres – 150.925kph
50 miles – 93.87mph
100 kilometres – 144.342kph
1 hour – 89.92mph

13 November 1925

Brooklands
Class F (600cc with Douglas)
Standing start kilometre – 66.54mph
Standing start mile – 71.51mph

(I am grateful to Dr Joe Bayley for his assistance in compiling these records)

PART TWO

Four Wheels

1932

20 August

Tourist Trophy Race   Retired after a crash

24 September

Brooklands 500   Retired on *Red Mongrel*

1933

11 March

Brooklands   1st in sprint on *Red Mongrel*

25 March

Donington (inaugural meeting)
2nd heat unsupercharged   2nd (probably Riley TT car)
up to 1500cc

2 May

Final International Trophy Race   Retired on *Red Mongrel*

June

BARC Whit Monday Meeting
Brooklands Gold Star   Retired on *Red Mongrel*
Cobham Senior Long Handicap   Unplaced

13 July

Mannin Beg   1st on Riley TT car

August

Brooklands 500   Retired on *Red Mongrel*
                                       (Riley TT car 3rd driven by
                                       Paul and Turner)
BARC Mountain Handicap, Brooklands 3rd

2 September

Shelsley Walsh Hill Climb   Unplaced

7 October

Donington
Up to 1100cc   2nd on Riley TT car
Up to 1500cc   Retired

1934

3 March

Brooklands

Mountain Handicap	3rd on Riley Nine
Walton Senior Mountain Handicap	2nd on Riley Nine (Broke Class G lap record at 71.15mph)

April

Brooklands Easter Meeting

Ripley Lightning Short Handicap	1st on Riley Nine
Ripley Senior Long Handicap	1st on Riley Nine
Mannin Beg	Retired on six-cylinder Riley after running out of fuel (leaking tank) (Cyril Paul finished third on Dixon's other Six)
Mannin Moar	Retired on six-cylinder Riley
Daily Dispatch 1000 Guineas sand race at Southport	4th

28 April

Junior Car Club International

Trophy Race Brooklands	Retired on Riley Six (Cyril Paul was 4th on Dixon's other Six)

17 June

Le Mans 24 hour race	3rd on Works Riley Six

July

British Empire Trophy Race Brooklands	Retired (Pat Fairfield drove one of Dixon's Riley Nines without being placed)

7 July

Donington 25-mile handicap	1st
Up to 1500cc	1st
Unsupercharged up to 3000cc	Retired
Last race of the day	Retired after serious crash

2 September

Ulster Tourist Trophy	Practised but did not race (Pat Fairfield finished third in class on a Dixon Riley Nine. Cyril Paul retired on Dixon's other Nine)

22 September

Brooklands 500	1st on Riley Six (Fairfield retired on Dixon Nine. Cyril Paul retired on *Red Mongrel*)

1935

March/April

BRDC Easter Meeting

10-lap Mountain Handicap	1st

April

Mannin Beg	2nd (only two finished)

6 May

Junior Car Club

Brooklands International Trophy Race	2nd

10 June

Brooklands 10-lap race	Unplaced (called before stewards)

June

Le Mans 24-hour race (Works team)	Retired after fire
BRDC British Empire Trophy	1st on six-cylinder Riley (Cyril Paul 3rd on Dixon's other Riley Six. Dobbs 8th on Nine) – Team prize

July

Donington Nuffield Trophy	4th on 1486cc four-cylinder Riley

7 September

Ulster Tourist Trophy	1st on 1486cc Four (probably Works car)

21 September

Brooklands 500	Retired (Brackenbury retired another Dixon Six. Dixon Nine driven by Hess and Rayson unplaced) – Team prize

29 September

Shelsley Walsh Hill Climb	Unplaced

1936

March

Brooklands British Empire Trophy	Retired after Handley (race co-driver) crashed

April

Brooklands Junior Car Club International

International Trophy Race	3rd on Nine

September

Ulster Tourist Trophy	1st on 1496cc Four (co-driver Dodson driving at the finish)

| Brooklands 500 | 1st on six-cylinder Riley (Wisdom and Daybell 8th on Dixon Six and Hobbs/Dobson 8th on Dixon Four) – Team prize |

BROOKLANDS RECORD ATTEMPTS

28 October 1932

International Class G – on *Red Mongrel*
50 kilometres – 109.16mph
50 miles – 110.37mph
100 kilometres – 110.78mph
One hour mph – 111.09mph
200 kilometres – 110.67mph
100 kilometres – 122.82mph
Six hours – 123.01mph
Twelve hours – 121.19mph
3000 kilometres – 120.17mph
2000 miles – 120.71mph

Class A (over eight litres):
1000 miles
2000 kilometres

RECORD BREAKING

April 1934

Montlhéry
Attempt on 24 hour World Land Speed Record with Napier-Railton – Retired before 24 hours completed

DIXON AND DOUGLAS
MOTORCYCLES 1928–1954

Dixon's renewed association with the Douglas Company in 1928 coincided with a significant event in the history of motor sport and the fortunes of Douglas Motors. On 19th February 1928, at High Beech, Epping Forest, a dirt track meeting was first held, the first serious event of its kind in the United Kingdom. The new sport was an instant success, the meeting having attracted an audience of 20,000 and there was immediate demand for suitable machines. Douglas, along with most other manufacturers of motor cycles was keen to fill the new niche in the market. This was one of the projects Dixon was involved in. A Dixon tuned engine for the dirt track bikes was available for an extra £10.00. This gave an extra 7bhp and was a worthwhile investment.

Dixon began working on new models immediately, partly with the 1928 TT in mind. He produced a new twin camshaft engine with enclosed push rods. The new machines had excepional performance, but as we shall see, did not shine in the TT. The camshafts were not overhead, and there has been speculation as to why the company did not experiment with this layout. It was rumoured that an overhead camshaft design was lost in the 1927 fire, and it may be that Dixon was content to make the pushrod models work as well as was possible without the cost and complication of overhead camshafts.

The 1928 Olympia show saw the results of Fred's efforts to improve the Douglas range. A wet sump lubrication system was used. Oil was delivered from a finned sump below the engine, and travelled to the mainshaft via a submerged rotary vane pump. A much larger silencer was fitted, together with black painted finned valve caps to improve cooling, flat top pistons with three rings, more substantial valve gear and provision for sliding the engine in the frame to assist with adjustment of the primary chain. The new model was designated the B/29. It had a new saddle type tank. The gear lever was fitted to the tank on a ratchet, with the pivot transferred to the lower tank rail. The solo machine cost £45. The A/28 was retained in the range to provide a cheaper alternative, but now called the A/29. Other machines in the range were also retained, with only the fitting of a saddle tank to differentiate them from previous models. Most effort was put into the TT machines. The dirt track machines were shown at Olympia, and were much admired for their purposeful lines.

The company's products shone in competition at home and abroad. RF Parkinson and CP Wood were successful on Douglas machines at the Welsh 100 event held on the Pendine Sands on machines prepared by Dixon.

The 1929 Olympia show, held in December, saw the appearance of the new Douglas S5 and S6 models. These were almost entirely the product of Fred's fertile brain, and became known as the Dixon-Douglas models. They were said to be the quietest and most flexible machines of their time. The company boasted that the machine would give two years service without major replacements. The engine had the familiar two cylinder horizontally opposed layout. Very little else was carried over from the earlier models. The engine was in line with the frame. Dry sump lubrication was used for the first time, without external pipes. The engine had very long valve guides, fitted to the cylinder barrels. The cylinder heads could be detached above the valve seating. The valve gear was completely enclosed by finned tappet covers and the induction system was cast in with the timing gear to assist in cold starts. A dynamo specially built for the Douglas range was driven by gearing from the crankshaft. The gearbox was similar to what had gone before, but could be supplied with a starting handle instead of the more usual kick-start. There was a central stand to assist with parking and repairs.

The new range was compatitively priced, with the 600cc SG model at £51.10s. There was a touring version at two pounds less, with the choice of footrests or footboards. The company continued to supply dirt track and competition machines. 730,000 motorcycles were in use in Great Britain by 1929, and the whole industry faced change. However, by 1929

Dixon was, as we shall see, once more ready to leave the Douglas company, to embark on a new racing career.

Dixon did not end his association with Douglas until almost the end of his life. Whether it was a wise or happy association is debatable, but the company and Dixon seem to have been drawn together. The association sprung up again after the war.

In 1947 Douglas produced a new range of machines based on the T35, with a transversely mounted horizontally opposed twin cylinder pushrod ohv engine and torsion bar rear suspension. Unfortunately, it suffered a series of frame failures, and had mediocre engine performance. Dixon was persuaded in 1950 to take in hand the development of the engine, and the much improved Mark III appeared. A major problem was in the camshaft design, which resulted in a valve overlap of 110 degrees. At his home in Reigate, Dixon designed a new camshaft which permitted an engine speed of 7500 rpm. He also strengthened the valve gear as the rockers had tended to twist. For months machines were taken to Fred's workshop for modification. He was also involved in the return, briefly, of the company to racing, working with Eddy Withers, an association which lasted until the 1954 Junior Clubman's TT race. This was the end of Dixon's involvement with the Douglas Company. The patents applied for jointly by Dixon and Douglas are further evidence of their collaboration and are detailed in Appendix 1.

BIBLIOGRAPHY

(Sources drawn on by the author and recommended for further Dixon study)

Periodicals and newspapers: Motorcycles
Classic Bike
Motor Cycling
The Con Rod
The Evening Gazette (Middlesbrough)
The Motor Cycle
The Northern Echo (Darlington)

Periodicals and newspapers: The Riley Years
Brooklands Society Journal
Bugantics
Classic and Sportscar
Classic Cars
Motor Racing
Motor Sport
Old Motor
Supercar Classics
The Autocar
The Automobile
The Evening Gazette
The Motor
The Northern Echo
The Riley Record
The Riley Register

Record Breaking
Motor Sport

Four-Wheel Drive & Engineering Exploits
Autosport
Motor Racing
Supercar Classics

Books
Clew, Jeff; *The Douglas Motorcycle, The Best Twin* (Haynes, 1981 – originally published as *The Best Twin* by Goose & Son, 1974)

F W Dixon; *Flying Fred – 1892–1956* (Stockton-on-Tees Museum Service, 1986)

Hartley, Peter; *Bikes at Brooklands in the Pioneer Years* (Goose & Son, 1973)

Hartley, Peter; *Brooklands Bikes of the Twenties* (Goose & Son, 1980)

Ward, Peter, and Cadell, Laurie (eds.); *Great British Bikes* (Macdonald & Co. Ltd. 1976)

Small, Gordon; *Sweet Dreams: The Life and Work of Rex McCandless* (Ulster Folk and Transport Museum)

The Ards TT (2nd. edition) (The Ulster Vintage Car Club, 1978)

Baldwin, Georgano & Sedgwick; *The World Guide to Automobiles – The Makers and their Marques* (Macdonald Orbis, 1974)

Birmingham, Dr A T; *Riley – the Production and Competition History of the pre-1939 Riley Motor Cars (2nd. edition.)* (Haynes, 1974)

Boddy, William (ed.); *The* Motorsport *Book of Donington* (Grenville Publishing Co. Ltd.)

Boddy, William; *The History of Brooklands Motor Course: 1906–1940* (Grenville Publishing Co. Ltd., (rev) 1979)

Chula (Prince Chula of Thailand); *Wheels at Speed – 1935* (Foulis & Co., 1949)

Conway, Hugh with Sauzay, Maurice; *Bugatti Magnum* (Haynes, 1989)

Fletcher, Rivers; *MG Past and Present (2nd edition)* (Haynes, 1985)

Hough, Richard; *Tourist Trophy: The History of Britain's Greatest Motor Race* (Hutchinson of London, 1957)

May, C A N; *Shelsley Walsh* (Foulis, 1946)

Mays, Raymond; *Split Seconds – My Racing Years* (Foulis, 1951)

Robson, Graham; *Riley Sports Cars: 1926–1938* (Haynes, 1986)

Styles, Dr David G; *As Old As The Industry: 1898–1969* (Dalton Watson)

Styles, Dr David G; *Sporting Rileys, the Forgotten Champions* (Dalton Watson, 1988)

Venables, David; *The Racing 1500s – A history of Voiturette Racing from 1931 to 1940* (Transport Bookman Publications, 1984)

Record Breaking

Posthumus, Cyril and Tremayne, David; *Land Speed Record: from 39.24mph to 600+mph* (Osprey Publishing, 1985)

Miscellaneous

Read, Cyril and Robin; *Goodwood – A Private View: Photographs 1949–1956* (Nelson & Saunders, 1985)

Middlesbrough and District Motor Club Jubilee Year Publication, 1955

Middlesbrough and District Motor Club Journal

Race Programmes

Supplement to BMCRC Programme, July 21 1923 (Brooklands Celebrities)

500 Miles Race, Brooklands, 16 September 1933

International Trophy Race, Brooklands, 28 April 1934

Seventh International Race, Brooklands 500-Mile Race, 21 September 1935

INDEX